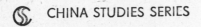

CHINA STUDIES SERIES

SMALL TOWNS IN CHINA
— FUNCTIONS, PROBLEMS & PROSPECTS

By Fei Hsiao Tung & Others

NEW WORLD PRESS · BEIJING

First Edition 1986

Cover design by Sun Chengwu

ISBN 0-8351-1529-1

Published by
NEW WORLD PRESS
24 Baiwanzhuang Road, Beijing, China

Printed by
FOREIGN LANGUAGES PRINTING HOUSE
19 West Chegongzhuang Road, Beijing, China

Distributed by
CHINA INTERNATIONAL BOOK TRADING CORPORATION
   (Guoji Shudian)
P.O. Box 399, Beijing, China

Printed in the People's Republic of China

CONTENTS

EDITOR'S NOTE   7

SMALL TOWNS, GREAT SIGNIFICANCE
— A Study of Small Towns in Wujiang County
Fei Hsiao Tung   9

PROBING DEEPER INTO SMALL TOWNS
— A Study of Small Towns in the Four Municipalities of
Southern Jiangsu
Fei Hsiao Tung   62

SMALL TOWNS IN NORTHERN JIANGSU
Fei Hsiao Tung   88

SMALL TOWNS IN CENTRAL JIANGSU
Fei Hsiao Tung   133

THE SHIFT OF SURPLUS AGRICULTURAL LABOUR
FORCE AT DIFFERENT LEVELS
— A Survey of Four Administrative Villages in Wujiang
County
Zhang Yulin   171

PEASANT WORKERS IN COUNTY TOWNS
— A Survey of Wujiang County
Zhang Yulin   196

THE RISING OF RURAL INDUSTRY AND PROSPERITY OF
TOWNS
— A Survey of the Town of Tangqiao in Shazhou County
Huang Bingfu, Xu Weirong and Wu Daqian   211

ECONOMIC CONNECTIONS BETWEEN A TOWN AND ITS
NEARBY CITIES
— A Case Study On Songling
Xu Dawei, Meng Chen and Zou Nonglian   227

RESEARCH OF THE DISTRIBUTION OF THE VILLAGES
AND TOWNS OF GAOCHUN COUNTY
Jin Qiming, Shen Guoming, Dong Xin and Lu Yuqi   248

GIVE FULL PLAY TO THE ROLE OF SMALL TOWNS
— An Investigation of Yiling Town in Jiangdu County
     Wu Rong, Wu Defu and Qian Guogeng 271

THE FORMATION AND DEVELOPMENT OF THE SILK
TOWN SHENGZE
     Ju Futian and Wu Dasheng 290

A PRELIMINARY STUDY ON THE DEVELOPMENT OF
TONGLI — AN ANCIENT CULTURAL TOWN
     Zhu Tonghua 316

FORMATION AND DEVELOPMENT OF A RURAL RE-
GIONAL COMMODITY CIRCULATION CENTRE — ZHEN-
ZE
     Zhang Yulin and Shen Guanbao 342

TABLES

Main Economic Statistics of Northern Jiangsu Compared with
the Provincial Total   93

Industrial Output Value and Its Proportion in the Four Counties of
Zhenjiang Municipality   135

Average County Industrial Output Value of Jiangsu's Various
Municipalities (1983)   136

The 1983 Output Value of Heavy and Light Industries in Seven
Cities of Jiangsu   138

Major Outside Contacts Kept by Township and Town Industries
in the Four Counties of Zhenjiang Municipality   139

Compositive Production Activities of Peasant Households in Waiyi
Village   177

A Comparison of Sex, Age and Education Among People of Different Trades in Waiyi Village   178-179

The Division of Labour Among the Households of Waiyi Village   181

Household Labour Division of the Three Comparison Villages   182

Family Sizes in Waiyi Village   185

Family Structure of Waiyi Village (1)   186

Family Structure of Waiyi Village (2)   186

Labour Distribution of Waiyi Village   191

Age Structure and Educational Levels of Shifted Agricultural Labourers at Different Levels   192

Town Population Fluctuations of Wujiang County   198

Age Structure of Zhenze's Peasant Workers   203

Comparative Educational Levels of Peasant Workers and Workers
of Town Residence   204

Time of Recruitment of Peasant Workers   204

Composition of Original Localities of Zhenze's Peasant Workers   207

A Sample Survey of Peasant Workers' Commuting Distances to
work   208

Economic Connections of Songling's Factories with Suzhou and
   Other Cities   228

Different Kinds of Co-operation Between Songling's Factories and
   Those in Suzhou   237

Average per Capita Fixed Assets of Various Suzhou Factories   238

The Variety of Commodities Available at Different Towns   253

1982 Sales Volume of Service Trade in Different Grade Towns
   in Gaochun County   257

Average Service Area and Radius in Different Grade Towns   257

Diagram of Rational Selling of Goods by Towns of Different
   Grades in Gaochun County   267

Residents Composition of Shengze   308

Leading Cadres in Tongli's Factories   329

Financial Sources of Tongli   341

General Situation of Zhenze's Privately-Owned Industry and
   Commerce   348

Comparative Commercial Statistics of Zhenze   350

Increase in Output and Output Value of Major Commodities in
   Zhenze Commune   354

Composition of Zhenze's Total Commodity Sales   358

Composition of the Volume of Retail Sales of Zhenze and the
   Zhenze Township   359

Changes in the Number of Commercial Establishments and
   Workers   359

Changes of Economic Results in Circulation Field   362

EDITOR'S NOTE

As the political, economic and cultural centres of rural China, currently accommodating nearly 80 percent and in earlier times an even larger proportion of the nation's population, small towns have a vital bearing on the overall social and economic life of China. They are essential to the solution of the country's emerging problems of population, employment, commodity production and circulation. Also depending much on the development of small towns are the rationalization of the nation's economic and administrative structure and the redivision of rural labour and trades. The construction of small towns has become ever more significant in China's present modernization drive to build a socialist society with Chinese characteristics.

The present book represents a most authentic and up-to-date study of the subject by Professor Fei Hsiao Tung, a Chinese authority in the field, and members of his research groups.

Professor Fei first became aware of the existence of small towns as an independent social entity and their far-reaching significance to the entire society during field study in the 1930s in Kaixian'gong Village in Wujiang County of southern Jiangsu Province. It had been his long-cherished hope that he could one day expand his research on individual villages to cover entire areas with small towns as their centres. However his chance for such a comprehensive and systematic study did not come until 1983. This research project on small towns is, therefore, his "dream come true".

Since the beginning of his studies in 1983, Professor Fei Hsiao Tung has led research groups on four investigative tours in the rural areas of Jiangsu Province, covering its vast areas in southern, central and northern sections. His two 1983 trips to southern Jiangsu, one of the most affluent areas of the country, include Wujiang County, which has the greatest number of small towns, and the four municipalities of Chang-zhou, Wuxi, Nantong and Suzhou. His early 1984 trip to northern Jiangsu, used to be a relatively underdeveloped area by the national standard, covers the five municipalities of Xu-zhou, Lianyungang, Yancheng, Huayin and Yangzhou. His trip to central Jiangsu in October 1984 covers the Nanjing-Zhenjiang-Yangzhou region, commonly known as the silver triangle. The four essays by Professor Fei Hsiao Tung in this book are based on the findings of the above-mentioned four investigation tours.

During the research, a standard was set that all studies must be based on first-hand information and on-the-spot in-vestigation. The procedure was to analyse collectively the conditions of the areas to be investigated to determine the concrete problems and research topics to be assigned to each individual and group accordingly.

The nine other papers included in the book were chosen personally by Professor Fei from among dozens of papers by individual researchers and groups. They are either case studies of small towns of different classifications or papers focused on specific problems or social phenomena.

The research has been a multi-disciplinary project which involves the participation of people engaged in social and natural sciences, university teachers and people from the rele-vant departments of the central government and the provincial, municipal and county levels. It is unprecedented in both the number of towns studied and the personnel involved. We are convinced that the book will be of great help both to specialists and the general reader in a better understanding of the social and economic life of China.

SMALL TOWNS, GREAT SIGNIFICANCE

— A Study of Small Towns in Wujiang County

Fei Hsiao Tung

In the late spring and early summer 1983, I conducted a month-long field study of the history and present situation of about a dozen small towns in Wujiang County, Jiangsu Province. I had initially planned to write a paper based on my findings concerning the various types and levels of these small towns, the vicissitudes they have undergone, and their distribution and development. However, upon returning to Beijing I found that my busy schedule did not afford me sufficient time to write the paper I had originally planned. Therefore, my presentation today is just a collection of impressions and afterthoughts about my stay.

It was first decided to convene the present symposium at the beginning of this year. Through the joint efforts of all present, we have not only been able to hold meetings as scheduled, but have also selected a few dozen amongst the research papers which were submitted as outstanding. Everything is difficult at the beginning, and to have achieved such excellent results in merely half a year was indeed no easy task.

These research papers are valuable because they are all concerned with the construction of small towns, and explore, from different angles, concrete problems encountered in the course of their development. I believe that the direction we have taken in research is correct. Our social sciences must make sure that their research is closely connected with China's social reality and will serve the nation's socialist modernization programme. However, historical experience tells us that fulfilling this task is no easy job. For quite a long period in the past, many of our social scientists, though well-versed in Marxist-Leninist theories and sincerely intent on doing a good job, failed to link their bookish theories with their actual work. This in turn has prevented our thinking from keeping pace with the changing realities. Therefore, when confronted with practical problems, we could not offer any realistic suggestions, but rather always fell back on our past practice or mechanically copied foreign experience. The price which we have paid for such incompetence is the extremely round-about course our work has taken.

However, people learn from their mistakes. We are now through with the errors of the past, and have begun to adopt the scientific attitude of combining theory with practice and seeking truth from facts, as has been advocated by Comrade Deng Xiaoping. It is only in this way that we can get to know China's actual characteristics.

I

In our study of small towns, we have from the very beginning broken away from the conventional pattern of going "from abstract concepts to abstract concepts". Rather, from the very start we have stressed conducting field studies and gradually deepening our understanding through carrying out on-the-spot investigations. We can say that our research on this subject was an experiment in combining theory with practice.

Understanding based on actual experience is certainly much more concrete and meaningful than that based on mere book knowledge. Although the papers included in this collection are a bit rough and perhaps not completely comprehensive in their analysis, yet all the facts they present objectively reflect reality. They are not theoretical deductions from abstract concepts, and still less arbitrary assumptions based on our imagination. In fact, the value of these papers lies in their objectivity. Being factual sketches of towns which they cover, they constitute a realiable historical record which will serve as valuable historical reference material decades or even hundreds of years from now. They are particularly valuable because they provide the basis for future studies, which will in turn represent their continuation.

Of course, it is impossible for people's subjective understanding to conform entirely with objective reality. As objective reality is constantly changing, people's understanding of it, even if imperfect, has to keep pace with such changes as well. Each new generation of scientists or social researchers furthers its predecessors' understanding of the world of reality. If one day we look back at our present findings concerning the small towns and find that this understanding was superficial and naive, this will only be evidence of progress in our understanding.

The study of small towns is a long-term research project. It is not only a major research project in China's Sixth Five-Year Plan, but it will be continued in the Seventh Five-Year Plan as well. The on-going study being carried out in southern Jiangsu is only the start of this long-term project. In order to extend our research, we must consider what the next step should be; we should make out a specific plan for the coming year and begin drawing up tentative plans for the Seventh Five-Year Plan.

In engaging in scientific study, the most dangerous tendency that people must guard against is to have one's view of the important overshadowed by the trivial, and to take a narrow view of things. We should keep in mind that both in terms of depth and scope, the research we have done on small towns this year is far from enough. Up to now, we have neither made any comprehensive examination of any specific small towns; nor have we gone beyond the limit of Wujiang County. We have merely examined, as if through a microscope, one "cell" of the entire subject of small towns, and have not even had a clear look at this. Hu Yaobang, General Secretary of the C.P.C. Central Committee, coming back from an inspection tour of northwest China, proposed to develop this vast area by expanding grazing land and carrying out afforestation. This proposal had a very eye-opening effect, as before this it had scarcely occurred to anyone that this area had such great development potential. The mere fact of China's being such a large country doesn't allow us to take a very narrow view of things. Even if the scope of our research extended to include the whole of Jiangsu Province in future, it is still a small spot to the whole country. In order not to be deceptively contented with our limited view, or try to substitute our limited experience of the part for the whole, we should always keep in mind the concrete position which Jiangsu occupies in the entire country, that of Suzhou in the province of Jiangsu, as well as that of Wujiang County in Suzhou Prefecture. We must therefore be aware of the limitedness of our present knowledge of the subject, and the special characteristics of the small towns of Wujiang County.

Though the part can never substitute the whole, it is nevertheless a portion of the whole. Despite their special features, the small towns of Wujiang County also possess the common characteristics of all small Chinese towns in general. If we can scientifically analyse the part in light of the whole, and properly handle the relationship of the two, then our studies of the part will, to some extent, reflect the basic features of the overall situation. Wujiang County is located in southern Jiangsu, one of China's most affluent areas. By taking Wujiang's small towns the object of investigation and making an in-depth analysis of their problems, we have perhaps touched the heart of China's small town problem. By this we mean that the present construction efforts in Wujiang's small towns point the way for the future development of other areas, and the problems which have arisen here might crop up in other areas in the future. Such being the case, our scientific analyses of the problems encountered during this investigation will surely provide useful reference material to those engaged in the construction of small towns in other areas of the country in the future.

In undertaking any scientific research, there should always be a clear objective as well as a plan for carrying it through. Similarly, to make headway in our research of small towns, we must in the first place draw up a specific plan. The focus of our studies should still be on the areas that we have investigated before. On the one hand, we will further elucidate the problems we have already touched upon, and on the other, we should check to see if there are any previous research topics which we overlooked. At the same time, we may set up new bases for investigation in areas of different types in order to make comparative analyses and obtain the index necessary to advance from qualitative analysis of the investigated areas to quantitative analysis of the small towns throughout the nation.

In actuality, the process of drawing up research plans is the process of defining the aim and the requirements of a given research project. Only when the aim and requirements of research are clearly defined, can concrete and workable plans be drawn up. Our symposium made new attempts in this connection. Apart from sociologists this symposium was also attended by people engaged in the study of various disciplines of both the social and natural sciences, as well as university teachers. Furthermore, we have also specially invited to our symposium people who actually work in small towns, people from the relevant departments of the central government, and people from the policy-research bodies at provincial, municipality, and county levels of Jiangsu Province. To consult people from such a variety of branches of learning, and have the participation of so many organizations and people from so many levels of government in one research project, has been a novel and encouraging experience for me.

Such wide-ranging co-operation has at least two strong points: in the first place, it provides us with an opportunity to hear many different opinions, thus widening the horizons of our thought. The second strong point is that it establishes close links between scientific study and the actual demands placed on it in practice. The former problem of theory losing touch with reality was attributable to both subjective attitudes of the individuals concerned as well as irrational organizational set-up, which resulted in a severe lack of exchange and communication between scientific research institutions and the various departments engaged in practical work. Therefore, intellectuals engaged in research turned their backs to one another, and those in practical work were completely separated from one another. As a result, the former were willing to put their knowledge into practice, but did not know where it could be used; while the latter, badly in need of scientific knowledge to guide their work, did not know where to acquire it. Now both sides have established direct contact with each other. People engaged in practical work present the scientific researchers with the problems which they encounter in their work, thereby helping them to clarify the aims of their research, rationalize their plans and give more practical value to the result of their research. Scientific researchers, on the other hand, by making the results of their research available to those engaged in actual work and offering them feasible proposals, ensure that the latter will be carried out according to objective laws, and that this work will have a scientific foundation.

It is my hope that our present symposium can put forward some concrete proposals as to how to effectively implement the policy of "vigorously developing small towns". That is, on the basis of our previous studies, to arrive at some kind of agreement concerning the solutions to the most urgent problems in the building of small towns, to be offered for the consideration of the policy-makers.

The realization of our modernization programme demands knowledge. That is to say, we need knowledge, the product of scientific research which reflects reality, to solve the various kinds of problems we may encounter during the course of the modernization process. To do this, there must be unimpeded communication between persons engaged in scientific research and social construction so that the problems which crop up in construction will be included in the research projects. Therefore research which accurately reflects these actual problems provides the policy-making bodies with advice concerning their solutions. The policy-making bodies will then, in light of the actual circumstances, make the appropriate policies which, when implemented by administrative organs and carried out by the masses, will solve the problems. However, the effectiveness of these policies and measures can only be determined as a result of putting them into practice. It is the rule rather than the exception that the resolution of the old problems gives rise to new problems. Gauging the effectiveness of these policies and investigating the occurrence of new problems create new topics for research. This shows that in promoting our modernization drive, scientific research, consultation, policy-making and practice form an interdependent circulatory system. These four elements are linked together closely, and interact continuously, in response to the constant demands for the study of new situations and the solution of new problems.

China's policy-making bodies are the leading organs of the Chinese Communist Party. The ever expanding scope of our modernization programme requires that the policy-makers have a penetrating understanding of the situations they must deal with. This is why it is now being demanded that cadres possess a wide range of intellectual knowledge. By emphasizing this, we have placed policy-making on a scientific basis. To take scientific research and consultation as necessary links in the entire system in fact embodies the essence of the Party's traditional mass line.

Scientific research and consultation, as necessary links in the system, are relatively independent of the other related links. The Party, in exercising its leadership, always follows the principle of seeking truth from facts. Therefore, its policies are drawn up on the basis of investigation and study of actual situations. For this reason, it has set up policy-study departments at all levels of the leading government bodies. This is a fine tradition of the Party.

There is no doubt that scientific research must serve politics. By this we mean that science and scientific research ought to help politicians to root their policies in reality. Nevertheless, the fundamental principle of scientific research of "seeking truth from facts" cannot completely eliminate the possibility of one-sidedness. Experts in fact tend to have an even more one-sided point of view than others. In order not to let our policy-making be distorted by such one-sidedness, there should be a middle link between the final policy-making and scientific research. Establishing such a middle link would mean employing the knowledge and research results of a variety of branches of learning to diagnose the same one problem, and on the basis of such group consultations, submit concrete, constructive proposals to the policy-making bodies. Of course, we as yet have had little experience in either organizing or conducting this kind of group consultation. However, I suggest that we experiment by setting up special consultation groups composed of deputies of both the National People's Congress and the Chinese People's Political Consultative Conference and other related specialists for the solution of important construction problems. Such consultation groups should identify themselves with the masses and approach the problems from the perspective of each different branch of learning, thus drawing a comprehensive picture of the whole. On the basis of such multi-faceted research, these groups should then make suggestions and report to the Party's leading bodies the true requirements and opinions of the masses, which they may then use as references in policy-making decisions.

After the policies are drawn up, the administrative departments are to put them into practice. In the process of implementing them, questions will inevitably arise concerning what effects they have had on practice and the changes which have taken place in objective reality, presenting new subjects for scientific research and study. Thus, the above-mentioned cycle repeats itself once again, namely, going from practice to scientific research, from study to consultation and from there finally to policy-making. The essence of this cycle has been summed up in the phrase "from the masses to the masses", which is the core principle of the Party's mass line method of exercising leadership.

The study of small towns is a comprehensive and long-term research project. It has already attracted the attention of people in different branches of learning and at different levels of government. With the passage of time and expansion of the scope of research, there will surely be even wider participation in the project. Therefore, some kind of organization is needed to co-ordinate their work and to facilitate communication between them. So, it is my hope that at the end of this conference an academic organization will be set up which will include all those who are willing to put their hearts into the study of small towns. As Jiangsu is the starting point of our research, I suggest that comrades from Jiangsu take the responsibility of establishing this organization, its name, structure and tasks to be decided upon later through collective discussions.

II

The problem of small towns has not been plucked from thin air, but has rather risen in the course of the development of practice. The problem has always existed, but we have not always recognized or understood the importance of it. I remember being told at a meeting in Tianjin early 1981, that during his inspection of Yunnan Province General Secretary Hu Yaobang noticed the dilapidated sight of the small market town of Banqiao Commune in Baoshan County. Subsequently, speaking at a meeting on the development of commodity economy, he pointed out that such development is impossible without first solving the problem of reviving the small towns. Without small towns, the political, economic and cultural work in the countryside will have no base of support. It is thus evident that the leaders of the Party Central Committee have long been aware of the significance of the small towns and intended to transform them into political, economic and cultural centres in the countryside. The construction of small

towns is of utmost importance in developing the rural economy and finding an outlet for our large population.

However, many people have not fully grasped the relationship between small towns and the rural economy, nor the
concept of small towns as the political, economic and cultural
centres of the countryside. This indicates that it is not so easy
to achieve common recognition of new problems which arise
in the course of social development. The process of understanding takes its own patterns. Usually people's understanding
of new things and new problems results from their direct experiences.

As for myself, back in my early years when I investigated
the rural areas, I strongly believed in the existence of a social and economic entity located in between the rural communities and the urban centres. This social entity is an organization mainly composed of the members of the rural population who are not engaged in farming. In terms of its geographical location, population, economy and surroundings, this
entity is both different and inseparable from the countryside.
I would like to term this socio-economic entity a "small
town".

However, such sweeping theoretical categorization tend to
cause people to lose sight of the differences and special
characteristics of things within the same category. This is also
true of our study of small towns. Should we start off with
one general concept, this would lead us to blindly mould all the
small towns into one stereotype and lose sight of the specific
characteristics and features of each individual small town.
Therefore, our research on small towns should begin with
the investigation of concrete examples, making a qualitative
analysis of each and classifying them into different types. In
the following portion of this essay I will discuss the five types
of small towns I saw in Wujiang County.

1. *Zhenze* — a town of the commodity collecting and
distributing type.

In 1936, I spent a month in Kaixian'gong doing field
study before I left for London to earn a Ph.D. I remember go-

ing to buy cigarettes at a five-and-ten store. To my surprise this small store did not sell cigarettes by the pack, but by the piece only. The shop owner told me that if I wanted to buy cigarettes by the pack I might ask the owner of the ferry-boat to help me. This caught my attention. With three to four hundred families and more than a thousand inhabitants, Kai-xian'gong was a big village in the region of Jiangsu, south of the Changjiang (Yangtze) River. But in such a large village there were only three or four shops, and their stock was so meagre and limited that they even had to sell goods like cigarettes by the piece. In those days, the villagers could by no means be self-sufficient. This made me wonder: where did they obtain their daily necessities? With this question in mind, I went to the ferry-boat and store owner mentioned above and inquired about this.

In fact the ferry-boat was just an ordinary engineless wooden junk with a cabin. It was employed to transport both people and commodities. The village, at the time, had a total of two such boats. Every morning, when the boats were rowed out of the village, people on both banks along the river would ask the boat-owners to help them purchase all sorts of goods in town: one might give him a bottle for some soyasauce and another a basket to carry back something else. The boat-owners noted all of their orders and the boats left the village with these empty bottles and baskets, heading for Zhenze, a small town six kilometres away from the village. As soon as the boat arrived at Zhenze, the apprentices from various stores, waiting on the bank, would rush up and compete to make a deal with ferry-owners. The ferry-owners, after settling all their business, would relax themselves with a cup of tea at a tea-house. In the afternoon, the apprentices sent back to the boat-owners their bottles and baskets filled with goods and the boats would then weigh anchor and return. The boats travelled to and fro between Zhenze and the village every day, also carrying passengers between the village and the town. However neither the passengers nor the beneficiaries of the ferry service paid the boat-owners a cent. Asking about their source of income, I was told that the ferry-boats transported the villagers' silk and grain to Zhenze Town for sale. At the end of each year, the silk and rice firms gave the boat-owners a certain amount of cash commission. Those sauce and pickle shops and groceries that had business contact with the ferry-owners also paid them money especially on New Year's Day or other festivals. All this combined to make quite a sizable annual income. These ferry-owners were agents in the rural commodity circulation, and played a very important role in rural economic activity. Later, I was also privileged with free boat rides to and from Zhenze, where I found two or three hundred boats anchored alongside the river, which were said to have come from other villages in vicinity. It was obvious that Zhenze was the commercial centre of the whole area.

I have recalled all this just to show that Zhenze was a commercial centre characterized by collecting the local produce and distributing manufactured products. It is absolutely indispensable for the peasants who sold their agricultural and sideline products in return for industrial products. The agricultural and sideline products produced by the peasants were sold in Zhenze; and the industrial consumer goods needed by the peasants were bought from Zhenze. With regard to the livelihood of the peasants in the surrounding areas, Zhenze was an indispensable economic centre. Collectively, the boatmen, apprentices, the rice and silk proprietors and grocerers formed a comprehensive commodity circulating network. The hundreds of ferry-boats, shuttling between Zhenze and its nearby villages played the vital role of linking up the town and the countryside. At one end of this ferry line was the town and at the other were countryside villages. The local people called those villages, which nourished Zhenze Town and at the same time fed on it, the town's "footholds". Without these "footholds", the town would have dried up economically; and without the town, its "footholds" would have ossified due to poor circulation. The relationship between the two was like the nucleus and cytoplasm: mutually indispensable to one another.

This proves that small town as a rural economic centre is not an empty concept. Half a century ago, Zhenze Town, as a commodity collecting and distributing town, triggered my curiosity and held great attraction to me. However, as I was conducting my field study alone and unaided at the time, I had to limit my research to the area within the boundaries of the village itself. Although I was keenly aware of the existence of small towns and of their strong influence on the villages, I was unable to extend my research to include the study of small towns. Ever since then, I had always hoped that one day I would have a chance to fulfil this wish. The chance came to me unexpectedly in 1981.

2. *Shengze* — a town of the specialized industrial type.

At present, Shengze Town is the town with the largest population and highest industrial output value in Wujiang County. The silk cloth exported from this town accounts for 10 per cent of the national total. Shengze is unquestionably a centre of silk industry, and is an example of the type of small town which possesses specialized industry.

Shengze's development started very early. As far back as Ming Dynasty its population was said to have reached over ten thousand. Then what was the basis of the town's early development? What did its population do for living? As a child I went to Shengze where I saw people standing at Jacquard looms, which had struck me as quite curious. In 1982 when I visited the town again, I inquired about the silk knitting workshops of the pre-1949 days and was told that at that time the town only had a few workshops, all of which were quite small, the largest of them having been equipped with only twenty old-fashioned looms. However, the town had many silk, brocade and rice firms. Since the town itself had only a limited capacity for silk production, this made me wonder: where had the silk and brocade firms obtained silk fabric? The research I carried out in seeking an answer to this question shed much light on the difference between the towns of Shengze and Zhenze. The silk and brocade firms in town had gotten their supplies mainly through "silk brokers", who served as middle men between the firms and the silk weavers. These firms first bought the silk they needed from the peasants through these brokers, and then distributed the silk together with necessary credits through these brokers to other peasants to weave into silk cloth, according to the firms' desired designs and specifications. The finished products were then collected by the brokers from the peasant households and sold to the firms. In this way, through their connections with the brokers, a silk cloth firm could have dozens, hundreds or even thousands of weavers in their employ at one time. Thus it was utterly impossible to have all these looms installed in town. Therefore, the difference between Zhenze and Shengze lies in the fact that unlike the former, Shengze was engaged not in collecting native produce and distributing industrial goods, but was rather the hub of the whole area in which the products of rural household handicraft industry were collected and distributed. Towns like Shengze, which were traditionally engaged in collecting and distributing handicraft products, merit further attention and study. The family-based textile industry served not only as the foundation of Shengze's development, but also for the development of Suzhou and Hangzhou areas. This tradition, with a history of nearly a thousand years, is still significant with regard to today's construction of the town. Once a foreign friend, amazed by the dexterity hands of Suzhou girls, remarked to me that their skills might well be applicable in the modern electronics industry, which requires highly accurate and precise work. As even foreigners have given so much thought to the benefits which could potentially be derived from our tradition of superb handicraft work, it would be indeed a shame if we ourselves turned a blind eye to them.

3. *Songling* — a town of the political centre type.

Songling has always been the political centre of Wujiang County, both in the days before and after the founding of the People's Republic in 1949. It is the seat of the county government. Since 1949, all the other old small towns in the county had been at a standstill or have shrunk, with the exception of Songling whose population has increased considerably as compared with the early post-1949 period.

Songling has long been the county seat. Formerly, under feudalism, the ruling landlord class had city walls and gates built to guard against peasants' uprisings and rebellions. Even county fairs and markets were forbidden inside the town. Therefore business transactions could only be conducted at Shengjiasha, outside its eastern gate. The inside of the town was reserved mainly for the two complementary organs of power: the local government offices, known as the yamen, and the temple of the town god. According to the popular religion of former days, the living were subject to the jurisdiction of the county government, represented by the feudal lords whose jails and execution grounds were located in the immediate vicinity, and the dead were ruled by the town god in his temple, assisted by the ox-and-horse faced demons of the nether world. Most of the residents in the town were either landlords or their vassals. The buildings inside the town were different from those of other places, in that they are lined on both sides with defensive walls several metres high, giving the town an aspect very much like that of a mediaeval European castle.

4. *Tongli* — the consumer type town.

Tongli, where my sister was born and where we lived for many years before moving to Songling, is located on the bank of the Grand Canal six kilometres away from Songling and 5.5 kilometres away from Tunzun Town, an important water communications centre between Suzhou and Shanghai. Tongli is surrounded by water on all sides, making it an island cut off from the outside world. Criss-crossed by rivers and linked up to rippling lakes and ponds, it is a town typical of this region of rivers and lakes. Before liberation, the town was only accessible by water, so all contacts with it had to be made by small boats. Strangers who were not familiar with the water-route would have to spend hours in this maze just to find their way in or out of this island town. Its geographical features of inaccessibility and isolation made the town an ideal refuge for the landlords and feudal bureaucrats; and in the pre-1949 days, it was the home of many such people. A statistical survey conducted during Land Reform showed that out of the town's total of two thousand households more than five hundred were landlord families. To make the island more aesthetically pleasing, they constructed gardens that are comparable in beauty to the famous ones in Suzhou. One of them is the "Tuisi" Garden, now under renovation, which is said to be the site of the well-known folk story "The Pearl Pagoda". Tongli used to be a consumer town which offered a variety of entertainment. At present, it is being turned into a tourist resort and has been a key cultural protectorate.

5. *Pingwang* — a town of the transportation type.

Pingwang is an important gateway between Jiangsu and Zhejiang provinces, leading to Suzhou in the north and Hangzhou in the south. Located in a position of strategic importance, the town suffered tremendous damages in wartime. From ancient Wu-Yue war rivalry in the Spring and Autumn Period (770-476 B.C.) to the local warlords' conflicts in modern times, Pingwang had always been a battlefield. During the War of Resistance Against Japan (1937-1945), it was almost laid waste by the Japanese invaders. In recent years Pingwang has become the crossroads of the main land and water traffic routes. The Grand Canal links up Suzhou and Hangzhou through the town. It has highways reaching Shanghai to the east, Zhejiang to the south and Nanjing and Anhui to the west. The town is the biggest communication centre in Wujiang County.

Pingwang's geographical position and transportation conditions give rise to the town's dual character. On the one hand, it is vulnerable to attack and destruction. Before 1949 the town experienced numerous ups and downs of this nature which deterred its development. On the other hand, due to its well developed transportation facilities and easy access to kinds of goods, it has all the right conditions for rapid economic development enabling it to recover from its repeated setbacks. Since the founding of the People's Republic of China and especially after the Third Plenary Session of the Eleventh C.P.C. Central Committee held in 1978, all of these advantages have been fully made use of in the town's economic development. Owing to its good transportation conditions, during the course of their expansion, several Shanghai factories settled on this town as the site for building their extensions. Pingwang thus stands out among all the small towns in Wujiang as the town with the highest speed of development.

However, it should be noted that the above-mentioned five different types of small towns are only tentative classifications in the qualitative analysis of small towns. They are furthermore limited only to the towns of Wujiang County which I am most familiar with. Without a doubt, further investigation would reveal other additional types. Small towns engaged mainly in fishery, for example, although small in terms of population, can be classified as an independent type in their own right. Apart from Wujiang County, the great variety of small towns all over China would certainly yield numerous additional types, like mining towns in mining areas. In many areas the commodity exchange centres where country fairs and all major local economic activities are held are still in the process of becoming stable towns. All of these need further investigation and study. So the five types I have listed here are by no means all inclusive.

The purpose of my classification of the small towns is to spotlight the individual characteristics of several specific small towns so that our concept of small towns will not stop at sweep-generalizations. But at the same time, while emphasizing the individuality of each small town, we should not ignore the common characteristic shared by the small towns either, that is all small towns are, regardless of their type, the political, economic and cultural centres of the countryside. The classification of small towns is based on this common characteristic, and is carried out according to their different individual traits. For instance, although Songling Town is most

conspicuously the county's political centre, at the same time
it also plays an important part in the economic and cultural life
of the nearby countryside. Similarly, although Zhenze is a
commodity collecting and distributing centre, and Shengze
the centre of local silk industry, they also serve respectively
as the political and cultural centres of their surrounding areas
as well. When I say that a certain town belongs to a certain
type, I am referring to its most outstanding trait.

Such classification brings to light the special characteristics
of each town which result from each town's particular course
of historical development and which decide the different approaches we must take towards each of them in their construction. Take the above-mentioned Tongli Town for example.
Formerly a refuge for landlords and retired bureaucrats, the
founding of socialist China put an end to its original economic
basis. Therefore, its economic development obviously cannot
follow Pingwang's model, as it lacks Pingwang's geographically advantageous location as the crossroad of the major water
and land routes. Nor can it follow Shengze's pattern, for it
doesn't have a traditional industry. However, unlike these two
afore-mentioned towns, Tongli has beautiful gardens and architecture typical of the region of rivers and lakes, and is criss-
crossed by rivers. It has all the necessary natural attributes
to be built into a garden-like town for convalescence and
tourism, a Victoria Island in China. The point I am trying to
make is that the classification of small towns according to
their individual characteristics will be conducive to deciding
the direction of future development of small towns.

III

The small towns in Wujiang County have undergone two
major stages of change since liberation, the early 1970s is the
dividing line between the two stages. The first stage was a
period of decline and recession in the small towns. During
this period, small towns gradually lost their basis of existence.
The situation did not improve until the early 1970s. The late

1970s, and especially the years after 1978, witnessed the rapid development and prosperity of small towns.

Between the 1950s and 1970s the total population of small towns in Wujiang County registered zero and sometimes even below-zero growth, while the population of the whole county increased rapidly. Shengze, for example, had a population of 22,000 in the early 1950s. In the following twenty years, its population kept falling, and the trend was not reversed until recently. By 1981, its population totalled only 26,000. If we take 22,000 as the base number, Shengze's total population should be no less than 40,000 today, according to the average national growth rate.

But Shengze's growth rate was by no means the lowest. Now let's turn to look at the population changes in the town of Tonglou, which is situated on the southern border of Wujiang County. Tonglou, known as Yanmu before liberation, is of the same type as Zhengze, and was formerly famous for its liquor and pork. Its population stood at 2,475 in 1952, 2,488 in 1962, 1,900 in 1972 and was 2,007 according to the 1982 census. There presents a decline of 19 per cent over the past thirty years.

The initial findings of our study show that this decline is attributable to many factors. In 1951, the year Land Reform was carried out, 60 shops in the town were closed as their owners returned to their native villages to till the land they had been apportioned during the reform. This resulted in about 150 people becoming farmers. In the same year, some twenty young men enlisted in the Chinese People's Volunteers and went to Korea, few of whom later returned to the town. Between 1952 and 1957, and especially during the socialist transformation of private commercial and industrial enterprises in 1956, another 200 people, most of whom were proprietors or apprentices, left the town. Among them, those with education went to work in the state enterprises in the nearby large or medium-sized cities, while those with one skill or another found employment in Shanghai suburbs and some county seats in Zhejiang Province. They were said to

be in pursuit of a new life, as they considered private businesses to be exploitative and felt it to be dishonourable even
to work in them. Then in 1958, when the nation went all out
to develop and assist agriculture, and in 1963, when city
workers and staff were encouraged to settle down in the
countryside, fifty more families left the town. Besides the
afore-mentioned outflow of population, the enrolment of young
people in colleges, high schools and vocational schools, the
recruitment of workers by other provinces and cities and high
school graduates' departure for the countryside resulted in
further decreases in the town's population.

Other small towns also experienced more or less the same
changes. Decrease in population is one of the indicators of
the decline of small towns. But what were the root causes of
their decline and what would be its consequences?

During the height of Agricultural Co-operative Movement
in 1957, I investigated the conditions at Kaixian'gong Village,
the results of which I discussed in my paper "Kaixian'gong
Revisited" (which is included in my book *Chinese Village
Close-up*). Although the peasants led a far better life than before the founding of new China, I found there that the traditional household side-line production had declined. The peasants told me that they had plenty to eat, but were short of
money. As a result of the nationwide implementation of a
policy one-sidedly emphasizing grain production little had
been done to restore the rural commodity economy in the two
decades which followed.

It was not until the early 1970s that the situation began to
change for the better as a result of the rise of commune- and
brigade-run industries. The Third Plenary Session of the Eleventh C.P.C. Central Committee in 1978 put into effect the
policy of developing a diversified rural economy, launching
the countryside on the road to all-round prosperity. When I
visited the village for the third time in 1981, instead of grum-
bling, my old friends talked to me about their incomes from
selling rabbit hair and asked me to help promote sales of the
products of their commune- and brigade-run factories. At

present, besides their commune- and brigade-run factories, the peasants also developed both collective and household sideline occupations, which enable them to exchange their own produce for money to buy what they need. Therefore, I was glad to have found that peasants not only had plenty to eat but also enough money to buy their daily necessities. Their being well fed, well clad, and having enough pocket money are undoubtedly specific indicators of the improvement of peasants' living standards and the thriving of the rural economy.

Linking together the changes I perceived during my two visits to Kaixian'gong and the fluctuations in the population of Tonglou, we can infer the causes and consequences of the decline of small towns. As grain production was taken as the key link of a single-sector economy, rural commodity production was completely neglected. Peasants, therefore, had very little goods to sell in the town markets, and the small towns virtually lost their economic basis as the collecting and distributing centres of the peasants' farm and sideline produce. Meanwhile, our efforts to turn all consumer cities and towns into producer ones and the nationalization of commerce seriously limited and curtailed the business activities of collective firms and private traders. Town dwellers who had to give up their former professions had to leave the towns to go hunt for jobs elsewhere. Thus, the towns could no longer sustain their populations. In a word, the "Left" deviationist policies of the period, based on the traditional ideology of one-sidedly emphasizing agriculture at the expense of commerce, was the root cause of the decline of small towns.

The decline of the small towns, in turn, severely hindered the development of their "footholds", that is, the agriculture and sideline occupations in the nearby countryside. Similarly, the lower the level of rural commodity economy sank, the more sharply the small towns which served as rural economic centres declined. Therefore, this vicious circle between the economics of the countryside and the towns was the inevitable outcome of the decline of the towns. Of course, the existence of this chain of causality still needs to be examined and proved in a nationwide perspective.

Here I will briefly comment about the problems of commercial channels. Before liberation, with the exception of salt, the circulation of all commodities between the countryside and towns was managed by private businessmen. After liberation, we adopted the system of state monopoly of purchase and marketing. Therefore, all products such as grain, edible oils, live pigs, silk cocoons and other major agricultural and side-line products as well as the means of agricultural production were brought into the state circulation channels. Departments handling grain, non-staple foods and import and export were set up at all administrative levels. At the county level, companies were set up with branches at all levels below it, right down to the villages.

This new circulation system severed the ties between those towns where there were no administrative organs and their surrounding rural areas. Nevertheless, before 1958, besides the state monopolized channels, there were still some other channels in the towns such as collectively-owned supply and marketing co-operatives, associated shops as well as specialized individual households.

The situation changed for the worse during the entire period from 1958, when the people's communes were established throughout the country, to 1976, when the cultural revolution came to an end, during which period collective and individual enterprises were severely restricted and constantly criticized. Even peasants selling a basket of eggs in the town would be criticized and considered to be "capitalist tails" (vestiges of capitalistic ideology) that ought to be "cut off". Under the policy of "utilizing, restricting and transforming private enterprises", many associated and co-operative shops were merged to form state-run commercial enterprises or state-run supply and marketing co-operatives. As a result only a few tea-houses and bakeries were left in some towns. The former collective supply and marketing co-operatives which the peasants had pooled together their money to establish were also brought under public ownership. In the end, almost all commodities were purchased and distributed in accordance with the administrative divisions, and the state-run commercial enterprises become the sole channel of commodity circulation.

The national unification of commerce brought about dramatic changes in the small towns. Towns where administrative departments were located enjoyed priority in access to the state commodity circulation channels in purchasing farm and sideline produce from the peasants as well as goods the peasants themselves needed. For this very reason, Songling Town, where the county government and commodity wholesale centre were located, was the sole exception to the general decline experienced by all the other small towns in Wujiang County. With the influx of cadres transferred from elsewhere to staff the newly added departments, its population remained quite stable and even increased a little. Those small towns with commune administrative offices, thanks to the state commercial establishments and the commune supply and marketing cooperatives, succeeded in struggling to remain above water.

But those lacking any administrative organs whatsoever were quite seriously depressed. In the Miaogang Commune, the towns of Lugang and Genglougang used to be commercial fishery ports along the southeastern bank of Taihu Lake like the town of Miaogang itself. Before liberation, during Lugang's heyday, its households were engaged in commercial business. Though not as big as Miaogang, its business scope still covered a total of over three square kilometres. Genglougang was a bit smaller, comprising only about twenty household-run small shops. After 1949, the district government and commune administrative offices were successively set up in Miaogang; and Lugang and Genglougang became Miaogang's subordinate township and brigade respectively, without any actual administrative offices set up in either of them. From 1956, the business enterprises in these two towns were gradually merged with the state-run enterprises in Miaogang, and most of their workers were transferred to work in the commune-run enterprises. During the period of the "cultural revolution" the market of Genglougang was completely swallowed up, and all that was left of this former fishery port was a deserted stone street and some shabby, hardly recognizable shop fronts. The entire town was reduced to a mere rural residential area. Lugang too lost most of its commercial business to Miaogang. However, Lugang, owing to its superior geographical location on the border of Qidu and Miaogang communes and with its "footholds" far from Miaogang, managed to remain a town with two commercial department stores, a tea-house and 30 commercial workers. Throughout the county most of the small towns which had no administrative offices were swallowed up. Places like Lugang, which, though incapacitated, still maintained their status as small towns, were few and far between.

Administrative control of the circulation of commodities inevitably made it difficult for the peasants to buy and to sell, but it gave much leeway to bureaucratic style of work in commercial enterprises. Peasants complained that the purchasing departments were always anxious and in a hurry when they wanted to obtain products, but at other times they would behave indifferently, and make little effort to try and find markets. The traditional multi-channelled rural commodity circulation system was replaced by the single channel of state commerce, which not only proved unsuitable to the rural commodity economy, but actually became an obstacle to rural economic development.

The nationalization of commerce was carried out under the rubric of "turning consumer cities into producer cities". This policy had a positive effect in promoting China's urban construction. But because we failed to come up with a correct understanding of the concepts of consumption and production, we therefore misunderstood the nature of small towns from the very start. In traditional Chinese thinking consumption was a rather indecent thing, being almost a synonym for laziness and living off other's fruit of labour, or, to use a modern term, exploitation. On the other hand, production, in a small-scale peasant economy, meant solid material production which excluded commodity circulation or exchange. In this way, on the one hand, the commodity circulation function of small towns was ignored, and on the other, their commercial activities were considered non-productive. The exploitation of the hired labourers by the landlord class and bureaucrats through commercial enterprises in town came to be regarded as the basic nature of all small towns. Gradually, the concepts of private commercial business activities, consumption and exploitation became interchangable, with the result that individual and collective commercial businesses in the small towns were either limited or suppressed entirely, greatly weakening the small towns' function as the commodity collecting and distributing centres of the rural areas.

However, industrial products or agricultural and sideline produce still had to circulate, and so a channel had to be created for this. Under the circumstances of all collective and individual commercial channels being blocked, there was no alternative but to nationalize the supply and marketing co-operatives and appoint the state-operated commercial enterprises as the sole circulation channels. Though the state commercial enterprises could monopolize the commodity circulation by administrative means, they could not provide employment for all those townspeople who had formerly worked in commercial business. Thus all those that were not employed by local state-run enterprises either had to find new jobs in Shanghai, Suzhou or other big and medium-sized cities and towns, as a great many did, or answer the government's call to settle down in the countryside to engage in material production. The new society would not permit the rise of a new generation of town idlers. In the end, those who remained behind in town were only the ill, the old, and the handicapped, who lived on their earnings from working in small handicraft industries, operated as sort of social welfare. This was demonstrated most clearly in the population changes of Tonglou Town, which showed that the disruption of its economic base both drained its population and blighted the town.

There are three additional points I would like to make. First, during the period of general decline of small towns, some towns in Wujiang County experienced exceptional growth. Wanping and Jinjiaba, for example, developed from rural villages into commercial towns. This was possible only because they were chosen as the seats of commune headquarters. Second, since the late 1950s, Wujiang's industry had developed a great deal as compared with the old days. For instance, Shengze's silk industry has developed from a group of household handicraft workshops into mechanized modern silk industry, complete with a series of specialized technological production processes. But these county industries are all under administration of the county industrial departments which have little connections with the small towns. Third, the decline of some small towns was attributable to natural disasters and geographical change. For example, Nanku, five kilometres to the southeast of Songling, used to be a major port on Taihu Lake in northwest Wujiang with a capacity for accommodating 300 to 400 fishing boats and waterweed collecting boats which went out every day. It was a prosperous commercial town. In 1949, the town was flooded and its shops damaged. With the establishment of the people's communes, a portion of the lake's banks were encircled for land reclamation, and as a result, Nanku was separated from the lake and lost its position as a port. This, together with administrative changes, further led to the disappearance of its market.

IV

Personally witnessing both the decline of small towns in the 1950s brought about by the termination of their function as rural commodity circulation centres and the one-sided emphasis on grain production in the countryside, as well as their quick recovery in the early 1980s after the revitalization of the peasant household sideline production, combined to produce the erroneous impression that their revival was the result of the development of rural commodity production in both agricultural and sideline occupations. However, the conclusion of my later investigations was that the major and direct cause of the revival of the small towns in Wujiang County was the rapid development of the commune- and brigade-run industries, and the acceleration of commodity circulation rather than the diversification of the rural economy.

Take for example the town of Xinta, bordering on the suburbs of Shanghai. In the period prior to 1975, it was restricted to grain production as its sole farming activity and pig-raising as its only permissible sideline production. As a result, its economy went downhill, with average annual income of its members fluctuating around 150 yuan. Lacking sufficient capital for the maintenance and repair of its houses, let alone for starting new capital construction, the town of Xinta became delapidated, many of its residential houses falling into disrepair, and its two narrow streets becoming increasingly dirty and shabby.

Since 1975 great changes have taken place in the town. Many new factories and houses have been built, together with a cinema capable of holding an audience of more than a thousand. The newly-completed residential district, with an 18-metre-wide street, gives the town a modern look. Since 1975 a total of over 3.5 million yuan (RMB) has been invested in capital construction, of which over 2.5 million, or 72 per cent of the total, came from the profits turned over to the commune by the thirteen commune-run factories.

Except for the oil pump factory, which grew out of the farm tools factory founded in 1958, the year of the Great Leap Forward, all the other commune-run factories were set up after 1975. According to 1982 statistics, three among these factories, the oil pump factory, light bulb factory and bus factory, have each an annual output value exceeding one million yuan. With its brigade-run factories included, the Xinta Commune boasts a total of 57 enterprises with a total annual output of 10.26 million yuan and a combined employment of 2,098 commune members, accounting for 17 per cent of the commune's total labour force. According to calculations based on the wages for commune members engaged in actual industrial production and on the profits put aside for year-end distribution to these workers, each of the commune's 20,000 members derived an average yearly income of 49 yuan from industry, accounting for 15 per cent of the average annual per capita income.

An analysis of the composition of the commune's output value that same year reveals that agricultural production accounted for 33 per cent, sideline production for 13 per cent and industrial production 54 per cent. In the commune's average annual per capita income of 327 yuan, agricultural production accounted for 190 yuan, industrial production for 49 yuan and household sideline production 88 yuan.

This demonstrates clearly that the establishment of commune- and brigade-run factories in the mid-1970s enabled Xinta to break away from the previous single-sector economic practice of engaging solely in grain production. The development of industry further opened up a major source of funds for capital construction in the town, increased the peasants' yearly income and provided jobs for nearly one-fifth of the labour force.

The situation in Xinta is quite typical, not only of Wujiang County but even of the whole area of southern Jiangsu Province. In summing up the positive role the commune- and brigade-run industry has played, all commune leaders stressed the following three points: it has provided employment opportunities, increased income and accelerated the construction of small towns. What was it that enabled commune- and brigade-run industry to spring up and develop so rapidly all over southern Jiangsu in the 1970s?

Due to its large population and insufficient arable land, southern Jiangsu is an area where agriculture and industry have historically long been closely linked together, each supplementing the other. Such mutual reinforcement has a long history in southern Jiangsu and resulted in its being rather affluent, as compared with other areas. The denser the population in a given area, the less average cultivated land there is per person. As a result, dense population concentration and economic development are mutually contradictory in an agricultural society.

Furthermore agricultural production is restricted by natural conditions and there have been harvest fluctuations even in high yield areas. Take Zhenze Township for example. 1979 was a year of bumper harvests there when its total agricultural output value reached 8,500,000 yuan while the figure was only 2,200,000 (as against the average figure of 6,000,000 yuan of the recent six years) in 1981 when the area suffered serious natural calamities. The per capita income of 1981 would have decreased sharply had it not been for the development of rural industry. While the yield per unit area has to be further increased, the capacity for such increase is limited, and there have been some cases in which increases in output have failed to bring about a rise in income.

The traditional economic pattern of supplementing agriculture with handicraft industry, which has been summed up as "men do the farming while women do the weaving", was an ingenious method devised by our ancestors to get around the seemingly impassible obstacle presented by a large population and insufficient arable land. This combination of agriculture and handicraft industry dates back several thousand years. As early as the 1930s, when I first investigated a village in this region, I found that quite a few peasant households derived half of their income from agriculture and half from handicraft industry. Indeed, in a place with such high population density and limited farm land as southern Jiangsu, it is impossible to get rich by farming alone. To really prosper, one must in addition develop the processing of farm and sideline products as well as the household handicraft industry.

In the eyes of modern people, the mutual supplementation and reinforcement of agriculture and industry is quite simple and natural, but from the point of view of our predecessors, it must have been a rather remarkable innovation. It would probably utterly exceed their expectations that we have now inherited this tradition and developed it on such an unprecedented scale. The commune- and brigade-run industries established nationwide today, which enable large numbers of rural people to engage in industrial production without leaving the countryside, are rooted right in this tradition. They are the inevitable result of the ever-growing contradiction between our large population and limited arable land.

Talking to rural cadres at the basic level about population growth during investigation I have conducted in the countryside during the past few years, I found that they invariably felt it to be a crushing pressure. Ever since those born in the post-liberation baby boom came of age and joined the rural labour force in the mid-60s, job shortages began to appear in the countryside. Since then, the annual growth rate of the rural labour force has been continuously rising, bringing in its wake the soaring cash value of the work points. But the annual rate of increase of grain production in the corresponding period kept dropping with each passing year. Around the 1970s, it seemed to have reached its maximum, and began fluctuating around the same level. At this point, the peasants began to contend for work points and the problem of surplus labour force became ever more prominent. Once a county Party secretary estimated that if the existing level of labour productivity remained unchanged and the present grain output didn't decrease, between one-third to one half of the county's total labour force would be left idle.

Such a big army of surplus labourers would constitute an irrepressible force for change. Once the conditions were ripe, it would burst free from all restricting fetters with great momentum and emancipate itself. This pressure was the very driving force behind the establishment of commune- and brigade-run industries.

However, population density, land shortage and the tradition of household handicraft industries supplementing agriculture were only inherent driving forces behind the rise of rural industry, certain external factors were also required to set the phenomenon in motion. The social conditions created by the "cultural revolution" provided just this set of external factors. The ten years of turmoil of the "cultural revolution" brought great losses to China, but I must say that in a certain sense, Wujiang County and perhaps even the entire southern

Jiangsu Province managed to find a silver lining in this dark cloud, as it was in this difficult period that the commune- and brigade-run industry arose and unexpectedly developed. This may at first sound implausible, but it will prove to be quite understandable if we probe into circumstances surrounding the emergence and development of a few such factories.

The establishment of industry requires materials, labour, money, equipment, technology and a market for its products. The countryside has an abundant supply of the required labour force, but where can its commune- and brigade-run industries come by the other four requirements? A chemical factory in Tonglou was indeed started from scratch in 1968, with the help of the father of a city youth who settled down in the commune that year. The father worked in a city chemical factory, and upon learning that a city chemical factory had failed to meet the urgent need of another factory for a certain chemical product, he helped the town of Tonglou get in touch with the latter factory and conclude a deal. In accordance with their agreement the factory supplied raw material, technology, equipment and even part of the funds the commune required to set up the chemical factory. Examples of this kind are typical of many of the rural factories in southern Jiangsu Province. People from the commune- and brigade-run factories told me that at that time factories in big and medium-sized cities offered to help communes in their vicinity set up factories.

Why was that? The reason was very simple. The normal production in big and medium-sized urban enterprises was interrupted when their workers began making "revolution". However, people cannot live without commodities. As the situation in the countryside was then relatively stable, the production of some commodities which could not be carried out in the cities was shifted to the countryside. In carrying out this shift, the urban educated youth and the cadres who went to settle in the countryside and the retired workers whose homes were there originally acted as go-betweens. Of course, few of them realized the far-reaching significance of their actions at the time. It was under these circumstances of production demands exceeding capacity and voluntary mediators stepping forward to bridge the gap between cities and the countryside that commune- and brigade-run industries first came into being. By the end of the "cultural revolution", the commune- and brigade-run factories had passed their most critical phase of development and entered a period of further expansion.

The development of industry was different from that of agriculture; the location of commune- and brigade-run factories, for instance, must be easily accessible to peasants going to work, on the one hand, and transportation facilities on the other. The dwindling former small towns fit all these requirements. In Wujiang County, the commune- and brigade-run factories were mainly located in towns where commune headquarters were seated. The towns directly administered by the county government were not under the jurisdiction of the communes, and therefore, commune- and brigade-run factories could not penetrate them, but rather has to set up operations in their periphery or areas close by them.

Within the seven towns directly under the administration of the county government in Wujiang co-exist two types of factories: county-run factories and township factories. The development of the former dates back to the 1950s and 1960s. These factories have played a positive role in providing a livelihood for some of the townspeople and employment opportunities for the nearby peasants. But their performance and management have little economic impact on the town itself, as they pay their taxes and submit their profits only to the state and the county government. The latter developed mainly out of the mini-handicraft industries which were staffed by the townsfolk who had stayed behind, and were run for social welfare purposes. Like the commune- and brigade-run factories, they developed during the "cultural revolution", when administrations at all levels had to look for their own financial resources.

In the later period of the "cultural revolution", all levels of administration, from the county to the brigade level, started vigorously setting up factories, extending their efforts to include even schools. Zhenze Middle School is one of the best middle schools in Jiangsu Province, and has produced quite a number of talented persons. But oddly enough, part of its achievement must be attributed to its production of medicine bottle corks, which played a key role in providing funds for the school's teaching equipment, the teachers' dormitories and students' food subsidies. Without these earnings from the school factory, the school principal simply could never have managed to run the school with only the insufficient funds he had been allotted.

This was likewise the case with both the commune and county administrations. As the entire country was suffering from the effects of the "Left" deviationist policies implemented during the "cultural revolution", they were short of funds to carry out any construction. Because of this shortage the county government managed to build only 10 kilometres of highway during the whole decade (not including roads built with funds supplied from above). Such being the case, how else could they get funds except by setting up their own industries? Despite the prohibitory "Left" rules and regulations against small, local industries at that time, administrations at various local levels started to seek their own means of opening up financial resources.

The Third Plenary Session of the Eleventh C.P.C. Central Committee not only put an end to the "Left" policies practised for many years but also advocated economic reforms, thus clearing the way for the long frustrated development of the commune- and brigade-run industries as well as other small rural industries, which resulted in their unprecedented growth. This shows that the recovery of the small towns in southern Jiangsu was the result of the rise of small rural industries, and especially the commune- and brigade-run industries.

The rural collective commerce has not yet really started to develop. As social scientists, we must not only look at the development and growth of small towns as a general phenomenon, but more importantly, we must examine in what specific areas the small towns have developed and prospered, and what effect their development has had on their relationship

with the countryside. So now I would like to switch from discussing the above-mentioned concrete changes in the small
towns in Wujiang County and return to the question of the
relationship between the small towns and the countryside,
examining such things as the current state of industry, commerce and service trade in these small towns, and making a
tentative exploration of the basic problem of how to really
transform the small towns into rural political, economic and
cultural centres.

V

Since the Third Plenary Session of the Eleventh C.P.C. Central Committee, urban industrial production has returned to
normal, and, after undergoing the readjustment, reform and
consolidation of the past few years, has even experienced rapid development. Thus two diametrically opposed views have
been raised concerning the future of the small town industries.
One holds that the stagnation of urban industrial production
during the "cultural revolution" created an opportunity for
the birth and growth of the small town industries, the revival
and development of which would, therefore, undoubtedly pose
a threat to the rural industries. The second view holds that the
two are complementary to each other, therefore, there is no
need to worry about the future of rural industry. Though different, these two views touch upon the same issue, namely, how
to approach and deal with the relationship between big urban
industries and the small rural commune- and brigade-run factories. As the issue has cropped up in the course of social
development, we should study it with an eye to the course of
its development.

It is true that the commune- and brigade-run factories are
confronted with a host of problems. As they came into being
spontaneously, most of their products have so far not yet been
included in the state plan and they are dependent on the market economy for obtaining raw materials and energy. Consequently, the resumption of production and constant expansion

of the large factories in the cities has created difficulties for the enterprises run by production brigades with respect to obtaining supplies of raw materials and energy, giving rise to a contradiction between the collective and the state.

This contradiction, unless solved properly, is a hotbed of "unhealthy tendencies". The heads of these enterprises or people in charge of their supply and marketing try by hook or crook to get supplies of raw materials and energy through "the back door" or by using pull. These enterprises have to find outlets for their products themselves, and many rural cadres are fairly ignorant of both the industrial market situation as well as supply and marketing. Consequently, there have been cases of their being fooled in business, cases of the blind production of products which turn out to be unsalable on the market, and cases of factories operating in an on-and-off manner. All this gives rise to the latent dangers of production suspension due to poor sales or lack of raw materials, and of operating at a loss or even going bankrupt.

Nevertheless, we must not blame this unstability on the regulatory role of the market, which plays a decisive part in rural industrial production. On the contrary, with regard to commune- and brigade-run factories we should find a way of making the market regulatory forces serve the steady development of industrial enterprises under socialism.

First of all, we must see that the subsequent resumption of production in the city factories did not affect the existence of all the small rural factories, which had already gained a firm footing in the countryside as it was more advantageous for some industries or certain part of some industries to be run by communes or production brigades. Favourable conditions exist in the countryside for the development of such small factories, such as availability of land to build factories on, more surplus labour, lower wages, relative ease of management and the willingness of the peasants to transfer from agriculture to industry. Therefore, we must not treat the commune- and brigade-run industry in a vague, general way, but rather proceed from the concrete realities of different types of factories. Here I will briefly introduce the three types of commune- and brigade-run factories I saw during my visit.

Quite a number of the commune- and brigade-run factories in Wujiang County are textile factories. As the region has a long tradition of engaging in the silk fabric handicraft and an abundant labour force, the labour-intensive textile industry should be very profitable here and have a ready and stable market. However, a large number of these silk factories turned to manufacturing synthetic fibres in the 1970s, when there was a seemingly insatiable demand for chemical fabrics and their supply was limited. But along with the rapid development of the synthetic fibre industry in the big cities and the changes in people's taste in recent years, Wujiang's commune- and brigade-run textile factories lost much of their markets. Faced with fierce competition from their urban counterparts, the sales agents of these small factories adopted the tactic of selling their products in remote and mountainous areas. Some have gone as far as the mountainous areas of Fujian, Anhui and Qinghai provinces. In spite of all this, these factories still incurred sizable losses when the prices for chemical fabric products were cut last year.

The vegetable processing factory in Miaogang is another type. Set up in 1980, it now has altogether thirty regular workers and produces various kinds of pickles, its main products being small cucumbers and rutabaga. The raw materials of the factory are all grown locally by the peasants. In 1982, the factory purchased a total of 1.1 million yuan worth of vegetables from the peasants, greatly benefiting these growers. The factory turns out both semi-processed and processed vegetables. The former are sold to Shanxi while the latter, besides being marketed locally, are sold to Shanghai, Suzhou and a number of Southeast Asian countries. Unlike its counterparts engaged in manufacturing textiles, this factory earns an annual profit of 150,000 yuan.

The third type of local rural factories I wish to introduce is the factory in the town of Pingwang which is affiliated with the Shanghai No. 3 Sewing Machine Factory. The factory was built with capital invested by the Shanghai No. 3 Sewing Machine Factory and Wujiang County Farm Tool Factory. With the former providing the raw materials, it produces the necessary components and does some assembling on the one hand, while also contracting with several commune- and brigade-run factories to manufacture the machine stands and bases for both the Shanghai No. 3 Sewing Machine Factory as well as itself. The production and management of this type of small factories is mapped out in line with the production plans of the Shanghai factory, from which it receives the necessary technological guidance. The profits of this affiliated factory are divided equally between the Shanghai factory and itself.

These perhaps are the three basic types of the existing commune- and brigade-run factories in Wujiang. The first is a type which mostly takes advantage of the abundant local labour force, but lacks both local supplies of raw material and a local market. With its present low technical level, lack of funds and backward means of information circulation, the main channel of which is still direct personal contact, instability in its production and marketing are inevitable. The second type of rural factory, apart from making use of ample local labour resources, is also privileged with a guaranteed local supply of raw materials as well as a fairly stable market. As this type of factory exploits its local advantages to the full, it is the most stable type of commune- and brigade-run industry. As is the case in the first type of factory, the materials used by the third type are not produced locally, but rather supplied by a big urban factory. Basically a subsidiary workshop of an expanded larger factory, it enjoys both stable production and market so long as it maintains close connections with the big factory.

The first type of factory accounts for the absolute majority of the small rural factories in Wujiang County; the second type are next most common, while only a few of the third type have been established. So, from the point of view of their overall make-up, the commune- and brigade-run factories in Wujiang County are still in a formative period.

The above classification of the commune- and brigade-run industry is intended to show that the development of commune- and brigade-run factories, which is subject to market regulation, must be oriented towards making full use of their geographical and local advantages. This is the only means by which they can achieve stability and growth. Therefore, the countryside should focus on the promotion of industries of the second type, that is, on the development of the food and non-staple food industries as well as light and textile industries which reflect the characteristics of each locality.

The first type of industry, which emerged as a result of the stagnation of production during the "cultural revolution" and which has serious problems in supply of raw materials and marketing, seems to have finished playing its role as a pioneer in small rural industries. Whether this kind of industry has a future depends much on the outcome of the structural reform of national industry as a whole.

However, the future of the third type is more promising. As high population density, the rising cost of land and urban salaries and serious pollution problems have pushed the development of certain urban industries to the limits, the expansion of large urban factories into the rural areas has become a general trend not only in China, but throughout the world. Besides expanding into the urban suburbs and rural areas of their own countries, big capitalist urban enterprises have begun even to find their way into the third world countries. Such expansion has sometimes resulted in environmental damage. But in a socialist country like ours such evil consequences can be avoided.

We advocate that large urban factories lend assistance to commune- and brigade-run factories, and that commune- and brigade-run factories help those even smaller collectively and individually run enterprises. This is actually a mutually beneficial practice. Large factories can lower their costs by entrusting small rural factories the production of certain of their spare parts and components, while the small rural factories can attain stability in production. A recent report revealed

that the commune- and brigade-run royal jelly processing factory at Yinling Commune divided the task of producing the
producer's packaging among all of its production teams, to
give them an opportunity to make some extra income. This is
an example of the socialist relations of mutual help and benefit among various industrial enterprises.

All industrial enterprises, big or small, must make efforts
to put an end to their current wasteful self-sufficiency oriented
set-ups. Along with the development of specialized production,
enterprises should extend its production into the suburban and
rural areas rather than concentrating themselves in the urban
areas. However, it should be stressed that such extension should
bring with it increased job opportunities and income, not
pollution. In fact, this kind of extension enables urban enterprises to concentrate on raising the quality of their products
and improving their management, thus increasing their profits.

Restructuring the present self-sufficiency oriented industrial enterprises is by no means a matter of formality. The first
and foremost question, we must consider in extending urban
enterprises into the countryside should be the livelihood of
the vast rural population who will be affected. We must bear
in mind the painful lessons of industrial development in the
Western countries, which brought widespread bankruptcy to
the countryside. Secondly, we must make sure that the administration and management of our enterprises conforms to China's
present conditions.

It is undeniable that our lack of experience in running large-
scale enterprises has resulted in many of our large state-run
enterprises operating at a loss. Even some of the commune-
and brigade-run factories which have expanded the scale of
their operations a little bit find themselves, as it were, like a
man on his first horse ride, who "once having mounted is
frightened but unable to dismount". For this reason, the sizes
of the commune- and brigade-run factories as well as their
management and administration must be maintained at a level
suitable to the present rural conditions. We must proceed on
this basis to train a large contingent of managerial personnel

through practice at the grass-roots level, preparing qualified personnel for China's further large-scale industrial development.

Commune- and brigade-run factories have a seemingly indomitable vitality. Once I visited a brigade-run factory, which at the time was operating at a loss. On inquiring about their future plans, I was told that the factory would continue operations, no matter whether or not it was profitable. As almost every household in the village had a member or two working in the factory, shutting down the factory would go against the grain of all the villagers, who would rather earn less than nothing at all. Such factories are the expanded or collectivized form of the traditional household handicraft industries, which calculated only their general income and were actually quite unfamiliar with the concept of salary. Therefore, even though strictly speaking the factory was operating in the red, the peasants' general income nevertheless increased, thanks to their wages from the factory. The determination to continue operating despite the loss fully demonstrates the inherent tenacity of China's rural commune- and brigade-run factories. Such a vitality is rooted in their rural handicraft origins, as well as the particular conditions of the Chinese countryside. They have enabled these factories to weather all unfavourable situations.

To continue operating the factory despite incurring losses, employing one worker from each family and granting equal job opportunities for all, all of this would seem to deviate from the principles of modern industrial management, which emphasizes profitability and hiring only the best qualified personnel. To realize the modernization of industry, improvements must be made in all of these areas. However, these are merely phenomena determined by China's particular rural conditions which are characterized by high population density, insufficient farmland and the traditional practice of supplementing industry with agriculture. It would be hardly possible to change them without first changing the basic social conditions. Therefore, the problem now is how to turn such a situation to the advantage of establishing a new industry.

At the core of Japanese principle of management is the traditional relationship of dependence, which can be summarized as "we take care of you all your life, so you must work for us till your last day". The traditional system of interpersonal relations in rural China is much wider and deeper than this. Of course, such relations have both a good and a bad side. We should analyse and investigate them, carefully noting to what extent they can be used to our purpose. We must never adopt a nihilistic attitude towards our past. To truly understand China's characteristics and carry out our programme of socialist modernization in accordance with them we must, first of all, conscientiously study China's past, as this is what determines its present and future.

VI

The development of rural industry is narrowing the gap between town and country and is alleviating urban population pressure. In those production brigades where the per capita income exceeds 500 yuan (RMB), the peasants enjoy practically the same standard of living as the city residents in food, clothing, and housing. And the development of collective economy has made it possible to start collective welfare facilities such as building local roads, subsidizing house construction, providing free medical care and establishing a retirement system for the aged, providing material encouragement to children going to school, improving the life of those who enjoy the "five guarantees",* all of which have consolidated the basis of socialism in the countryside and have made the peasants more collective-oriented. The past few years have witnessed city population going back to the countryside in the areas around Shanghai, and the girls who were reluctant to marry peasant youths have begun to change their minds.

---

* The five guarantees are food, clothing, medical care, housing and burial expenses provided to childless and infirm old persons.

As a result of the change in rural economic structure, a large number of peasants formerly engaged in farming have gone over to the rural industrial sector, and there have appeared labourers who are concurrently engaged in both agriculture and industry. They are known as "peasant workers". They live in the countryside, work in the small factories run by production brigades in normal times, look after household sideline occupation in their spare time and do farm work during the busy seasons. Among their family members, there are both people engaged in agriculture and people engaged in industry, constituting a unit of subsistence that combines agriculture and industry. Such a combination facilitates the development both of industry and of agriculture. On the one hand, it provides cheap labour needed in the initial stage of rural industrialization and reduces industrial costs, and on the other, it absorbs surplus labour in the countryside and facilitates agriculture mechanization.

According to our study, during the last five or six years, the actual population of the small towns we investigated has increased by one-third. The most tiring and heaviest jobs, and those with worst working conditions are usually done by the peasants. In fact, they have become new members of the working class. Yet most of them still do not have the status of permanent registered town resident. Incomplete 1982 statistics shows that 5.27 million peasants were engaged in industrial production in Jiangsu that year, while the total urban labour force with registered permanent resident status that year numbered 6.06 million. In other words, within the urban labour force, the total number of peasant workers and that of workers with status of registered permanent town residents are drawing closer. At present, the former are actually shouldering over one-third of industrial production tasks of the small towns. However, without the status of permanent registered urban residents, they lack many of the benefits their townsfolk counterparts enjoy. As an ever-growing labour force, playing an increasingly larger role in the development of small town industry, questions concerning their social status as well as their living and working conditions deserve immediate attention and call for further research. Theirs is a situation unprecedented in China's industrial history, and the question as to what role they will play in the China's industrial development is a matter of significance.

The development of rural industry in southern Jiangsu Province has brought about social changes in many respects. The rate of population growth has never exceeded 10 per thousand since 1974 and it dropped to below 3 per thousand in 1979, though it has risen a bit in the past two or three years. The people in this area, who used to control population growth by infanticide, have now adopted modern contraceptive measures, and there is little obstruction in family planning. In the past few years, the proportion between new-born male and female infants has become normal as against the previous case of males exceeding females. Most couples prefer to have two children and it is rather difficult to persuade them to have only one. However, most married women working in the rural factories have no objection to having only one child, and neither do the working couples living in towns.

There is little population flow in the countryside. People moving in or out of Kaixian'gong Village, for instance, constitute only less than 1 per cent. Young people tend to find their spouses in their own village. The outflow population are mostly people who go out to find jobs without changing their residence registration. There have been more young people willing to stay in their villages as a result of improved living conditions in recent years.

With this improvement in their lives, the peasants' main desire now is to build houses and have more furniture. Among the 250 families in Kaixian'gong Village (medium low living standard) 50 rooms were repaired within a year at the cost of 1,000 yuan (RMB) per room. Two-storey houses of six rooms each have been built in Jinxing No. 2 Brigade (high living standard). And the Nongchuang Brigade (top living standard) has provided subsidies to all its members for building two-storey houses of 24 rooms each, all of which are to be completed within two years.

Generally speaking, the peasants build houses before their children get married and the cost of the houses is part of the expenditure for the wedding. A bridal chamber is generally furnished at the cost of around 2,000 yuan (RMB). The call to hold thrifty weddings has not been very effective in the countryside. Cremation is now an accepted practice, but the ashes of the dead are still buried in the land originally belonging to him. There have been more disputes in recent years with respect to the obligation of supporting the elders or between mothers-in-law and the daughters-in-law, which shows that family relations are undergoing changes. It is not rare that two generations living in the same house have their meals separately. There are fewer superstitious activities and the Kitchen God in each family has been removed. However, there are still people who worship gods or Buddha.

Some social problems still exist at present. The spare time life of the young people is rather dull. They have only a limited education and consequently their interests are narrow. There are no organized recreational activities, and few films are shown in a village during the year. Because power is frequently cut off, television is not very attractive either. Public order in the countryside is on the whole good, though there have been some cases of hooliganism. The gap between the young and the old is widening, which is quite obvious in women's dress. Old women still wear traditional style dress, and middle-aged women continue to wrap their heads with towels, but most young girls, and especially those working in the rural factories, have begun to wave their hair and dress in a style which is practically the same as that of young women in cities and towns.

VII

The small towns, as the rural centres for collecting farm and sideline produce and distributing industrial goods, are closely linked with rural economic development. At present, one of the major tasks facing us is to clarify the various links and barriers in commodity circulation between the small towns and their surrounding villages, so as to unclog the circulation channels.

By the "links" in commodity circulation, we mean the different intermediaries the commodities must pass through before they finally reach the consumers. Take for example a shipment of a certain industrial product produced in a factory in Shanghai. It is first transported to Suzhou, where the commercial department there allocates it to Wujiang County. Then the county's commercial department reallocates it to the township. The township supply and marketing co-operative then sells it wholesale to the retail stores, where, at long last, it finally reaches the consumers. Thus, the shipment must pass through a total of five intermediaries. By the same token, the farm and sideline products also go through a similarly complex procedure from the opposite direction in being shipped from the rural villages to the cities. In the following, we will examine each of the links the commodities have to pass through, and specific effect each link has on commodity circulation.

Let us leave big and medium-sized cities aside for the moment and have a look at the commodity circulation links between small towns and the countryside. A closer look at the concrete case of each small town reveals that though they are generally categorized as small towns, they actually differ from one another in terms of their respective sizes and administrative levels.

My classification of small towns in part II shows that different types of small towns play different roles. Even small towns of the same type may play different roles and cannot be treated as invariably the same. Zhenze and Miaogang, for instance, are both collecting and distributing centres for farm and sideline products, but Zhenze's scope of commercial activity is much larger than that of Miaogang. Therefore, the difference in their roles, and consequently the extent of their influence, are reflections of the multi-level administrative system.

In the past, the population size of a town determined its level in the social hierarchy. At present, however, this is no longer the case in deciding the commercial functions of a small town. The multi-level administrative system is now a decisive factor in the process of commodity circulation. In such a system, the administrative location of a small town determines very much its role in commodity circulation.

The small towns in Wujiang County can be divided into three levels and five degrees, based on their administrative locations. The first level includes the seven towns directly under the jurisdiction of the county government. Each of these seven small towns has commercial departments set up by the town and nearby communes. Among these, the county seat, Songling, also has commercial departments set up by the county government.

The second level is composed of 16 commune towns where commune commercial departments are located. The three towns of Bache, Tongluo and Hengshan whose commercial population is close to that of towns under county jurisdiction, also have county commercial departments, their scope of management exceeding that of the respective communes in which they are located.

The 12 brigade towns (or village towns) constitute the third level, having no commercial administrative departments whatsoever. From this we can see that the commodity circulation links are based on the different levels of administrative organizations. However the actual flow of commodities through these links is more complicated than it appears to be.

Kaixian'gong Village, for example, has a small shop which sells matches, sweets, cigarettes, wine, soy sauce, salt and other daily necessities. When I visited it, I noted three aluminium pans which, I was told, had been on the shelf for a whole year. In response to my query as to whether or not the villagers used aluminium pans, I was told that they did, but did not buy them here. In purchasing durable goods such as pans, which will last them several years, they need more alternatives to choose from than the shop can offer. So when they are in need of such items, they go to Zhenze or Miaogang to buy them. When the young people in the village get married, they go to Shanghai or Suzhou to buy the things they need for decorating the wedding chamber.

In general, the peasants' demands for various daily necessities are met separately by towns at different levels. Ordinarily, the peasants get things like edible oil, salt, soy sauce and vinegar from their village shops. A village town usually has fewer than ten such shops, which serve a radius of one kilometre. Such daily necessities as thermos flasks, washing basins, and other low-grade durable goods, are generally supplied by the commune towns or the towns directly under the county jurisdiction. Each commune town usually has 10 to 50 shops, with a total service radius of about three kilometres. As goods of the same type are generally sold by only one shop in the commune towns, they are quite limited both in variety and quality. In towns directly under the county jurisdiction, however, the same type of goods are sold by two or more shops, offering the peasants a greater variety to choose from. A county town usually has 50 to 100 shops, which serve an area of about five kilometres.

The sales scope of small towns at higher levels overlaps with that of the small towns at lower levels. That is to say, the small towns at higher levels not only deal in commodities that are excluded from the business dealings of the small towns at lower levels, but also in those items included in the business scope of these latter small towns. For instance, if the peasants from the commune towns of Miaogang, Qidu and Badu as well as those from their subordinate villages all go to Zhenze to buy aluminium pans, the scope of Zhenze's sales of aluminium pans then includes all of its surrounding commune towns and villages. But Zhenze not only sells aluminium pans, but also sells edible oil, salt, soy sauce and vinegar. However the scope of its sales of these things is hardly any bigger than that of a village town like Lugang, being limited to the residents within the radius of one kilometre. This business scope is actually the town's "foothold" as the local people usually refer to it. A town's "foothold" is never a regular circle. Rather, as has been shown, every commodity has its own "foothold", and a small town has a great many commercial "footholds" with different radiuses. The actual level of any given small town is determined by the radii of its commercial "footholds".

Commercial establishments should be distributed in small towns in such a way so as to enable the peasants to spend the least amount of time and money to get the most satisfactory goods. Therefore, the shops should be clear about what kinds of goods they should stock and in what quantity. Otherwise, they will run short of goods in great demand, while unpopular items will pile up in their warehouses.

It is quite obvious that the rationalization of circulation links is the prerequisite for smooth commodity circulation. The realization of such rationalization calls for further careful study.

But unclogging the commodity circulation channels is even more important. In the last few years, the revived rural fairs have done a thriving business in the small towns of Wujiang County. On each market day, you can see peasants carrying shoulder poles loaded with their farm and sideline produce to the fair, and pedlars' stands lining the streets, as the entire town bustles with activity. In Zhenze, plastic-tiled booths have been built along the market place so that people selling or buying can seek shelter in the event it rains. This is praiseworthy. However, these markets are still in a primitive state. The peasants just sell what they have carried to town on market days. They may have to wait for half a day to sell a basket of eggs. This backward state is, to my opinion, the major problem hindering the further development of small towns.

How should commodity circulation be improved in the small towns? A short time ago, I received a letter from some friends in Songling, asking me to help them buy a truck to transport their mushrooms to Suzhou. In 1981, I brought back to my hometown some mushroom spores given by an Australian friend. The next year, the staff in the agrotechnical station of Wujiang County and Songling Town succeeded growing this type of mushroom, pleurotus ostreatus, and introduced it to the peasants, giving it the pretty name "phoenix tail". Because of its high nutritive and economic value as well as its easy cultivability, it quickly became a very popular sideline product in the rural areas and a favourite food in Suzhou, Shanghai and other cities. But transporting the crop still stands out as a serious problem.

It dawned upon me that new circulation channels must opened up for new commodities. The development of new commodities calls for and stimulates people to create new channels. As it is difficult to do away with the existing barriers in circulation, we should support and encourage the producers to organize themselves to try and do so. All success comes from trial and error. The key to the vigorous development of small towns lies in actively seeking and experimenting with new approaches to development.

This also convinced me that it is imperative to thoroughly study the question of scale in rural commodity production. The rapid increase in the output of their mushrooms prompted the peasants to buy trucks to solve the circulation problem. If local commodity production (excluding that of the commune- and brigade-run factories) was insufficient to satisfy the market demands of the residents of the nearby towns and communes, the peasants would never have abandoned their shoulder poles and buckets in favour of motorized transportation.

In fact the reason that the small town commerce develops more slowly than that of the commune- and brigade-run industries is that the existing commercial circulation channels have not become strong enough to break the monopoly in commodity circulation.

At present, the rural economy is in the midst of evolving from the more elementary stage contract responsibility system for production to the higher stage of a diversified economy featuring specialized production. This is sure to accelerate the rural commodity production in a big way and fundamentally reshuffle the present stagnant situation. We must consciously accustom ourselves to and promote this development, and endeavour which will lead us to a bright future.

VIII

Now I would like to turn to the question of how to transform small towns into the service, culture, and education centres of the countryside.

During my fourth visit to Kaixian'gong Village, the cinema in the town of Zhenze was showing *Shaolin Temple*, a popular *kungfu* film. Peasants from the nearby villages all rowed their families to the town to see the film. The film ran for a whole week to capacity audiences and earned about 10,000 yuan for the cinema. When peasants go to town to see films they always treat themselves to some dim sum and do some shopping. So during the week when the movie was shown the business volume of the town's shops increased by 60,000 yuan. This vivid example illustrates the tremendous potential of service trades in small towns. It is not that the peasants do not have a demand for a modern social life, but rather that we are not sensitive to their demand. This is the root cause of the fact that the variety, standard and quality of rural services falls far short of demand.

One of the new service items in small towns is hair perming for rural women. As recently as my third visit to Kaixiangong in 1981, girls with coiffured hair were still rarely seen. But on my fourth and fifth visits, I noticed more and more young women with stylish hair-dos. On my sixth visit this year, almost all young women, whether they were workers in the brigade factories or peasants in the fields, had their hair curled. I was told that most of them had their hair done by the hairdressers at Miaogang or Zhenze, and each treatment cost two yuan. I was also told that during major festivals the hairdressers in these towns have to stay open round the clock. So, in styling hair, Miaogang and Zhenze have become service centres for rural women.

In the past, tea-houses in small towns functioned virtually as the information exchange centres for all the nearby villages. In these places, all sorts of news of cities, towns and villages were talked about and spread to the surrounding villages. They were where peasants sought advice from one another, on matters ranging from farming techniques to match-making. Are the tea-houses still ideal places for information exchanges and mutual consultation in the rural areas? Are there any other suitable channels for such activities? Under the situation of universal implementation of production responsibility system and simultaneous development of agriculture, industry and family sidelines, what sort of services do the peasants really need and how should these needs be satisfied? These questions all call for urgent study.

In terms of social life with the exception of cinemas, the towns have almost no cultural facilities to offer the rural folk. Young people seldom go to the tea-houses, and there are hardly any organized recreational or sports activities. When rural youth come to town, they have no place for dating. The severity of this lack is illustrated by the fact that last year, when Songling built a park, it immediately filled up with young people.

As the young people have almost no social life, they barely know anyone outside the circle of those with whom they live and work. As a result, their number of choices for spouses is highly limited, and so they generally marry within this limited circle of acquaintances. I was told that in some out-of-way mountain villages the number of retarded children is increasing, probably as a result of generations of in-breeding. Therefore it is extremely important to change the present situation.

The call to transform small towns into cultural centres must not remain a mere slogan. As young people are badly in need of social life, small towns should build cultural centres to meet this need. Apart from their function as commercial centres, the small towns should also provide the peasants with forums where they can meet with each other and exchange information.

I was particularly disappointed with the educational level in Wujiang. Jiangsu Province's illiteracy rate is higher than the national average, and Wujiang County's is the highest in Jiangsu. Generally speaking, an area's economic level should be in direct proportion with its educational level. But here in Wujiang it is the other way round. This abnormal phenomenon raises some questions. Why do people need study? In the countryside, what difference does it make between literate and illiterate? When the illiterate can make more money than the educated, is education necessary?

One day when I was taking a walk in Miaogang on the bank of Taihu Lake, I met and asked several fishermen of different ages whether they know how to read and write. They all shook their heads. The elderly among them were all experienced fishermen and the younger were learning how to fish with the elderly. They told me that their income in recent years was much higher than that of the peasants.

After talking with them, I learned why they could not read. These people have been fishing on Taihu Lake for many years and even for generations. To be a successful fisherman requires a rich knowledge of the locality's natural and geographical conditions such as the climate, the winds and the location of the shoals. This knowledge which they use to make their living is gained not from books or classrooms but from their elders and their own experiences. Therefore to become a really good fisherman one has to commence learning and go on boat with his elders at an early age. This being the case, they argued, why spend several years in school to learn a few thousand characters which have nothing to do with their livelihood? Besides if they do go to school instead of learning the trade, it would make it all the more difficult to start all from the beginning after the school. So they decided they'd rather learn to make a living than go to school.

However, the improvement of fishing techniques makes artificial breeding necessary. Fish breeders need to know about the temperature, humidity, the oxygen content of water and so on. This knowledge, unlike natural fishing, can never be learned without knowing how to read and write. The transformation of the natural fishermen plying their trade on Taihu Lake into fish pond managers represents the evolution of fish production from its primitive mode to the modern stage of artificial breeding. Such a development when it takes place will necessitate that the fishermen who formerly regarded learning useless to look upon education as being indispensable.

I returned from my walk with a deeper understanding of the problem of eliminating illiteracy. I realized that education can never be universalized without the development of productive forces. To study the problems of present rural education from this prospective, one may find that the rapid development of productive forces in the rural areas not only makes universalization of education necessary, but is making it possible. I further realized that whether the peasants' needs for education can be met or not depends on the content of the education we provide. Therefore, transforming small towns into the cultural and educational centres in the countryside presents us with many new and challenging problems.

PROBING DEEPER INTO SMALL TOWNS

— A Study of the Small Towns in the Four Municipalities of Southern Jiangsu

Fei Hsiao Tung

I

My study of small towns developed from my more basic research on villages. On my third visit to Kaixian'gong Village in 1981, I had limited my observations to the bounds of one village only. When I toured the village a fourth time at the end of the year, however, I aimed to "climb one storey higher", and study small towns in their role as political, economic and cultural centres of the countryside. I had visited about a dozen small towns in Wujiang County and found that they were reviving from their previous state of decline and beginning to flourish. Over the past 30 years, there had been an outflow of population in all but a few small towns. The rate of their population growth had been low, and in some towns the population had even fallen.

Nevertheless, a change took place after the Third Plenary Session of the Eleventh C.P.C. Central Committee held in December 1978. Large numbers of people moved back to and resettled in these small towns. In some towns, the actual population was one-third larger than that indicated by household registration figures. Since many new problems were appearing in small towns, I decided to make them the focus of my investigation work in 1982. In this decision, I had the support of the C.P.C. Provincial Committee of Jiangsu, which had recently held an urban-work conference in Changzhou, at which proposals to develop small towns were put forward. So we happened to "see eye to eye". As a result, the Institute of Sociology of the Chinese Academy of Social Sciences and the Sociology Institute of Jiangsu Province jointly organized a Small Towns Investigation and Study Team to begin work on the subject.

To probe deeply into the new subject, we adopted the method of "dissecting a sparrow". We chose as our pilot "sparrow" Wujiang County, which had the greatest number of small towns. We drew up an investigation outline covering classification, level, rise and decline, layout and development. Our work proceeded in two stages. First we consulted Party and government cadres at various levels, to gain an initial understanding of the conditions in the county and the various small towns, and to learn of the problems they had already detected, then we divided the team and assigned each member a specific research subject in a specific town of a certain classification and level. All members went to small towns and carried out observations on the spot. We met to report our findings in autumn last year. From September 21-27, 1983, we also held a series of academic discussions in Nanjing on a wide range of subjects related to our research. Personnel from related central government departments, policy researchers from the Jiangsu Provincial Party Committee, leading cadres of cities, counties and towns in the province, and specialists from research institutes and institutions of higher learning. During these discussions, I delivered a speech entitled "Small Towns, Great Significance".

In 1983, the National Committee of the People's Political Consultative Conference organized a Small Towns Investigation Team consisting of various specialists from Beijing and Nanjing. Between November 11 and December 6 members of the team toured the four municipalities of Changzhou, Wuxi, Nantong and Suzhou, as well as several counties and towns in Jiangsu Province, and held discussions on the views and problems raised at the Nanjing symposium on small towns. I wrote this article on the basis of my speech made at the summing-up meeting in Suzhou. Below I shall give an outline of what I learned from the November-December visit.

II

The fourishing of the rural economy has brought with it the resurgence of small towns. In the five years since the Third Plenary Session of the Eleventh C.P.C. Central Committee, various new economic policies have been implemented in rural China, which, with few exceptions, have resulted in general and remarkable increases in agricultural production throughout the country. Chinese peasants are well off — this is obvious to all. The four municipalities we toured — Suzhou, Wuxi, Changzhou and Nantong — have stood in the forefront of rural economic development in Jiangsu Province in recent years. Furthermore Jiangsu leads all other Chinese provinces in economic development. It established two national records in 1982, by producing 28.55 million tons of grain and an industrial output value of 50,200 million yuan. These records were further improved in 1983, when Jiangsu produced 30.5 million tons of grain and 82,400 million yuan in industrial output value, as well as registering a record revenue of 7,200 million yuan.

At the time of our investigation, production units in the countryside had not closed their accounts for 1983. The agro-industrial department of the provincial Party committee provided us with the following statistics:

On average, each peasant in Jiangsu Province earned 309 yuan in 1982, 154 yuan more than (or double) the 1978 figure. In the four years between 1978 and 1982, the province record-ed an average annual increase of more than four per cent in the output of grain, cotton and edible oil, as well as an annual increase of more than 10 per cent in major rural sidelines. Rural industries run by people's communes and production brigades also doubled their output value in the same four years. By 1982 they accounted for 42 per cent of total rural industrial and agricultural output value (industries run by production teams are reckoned as agriculture), and one-quarter of the total industrial output value of the province.

In the areas where we carried out our investigations, peasants were enthusiastically building new homes. The countryside had taken on an entirely new look. On the north bank of the Changjiang River, we used to see only thatched huts, but now these had been replaced by tiled-roofed, brick houses. Peasants in Suzhou, Wuxi and Changzhou south of the river had begun to replace brick houses with two-storey villas. In some places, we saw rows of villas with flower-filled balconies, that stretched for several kilometres. Department stores, cinemas, cultural centres, bookstores and other new buildings mushroomed on the sides of wide roads. Some production brigades had begun to build public bathhouses. The rising towns made old suburban Shanghai pale in comparison.

We called on a young peasant at his brand-new three-storey home in Qianzhou Township, Wuxi County. He told us he had spent 10,000 yuan for his new house. In the past few years, he and his wife, who worked in a textile-machinery workshop run by their production team, had earned about 4,000 yuan each year. After deducting living expenses for their family of three, they had saved between 2,500 and 3,000 yuan a year. Families like this were very common in the area.

The vogue for new and better homes in this "land of rice and fish" reflected the desires of peasants who were becoming well to do. Some peasants built very spacious houses, reserving room for family sidelines. They could not spend all their income from commodity production. Rural savings in Jiangsu Province totalled 2,000 million yuan at the end of 1982. In Suzhou Municipality, the average peasant deposited 78.9 yuan in the bank. There is reason to believe he kept more than this sum in his pocket, however. According to traditional ideas, peasants liked to turn their surplus income into safe immovable property hence the impetus to the building of new homes. But whatever the circumstances, the appearance of large numbers of well-to-do families in villages close to the four cities was a heartening sight.

The major factor in promoting the prosperity of peasants in these areas has been the change in the structure of the rural economy. Jiangsu Province has achieved annual increases in agricultural, farm-sideline and industrial production in recent years. Agricultural output registered the smallest annual growth rate, four per cent. Rural industry run by people's communes and production brigades recorded the greatest growth rate, about 90 per cent. This means that the proportion of peasant income derived from agriculture has grown steadily smaller while that from industry has steadily increased. In the four municipalities where we conducted investigations, the industrial output value of each county accounted for almost half, or more than half, of its total output value. In the three municipalities south of the Changjiang River, in particular, the industrial output value of most counties exceeded 70 per cent of the total output value. Wuxi, Changzhou and Jiangyin counties each recorded a gross industrial and agricultural output value of more than 2,000 million yuan in 1983, of which agro-output value accounted for only 10 to 20 per cent. According to 1983 statistics, seven townships in Jiangsu Province — Tangqiao, Leyu, Qianzhou, Yuqi, Zhouzhuang, Huashi and Huanghang — registered a gross industrial-agricultural output value of more than 100 million yuan. Industrial output value accounted for 90 per cent of the sum. It was a universal truth that peasants depended on industry to get rich.

It is worthy of special note that while the proportion of agricultural income continued to fall in these well-to-do villages, its absolute value kept on growing at a pace faster than in those villages where industry was undeveloped. This should be recorded in letters of gold because it shows a novel characteristic of China's socialist construction: Industrialization at the grassroots of Chinese society has taken place and developed on the basis of agricultural prosperity and, in turn, has promoted the expansion of agriculture, helping it to embark on the course of modernization.

The significance of this characteristic becomes clear if we contrast China's situation with the history of industrialization in the West. During the early days of industrialization in Europe, as machinery plants concentrated in the cities flourished, villages went bankrupt. Having lost their land, farmers left their native villages and flocked into the cities to swell the ranks of the reserve army of labour for burgeoning industry. Thus modern industries in capitalist countries grew at the expense of villages. This was the road of capitalist industrialization in the West.

China took a completely different road under socialism. On the basis of flourishing agriculture, Chinese peasants are running collectively-owned rural industries. These rural industries are aimed at strengthening, aiding and promoting the agricultural economy. As a result, agriculture, farm-sidelines and industry develop hand in hand, paving the way for constantly increasing prosperity in the countryside. Viewed in the context of concrete historical development, this road to industrialization is no deduction from theory, but a creation of the Chinese peasants derived from practice. Years of verification through practice have confirmed that the policy of "Hundreds of millions of peasants leave their land but not their villages to run rural industries" is one of strategic significance that fully accords with the current conditions of China.

III

Our investigation of small towns in Wujiang County showed their revival was due to the burgeoning of rural industry. Our latest visit to the four municipalities confirmed this as a common characteristic of this area.

We were told that although rural industries came into being in the early and mid 1970s in southern Jiangsu Province, they were "surreptitiously run" by the peasants. The number of factories was small as was their scale. It was only after 1978 that rural industries mushroomed everywhere. For example, the Qianzhou People's Commune in Wuxi County had only one factory — a farm-machinery plant — in 1970. With a total of 12 workers, the plant turned out products worth only 1.5 million yuan that year. In 1982, however, the commune's industries recorded a gross output value of 73.88 million yuan, or 49 times the 1970 output. Now more than 7,700 peasants in the commune have become workers. Since 1978, rural industries in Wuxi Municipality have achieved an annual growth rate of 23 per cent in gross output value and seven per cent in total profit.

The explanation for such rapid development of rural industries as I pointed out earlier can be found only in the intrinsic relation between rural industries and agriculture. Southern Jiangsu is an area with a long history of land development. The expanding agricultural economy attracted large numbers of people, who formed an increasingly dense population. To solve the problem of a large population in a small area of farmland, and to maintain the wealth of this "paradise", the inhabitants long ago took to producing household handicrafts on the basis of the steady development of agriculture. The legend "the Cowherd and the Girl Weaver" reflects the division of labour between husband and wife and the organic combination of farming and handicrafts within a family. This is a historical summing-up of how agriculture and industry complement each other in southern Jiangsu where the population is immense and the area of land small.

After the People's Republic of China was founded in 1949, individual household farming in southern Jiangsu took the road of the collective economy. This emancipated the production forces of agriculture to an unprecedented degree. But, the population of the area went through a period of uncontrolled growth, and the conflict between a big population and a small area of land grew sharper and sharper. In the early 1970s, arable land in the four municipalities averaged about one *mu* per capita. Moreover, rural economic policies were influenced by "Left" tendencies in the pre-1978 period. The policy of "taking grain as the key link" resulted in the exclusive production of grain, which destroyed the traditional structure of agriculture and industry complementing each other. The growing labour force had no alternative but to carry out intensified exploitation of limited land at multiplying cost. As a result, they increased their grain output but not their income. According to statistics of Suzhou Municipality, pure agricultural income averaged about 100 yuan per capita since the mid-1970s.

In my article "Small Towns, Great Significance", I explained how Jiangsu Province was obliged to develop rural industries in the ten years of turbulence of the "cultural revolution". Surplus village labour seeking a means to supplement its income was the intrinsic factor in the appearance and development of rural industries. According to our investigation in the four municipalities this time, if each peasant farms an average of four *mu* of land, there would be surplus labour amounting to one-third of the total rural labour force. The five counties of Suzhou Municipality alone would have a surplus labour force 1.2 million strong, or half of the total rural labour force of the municipality. This huge surplus of labour, which was engulfed in the "big pot" of equalitarianism, would become a new rural productive force if employed in rural factories.

Since the Third Plenary Session of the Eleventh Central Committee of the Communist Party established the rural system of contracting production quotas to households, every village family has found it can spare hands from its small farm to make money by other methods. As a result, rural industries have emerged everywhere. Therefore, we can say that rural industries are a product of surplus rural manpower combining a new means of labour with a new subject of labour. They are set up by peasants relying on their collective strength. They do not undermine agriculture and farm-sidelines, which form their foundation, but add to the state revenue and support, subsidize and maintain agriculture. This has formed the new path for China's industrialization which I mentioned in the preceding section.

In 1983, rural industries in Jiangsu Province paid state taxes amounting to 1,100 million yuan, or one-eighth of the total financial revenue of the province. In the four years from 1979 to 1982, more than 20 per cent of the profit made by rural industries was spent on buying farm machines, carrying out farmland capital construction and providing collective welfare facilities. This sum totalled 1,450 million yuan, equal to the total state investment in agriculture, forestry, water conservancy and meteorology in the province for the same period of time. In the same four years, total wages and profits of the rural industries amounted to 5,990 million yuan including 1,790 million yuan for 1982 alone (this averaged 35 yuan per capita for the rural population of the province).

A leader of Suzhou Municipality said, "The growth of industries here has enabled us to rely on industry to support agriculture, to arouse enthusiasm in farmers for production and to promote the continual development of agricultural production. In 1982, the peasants in the five counties of the municipality received an average per capita income of 255 yuan from the collective economy, of which 130 yuan came from rural industries. In fact, rural industries have helped the state make up for the difference between the price and value of grain under the circumstances of insufficient macroscopic regulation by the state. We have to accept this task, so we must run rural industries."

The above statistics show how rural industries in southern Jiangsu have contributed to the consolidation and growth of agriculture and farm-sidelines and to the prosperity of the countryside as a whole. During our investigations, we saw that wherever rural industries were well managed, they gave great support to agriculture and sidelines, which grew rapidly. This was not accidental, but an inevitable result.

The role played by rural industries in subsidizing farming and promoting the all-round development of agriculture, sidelines and industry is similar to that historically played by peasant household handicrafts. In a sense, we can say rural industries have their roots in the tradition of farming and handicrafts complementing each other. Nevertheless, in the new era, the complementary action is no longer confined to a single family, but operates on the collective economy. In the socialist era, the tradition has undergone historical change by passing from couples of "tilling men and weaving women" to the comprehensive development of agriculture, farm-sidelines and industry in whole villages and townships. This has rapidly transformed the villages, ensuring the prosperity of the peasants. During our tour of the four municipalities, we often heard cadres and peasants alike say this: "Agriculture gives us a bowl of rice and sidelines give us our dishes. Industries change the appearance of the countryside." They meant that whereas well-developed agriculture and sidelines could feed and clothe them and offer them a little spare money, only rural industries could lay solid foundations for prosperity in the countryside. This is what the cadres at all levels and the peasants have learned through their own experience. They are taking the same action voluntarily, ready to "share weal and woe".

A leading comrade of Suzhou Municipality said to us, "It's absolutely impossible for us to turn back and return the labour force of hundreds of thousands to their households, tying each person to one *mu* of land."

IV

Not only are rural industries intrinsically related to agriculture historically, they are also becoming increasingly closely linked with the economic systems in large and medium-sized cities. During the century in which old Shanghai was a foreign trading port, foreign capital and Chinese bureaucrat-comprador capital extended their blood-suckers into the villages in southern Jiangsu along the Shanghai-Nanjing Railway. Peasant household handicrafts were the first to fall victim after which agriculture was also struck down. Finally the peasants reluctantly sold their land and went to look for jobs in Shanghai, thus China followed a semi-colonial, Western capitalist-style road to industrialization.

As Chinese villages went bankrupt before the founding of new China, peasants fled to the cities and worked in factories where they learned modern techniques. Today they are activists in running and expanding rural industries. We were told in Wuxi that half of the blacksmiths in Shanghai before liberation came from Wuxi. They formed a "Wuxi group" in Shanghai's engineering industry. They had been village peasants who moved to Shanghai. Unlike the workers in Western countries, most Chinese peasant-workers moved to the cities without bringing their families along. They earned money in the cities and sent it to support their families in the countryside. This tradition remains unchanged today as "the lotus root snaps but its fibres stay joined". We toured 28 rural plants, all of which were established with the help of various rural "connections". Most of them were initiated by retired workers or cadres who, having rural connections, acted as go-betweens or supplied the enterprises with the necessary technical know-how. Rural connections were a catalytic agent for the development of rural industries, which then gradually established closer and closer relations with large and medium-sized cities after 1978.

In Hutang Town in Changzhou Municipality, we found a commune-run diesel engine plant making spare parts for a state diesel engine plant in Changzhou. We were told that in recent years the state plant was unable to expand production to meet increasing orders because of restrictions on land, capital and employee quotas within the city. Through certain connections, it got in touch with the commune-run plant and placed the extra orders with it. The two plants formed a "dragon-like" coordinated process. The "dragon's head" was the state plant which made the key parts and assembled the engines in the city. The commune-plant, being the "dragon's tail", produced the other spare parts in the rural town. Inspecting the rural industries in Wuxi and Suzhou municipalities, we saw that many of their products, such as clothing and hydraulic standardized pieces, carry Shanghai trademarks. This was because a number of urban plants had begun to manufacture expensive, advanced and sophisticated products and were not able to continue the production of old products still demanded by the market. Thus they transferred the order for the old products together with their technology to rural industries. This was known as "casting off the slough" as a cicada does.

Both "casting off the slough" and the "dragon-like" process are forms of co-operation between urban and rural industries. There are numerous forms, which can be summarized as follows: (1) Rural plants funded by joint investment with products or profit shared by both parties; (2) By way of "casting off the slough", each party turns out different products; (3) Rural processing of products to order with material supplied by the urban party; (4) Co-operation with technical aid to rural party at a charge; (5) Funding aid to rural party with compensation; and (6) Transfer of technology or patent right to rural party.

Whether such classification is comprehensive and scientific requires further research, but it shows that urban and rural industries have been cementing closer and closer ties as a result of economic readjustment and development after 1978. Comprehensive economic and technical co-operation is gradually replacing contacts through a few "connections".

We could clearly see that most rural industries in the four municipalities had developed economic and technical co-operation with Shanghai, while a smaller number was linked up with Changzhou, Suzhou, Wuxi and Nantong. This indicates that the economic development of Shanghai had a great impact on the economy of rural industries and the whole surrounding area, playing the part of an economic centre. Among the more than 2,000 rural factories in Wuxi County, 709 were linked up with major plants in large and medium-sized cities such as Shanghai and Wuxi. They co-operated in a total of 895 items, most of them involving plants in the two cities. Therefore, rural industries depended on urban industry, which regarded them as rear bases. This interdependence has been growing. Since their reorganization in 1980 and 1982, in particular, rural industries have held a position in the industrial system in cities. For example, the Jinfeng Commune Glassworks in Shazhou County turns out 300,000 standard cases of glass for civilian use a year under the help of the Yaohua Glassworks in Shanghai. It is one of the major producers in east China.

It is said that plants in Shanghai, Wuxi and other cities have requested the related rural industries to "remain heart to heart and be of one mind with us and never change your minds". Therefore, we can say the rural industries in southern Jiangsu have in fact formed a component part of the industrial system in cities. Neither can do without the other. The close relationship between the two is a natural result of the development of the regional economy.

In southern Jiangsu Province, urban industry, rural industry and agriculture and farm-sidelines constitute a harmonious whole, forming an enormous economic system. This is a system for realizing industrialization of the countryside in a socialist society. It presents a new pattern of industrialization in China, where "big fish help small fish, and small fish help shrimps". Details of the connections between various parts of the system remain to be studied further. Nevertheless, the different roles played by each part is obvious. Actual facts in southern Jiangsu show that a regional economic system has taken embryonic form there, with each part of the system playing its role. The so-called regional economic system means an economic pattern adapted to a special area. Outside the area, the development pattern changes. When we toured Jintan County in Changzhou Municipality and Rugao County in Nantong Municipality, we could clearly see that they lie on the edge of the Shanghai economic zone, because the economic development there has many characteristics different from the pattern of the entire southern Jiangsu region.

At present, rural industries are faced with quite a few pressing problems and difficulties. Most common among them are as follows: (1) Sources of energy and raw materials are not well planned. A number of rural plants frequently have to suspend production. Leaders of several counties are constantly racking their brains and travelling long distances in search of coal and steel supplies; (2) There is a shortage of technicians and skilled personnel; (3) Environmental pollution is not well controlled and labour protection is lacking; and (4) Many worry that rural industries will face problems when the current favourable low tax rate is nullified.

Leaders of Suzhou Municipality said it is essential to support rural industries. For example, their supply of raw materials and energy and the sale of their products should be included in state plan if possible. They should be favoured with low-interest loans. Funds to support and subsidize agriculture should be made tax deductible. A number of graduates from universities, colleges and specialized schools should be sent to rural plants each year to strengthen their technical force. These problems require further investigation and study before we can find practical solutions suitable to local conditions.

V

As they grow, rural industries provide large numbers of jobs for rural surplus labour. According to statistics of Wuxi Municipality, the payroll of rural industries and other businesses involves 34 per cent of the total rural labour force in the municipality. This holds true for the other three munici-palities. This means that in the southern Jiangsu region, one-third of the total rural labour force has given up farm work. In the whole province, there are more than four million people working in rural factories, nearly equal to the total number of workers who have residence registration in cities and towns. As the population of small towns dwindled in past years, enterprises run by county and town authorities became short of labour and employed a considerable number of informal workers, most of them coming from villages. According to statistics of the provincial labour bureau, businesses and depart-ments in cities and towns all over the province recruited a total of 990,000 rural workers in 1982, excluding those who processed products for them outside. To a certain extent this helped ease the pressure of a huge population in the villages and also helped a section of the peasants to engage in industrial production with new means of labour. Hence a unique labour force was formed in the countryside of Jiangsu Province.

Members of this labour force are known by different names in different places. They are variously called "peasant-workers", "worker commune members", "worker-and-peasant personnel", and so on. But whatever the appellation it embodies the same meaning — they are simultaneously both peasants and workers. They are unique in that they hold concurrent jobs. Nevertheless, the volume of surplus labour in the villages actually changes with the farming seasons. There is a small surplus during busy farming seasons and an enormous surplus in slack seasons. Therefore, when surplus labour engages in industrial production, it is necessary to ensure that it can also engage in farming at the required times in order to maintain the stability of agriculture. Hence holding concurrent jobs is essential to the harmonious development of the rural economy.

Although the technical level is low in rural southern Jiangsu, the sharp conflict between a dense population and a small area of land brings about a huge surplus of labour. Therefore, the transfer of surplus labour to industry, commerce, building, transportation and service trades is a good thing. This is also essential to the long-term development of the socialist countryside. County and township leaders have discarded their former view that villages can absorb unlimited labour. They are making efforts to find jobs for surplus labour and open new channels for production. This is praiseworthy.

The rural plants we visited often recruited one worker from each peasant family. This seems to be inconsistent with the principle of picking the best workers, but it suits the specific circumstances of the countryside. We were told that in this way all peasant families could increase their income by approximately the same amount and it is to the advantage of those doing two trades. Each family sent one member to work in a factory while the other members remained at home to engage in farming. The worker helped with farm work when off duty. A woman director of the Xinguang Towel Factory in Hutang Town was such a concurrent-job holder. She efficiently ran the factory, leading 1,800 workers, all of whom held concurrent jobs. She and her workers returned home to do farm work in the evening and on holidays.

Therefore, on the basis of the collective economy, industrial and agricultural labour are combined in each family, and each family becomes an agro-industrial household. Such families account for 80 per cent of the total peasant households in the four cities. In the counties of Wuxi, Changshou, Jiangyin, Shazhou and Wujin, where rural industries are well developed, almost all peasant households are concurrent-job holders, with the exception of a small number enjoying the five guarantees.

The concurrent-job holders engage in industrial work to different degrees depending on factory rules, work hours, kinds of work and family manpower. They primarily fall into three categories: (1) Families mainly engaged in farming which also process products for factories at home. Some family members do embroidery, knitting or weaving in their spare time; (2) Families with members working in factories that do not operate all the year round or that are close to their homes. When off duty, the workers go home to do farm work. They stop their factory work during busy farming seasons when they spend all of their time on their farms; and (3) Families primarily doing industrial work. Some members work far away in county-seats or towns. They board at the factories and come home only at weekends to do a little farm work.

Such differences between concurrent-job holders show how peasants gradually become workers. As the production forces of industry and agriculture advance to a higher level, more and more peasants join the ranks of concurrent-job holders, who spend more and more time on industry. During our investigations, we could see no essential difference between most of the concurrent-job workers and urban workers; both are linked with advanced production forces. The peasant-workers are fulfilling one-third of the industrial production in small towns. They are doing the same jobs as are workers with residence registration in the towns and are esteemed for their capacity for hard work. Many of them have formed production backbones indispensable to their plants. Some have become informal "technicians", "engineers" or competent management personnel. In fact, they are new workers born in villages, part of the upcoming generation of the Chinese working class.

Nevertheless, these peasant-workers have their residence registration in villages and depend on farming for their food. They do not enjoy as high a wage or as many welfare benefits as do other workers. Their working conditions are poor, and they are not entitled to join trade unions. Local cadres hold that village residence registration is no ground for denying trade union access to peasant-workers who spend most of their time working in factories. They demand that trade unions admit these new workers who are closely linked with villages and improve their wages and working conditions. This is a new problem arising from structural changes in rural society in southern Jiangsu Province.

The emergence of a contingent of concurrent-job holders has not only had a great impact on social structure, but has changed the distribution of population. Southern Jiangsu has a dense population, which was not equitably distributed. Over the years the flow of population moved in two opposing directions: there was the natural population flow into large and medium-sized cities, and the forced evacuation of the population from cities and towns to villages according to policy. The two-way movement of population led to a population explosion in large and medium-sized cities and a huge labour surplus in villages. At the same time, the population of towns and county-seats lying between cities and villages generally dwindled. A pictorial representation of the situation would be like a gourd, narrow in the middle and big at the ends.

Since 1978, most of the industries run by counties, towns, people's communes and production brigades have developed rapidly in small towns and county-seats. A large amount of surplus manpower from the villages moved to these small towns to work in factories. This has increased the population of the towns and brought changes to their social structure. Qing-yang Town, for example, had a population of 5,500 in the early

1950s. In the ten years to 1960, the population grew to 5,885, a seven per cent increase. In the 1970s, however, industries in the town began to recruit workers from villages and its population reached 15,366 at the end of 1982, of which 5,114 or 33 per cent of the total population were peasant-workers. Another example is Wujin County, whose 63 small towns today have a total population of 250,000, of which 70,000 are non-peasants accounting for 28 per cent of the total, while 100,000 are peasant-workers accounting for 40 per cent of the total.

The proportion of peasant-workers to registered urban residents found in Qingyang Town and Wujin County is common throughout southern Jiangsu. Therefore, residence registration does not represent the true population of towns and county-seats in the area. The great majority of peasant-workers still lodge in villages, moving back and forth each day between villages and towns like pendulums. This is how county-seats and towns control the rush of rural surplus labour to large and medium cities. Like dams standing one after the other, townships, county towns and county-seats stem the flow of people, relieving the population pressure in cities.

In the process of investigation, we also found that these areas send labour service teams to other provinces. As a result, their copious reservoir of manpower and technical skill is linked up with development and construction in frontier provinces. Nantong Municipality alone has dispatched rural collective building teams totalling 130,000 men to Heilongjiang Province and the autonomous regions of Inner-Mongolia and Xinjiang. These teams have won praise for the high speed and good quality of their work. The building workers do not take their families with them and are not particular about living conditions. They often complete one year's work in ten months, then come home to help with farming. After celebrating the lunar New Year Festival, they go out to join the building teams again. As well as sending out labour service teams, the three municipalities of Wuxi, Nantong and Changzhou carry out economic and technical co-operation with frontier areas on a mutual-benefit basis.

Two population movements are changing the irrational distribution of the population: (1) Part of the working population is moving out of villages to settle in small towns. These workers are known as "persons leaving their land but not their villages"; and (2) Another part goes to distant places in organized service teams to do periodical stints. These workers are known as "persons leaving their villages but keeping their homes in mind". In the whole province of Jiangsu, "persons leaving their land but not their villages" total more than four million, while "persons leaving their villages but keeping their homes in mind" total one million. These two forms of population movement should be studied as a method of solving China's population problem.

VI

All the small towns in the four cities we investigated, historically functioned as commodity circulation centres, and the overwhelming majority of them were once commercial towns. Before 1978, a single-product economy prevailed in the countryside, while state-owned enterprises monopolized the circulation of commodities, forming a mono-channel and blocking up other channels. As a result, business suffered a recession and small towns fell into a decline. Rural industries came into being in the 1970s and flourished after 1978, laying the foundation for the economic development of small towns. At the same time, the purchase of raw materials for industry and the sale of finished products urgently called for more circulation channels. As a diversified agricultural economy grew, the village economy gradually passed from self-supporting production into commodity production. The existing mono-channel failed to meet the new needs and under such pressure, business activities in the small towns have begun to adopt changes.

At present, great efforts should be made to widen circulation channels, which will otherwise bottleneck further economic growth in the countryside. Current trade in small towns generally involves three economic components — state-owned, collective and individual enterprises, and there are now seven or eight circulation channels: state companies, supply and marketing co-operatives, collective trade agencies, retail departments of factories in townships and towns, diversified economy service companies, individual household shops and country fairs. The most marked development has been in country fair trading, which involves long-distance transportation of farm and sideline products. According to statistics of the provincial Supply and Marketing Co-operative, the volume of business done by country fairs in 1978 totalled 810 million yuan, accounting for only eight per cent of total retail trade. In 1982, however, it rose to 2,220 million yuan, or 13 per cent of total retail trade. We were told that although the area of country fairs has been constantly expanded and numerous new booths have been erected, these expansions are insufficient to meet the requirements of the market. Former morning fairs have become all-day fairs. Periodical fairs have become daily fairs. The briskness of country fairs trading is a sign of the flourishing of the diversified economy in the countryside and also reveals the unsuitable factors in the original state-run and collective trade channels. For example, Hai'an County in Nantong Municipality raised 6.8 million chickens last year, but state commercial departments were incapable of handling all the purchasing, storing and transporting, so more than 10,000 traders came to help. Each trader carried a few dozen chickens on his bicycle to Nanjing and Shanghai and sold them there.

This leads up to two major problems in the circulation of commodities today.

The first problem is to open to the domestic market a new collective trade channel, closely connected with the interest of the producers. Peasant households in Wujiang County have been famous over the years for breeding long-hair rabbits. The price of rabbit fur fell drastically last year, and as a result peasants killed their rabbits and ate the meat. The chickens had better fortune for they did after all provide the city folk with delicacies. Rabbit fur is purchased by state companies and shipped abroad, whereas chickens are transported by individual or collective traders and sold on the domestic market. Therefore, if we do not open up the domestic market and if purchasing departments remain out of step with producers, it will be impossible to maintain a stable commodity rate of farm and sideline products, major economic development is out of the question, and the market would be limited to bustling country fairs. Hence the state commercial departments must always bear the large numbers of domestic consumers in mind and link their own interests with those of the producers. Only then can they effect true reforms. It seems that if we want to promote commodity circulation we should lay special emphasis on opening new collective transport and sales channels run jointly by producers.

The second problem is that of co-ordination between regulation by plan and regulation by the market. There is a growing imbalance between the energy and raw materials requirements of rural industries in small towns on one hand and the supply according to the state plan on the other. Quite a number of local leaders told us that small towns formerly played the part of transporting farm and sideline products to cities and supplying villages with urban industrial goods. Today they have become part of the city-village economic system, which has caused a tremendous change in the commodities exchanged. Not only do greater quantities of industrial goods for daily use now go from cities through the small towns to the countryside, but there are also large quantities of raw materials, fuel and various equipment of various kinds going to rural industries in small towns. In the opposite direction, small towns not only ship farm and sideline products, but also a greater quantity of various industrial products, especially textiles and machinery goods to the cities.

This calls for planned division of labour between the city and the countryside on focal points of economic development. Nevertheless, apart from the materials they obtain according to indirect plans from urban factories to which they are linked, rural industries today depend on the market for 70 per cent of their supply of raw materials and energy. Twelve major farm and sideline products are purchased by state commercial departments and transported to cities: these are grain, edible oil, silkworm cocoons, hogs, poultry, eggs, leather, fur, bones, cotton, fruit and tea. Most of them serve as raw materials for city industries. Facing such a great imbalance between planned supply and market supply, rural industries must deal with a host of difficulties if they are to survive and develop. Therefore, rural leaders express the hope that on the basis of division of labour between urban and rural industries, state enterprises will relinquish some varieties or certain quantities of appropriate farm and sideline products to rural industries as their planned supply. Rural industries should also be provided with appropriate amounts of other raw materials and fuels according to plan.

VII

Former commercial towns have now turned into political, economic and cultural centres combining industry and commerce and linking cities to the countryside. This has brought forth many new problems regarding the reconstruction of small towns.

The first problem is where to get funds for the reconstruction. Among the 18 small towns we have toured, the nine township towns have a greater number of new buildings than the county towns (excluding the county-seats), while the county towns carry out construction on a larger scale. This is because the county towns lack construction funds. Although the state and the provincial government have clearly stipulated that local industrial and commercial surtax, public utilities surtax and real estate surtax should be used for small town construction, the funds they provide are too small to be of any help. In Suzhou Municipality, for example, the sum from these three sources amounts to two million yuan, which is divided between 18 county towns, giving each town only 110,000 yuan. But the greater part of the sum is spent on construction in county-seats, while other towns get only a few tens of thousand yuan each. Many leaders of county towns say their share is not enough even for repairing unsafe buildings in the town. Construction is out of the question. The leadership of a county town is at the same level as the township government in the town. It has no control over either enterprises owned by the people or collective county enterprises in the town. Some leaders of county towns told us that they had formerly collected funds from these enterprises to repair streets, roads and bridges, but these funds were now refused them on the grounds that they were "levying contributions at random". They believed that the leadership of the enterprises distorted the related documents.

"We must carry out construction in small towns," they said, "and construction needs funds. We must depend on the collective for funds, and not on state finance. Therefore, those with power should do their duty. All businesses must contribute to the funds according to the extent to which they will benefit. This is a feasible way to raise funds for construction. It follows the principle of 'relying on the people to build their own towns'."

The second problem is designing a construction plan. Architects in our investigation team hold that current construction in small towns lacks overall planning. Each builder makes his own policy and uses every inch of available space. This must be corrected. Our architects proposed that small towns should be built into rural development centres, which should be divided into different types and orders. The layout of a town must be reasonable, taking into account land development for multiple purposes, local features and the spirit of the times.

We suggest that the Building Bureau of Jiangsu Province make designs for the reconstruction of small towns, with the assistance of the Architecture Department of Qinghua University and the Architectural Engineering Department of Nanjing

Engineering College. They could choose one or two small towns, such as Lili Town and Dongjiang Town, and produce specific pilot designs.

With regard to the economic development, commercial circulation and construction layout of small towns, there are many problems involving the administrative system. The current administrative system of small towns in this region is as follows: In a county-seat, there are the county government, town government and district or township government, which are at the same level or different levels. In a county town other than the county-seat, there are the town government and district government or township government, which function at the same level. In key township towns, there are district and township governments and in ordinary township towns, there are township governments. There are no governments in naturally-formed fair centres or rising industrial centres of production brigades.

Among the above-mentioned county-seats and towns at various levels, non-county-seat towns under the county government experience the sharpest conflicts within the current administrative system. Several systems of administration exist side by side in these towns, artificially partitioning cities from villages at the expense of their harmonious economic growth. As the leadership of Jiangsu Province puts more counties under the administration of municipalities, this problem of partitioned administration should move towards solution. Lili Town in Wujiang County has successfully experimented with merging the town and township governments and putting villages under the town administration. Such a reform strengthens the combination of town and village economy. It benefits the unified planning of town construction and shatters the manor-like closed-door system. Moreover, it contributes to the overall organization of rural labour and overall planning of public facilities. However, since the people's communes have much greater economic strength than the towns, after the town-village merger, part of the profit gained by factories originally run by communes and brigades will have to be used to build the towns. What improvement the villages will enjoy is still not obvious. This remains to be determined through the further summing-up of practical experience.

Another problem is how to strengthen the leadership of each area and gradually do away with dual administration by government departments and area administration. At present, county-run businesses in small towns are nominally led by both county government departments and town administration offices. In fact, they accept only the leadership of departments and ignore town leadership. This leads to the practice of the government running factories and factories running society. Solving this problem requires further research.

Apart from this, reform should be effected in the administrative system to speed up the development of those small towns with special resources or particular value as tourist centres. For example, Dingshu Town in Yixing County is a ceramics centre whose fame equals that of Jingde Town in Jiangxi Province. It has a population of 70,000, but is on the same administrative level as a people's commune under the county government, and is the site of the Dingshu Town government, the Dingshu district government and the Zhoushu township government. All this seriously holds back the development of the town. Such a ceramics centre renowned in China and abroad could be upgraded to the status of a city on a level with a county and put under the direct administration of Wuxi Municipality. Since Yixing County is short of funds, it could receive subsidies from towns belonging to the municipality.

*   *   *

After spending nearly one month in the four municipalities of Suzhou, Wuxi, Changzhou and Nantong, we feel that small towns are a major issue. Research into this subject is closely related to finding a path to modernization suitable for China. Researchers and practical workers in our investigation team are gratified by the co-operation given us and we sincerely thank the leading agencies of Jiangsu Province and related municipalities for their support. We know we have spent only a short period of time on our investigation and have had only a passing glance at things. We still lack a good knowledge of several issues, while our research on many subjects is still in the preliminary stages. We have toured only small towns on the banks of the Changjiang River in Jiangsu Province, and have not yet made investigations in northern Jiangsu, which has enormous potential and is developing rapidly. The facts we have collected this time and the views we have arrived at have their limitations.

Therefore, investigations into small towns in Jiangsu Province have not ended. Past investigations were only a first-stage exploration. To form a comprehensive picture of small towns across Jiangsu in comparison with the economic pattern we have found in the latest investigations, we are crossing the Changjiang and Huaihe rivers to the north and touring small towns in the four cities of Xuzhou, Huaiyin, Yancheng and Yangzhou. We hope our exploration will help open up new prospects for socialist construction.

SMALL TOWNS IN NORTHERN JIANGSU

Fei Hsiao Tung

After concluding the survey of small towns in four municipalities in southern Jiangsu Province in December 1982, we decided on going to northern Jiangsu to continue with the work of surveying small towns in Jiangsu Province. Our party reached Xuzhou on April 21, 1984, and, on the advice of the provincial Party committee, we toured the five municipalities of Xuzhou, Lianyungang, Yancheng, Huaiyin and Yangzhou. During the 1,500 km. trip, we travelled across 20 counties and stopped to survey in nine counties, two fairs, nine rural enterprises, one seaport and a key water conservancy project.

Our party arrived at Nanjing on May 10 at the end of the 20-day tour. In such a short time, we could only get a "fleeting glimpse of flowers on a trotting horse" in our effort to pave the way for a survey of northern Jiangsu Province. However, members of our advance party, who had gone there ahead of us, had worked together with research workers of the municipalities to make some investigation first. As a result, we were able to obtain some quite systematic data whenever we arrived at a given spot. Following discussion with leading local officials and observations in selected important places, we gained some idea of the situation in northern Jiangsu Province.

I

As a regional concept, "northern Jiangsu" is not very clearly defined. If the Changjiang (Yangtze) River is taken as a demarcation line to split Jiangsu Province into two — the northern and southern parts, then that big chunk of territory north of the Changjiang River not only includes the five municipalities of Xuzhou, Lianyungang, Yancheng, Huaiyin and Yangzhou, but also the Nantong Municipality and part of Nanjing city itself. However, it is generally accepted today that northern Jiangsu only embraces the aforementioned five municipalities. The "southern Jiangsu" we surveyed last year, which covers only the four municipalities of Suzhou, Wuxi, Changzhou and Nantong, also differs from the geographically accepted concept. Nantong Municipality, situated north of the Changjiang River, has been lumped, together with the municipalities of Suzhou, Wuxi and Changzhou, south of the river, into one area because they have something identical in their economic development. Some people have put these four municipalities into the Shanghai Economic Zone; I agree with the idea. But if the matter is given more thought, it can be seen that the northern part of the Nantong Municipality that includes Hai'an and Rudong counties is not very much influenced economically by Shanghai. This is the case with Jintan and Liyang counties in the western part of the Changzhou Municipality and Yixing County of the Wuxi Municipality.

According to a rough estimate we have made, the Shanghai Economic Zone sprawls over an area within a radius of only 150 km. from the centre of Shanghai. Up till now consensus is still lacking on how to map out the economically developed areas within Jiangsu Province. But I am inclined to have a "central Jiangsu" marked out between southern and northern Jiangsu to embrace a part of the Yangzhou Municipality on the bank of the Changjiang, the municipalities of Nanjing and Zhenjiang and even the southern and western parts of the Nantong Municipality. It is good to raise this question because we realize that economic development is uneven in different parts of the province and economic development zones with different characteristics should be treated differently in various ways. However, the present investigation can in no way provide the basis for solving this problem, as it does not cover the aforementioned "central Jiangsu".

For a long time in the past, my views on the differences between northern and southern Jiangsu were not in conformity
with reality. And in my head still lingers the prejudice against
northern Jiangsu, which was prevalent among people in the old
days. As a result I used to regard northern Jiangsu as a poor,
backward land without a future.

The economic backwardness of northern Jiangsu and the ex-
treme poverty of its people existed only in the century or so before the inception of the People's Republic of China in 1949.
Northern Jiangsu was an area with a flourishing economy before imperialist powers invaded China. What has impressed
me most on the recent tour there is that northern Jiangsu had,
in the Ming and Qing periods, given birth to a galaxy of authors
of very popular novels. While in Huai'an, we visited the residence of Wu Cheng'en (1499-1582), author of *Pilgrimage to the
West*. And in Lianyungang we toured a place which legend
has it was the mountain of fruit and flowers in the "kingdom"
of Monkey King. In Xinghua, we went to have a look at the
study of Shi Nai'an, author of *Outlaws of the Marshes*, who
lived in the later part of the Yuan Dynasty and the early period
of the Ming Dynasty. On arriving at Ganyu, we were told that
this was where Wu Jingzi (1701-54), who wrote *The Scholars*,
had his schooling in his childhood. While resting in the town
of Banpu, south of Lianyungang, we heard that this town was
where Li Ruzhen (1763-1820) wrote the novel *Flowers in the
Mirror*. The handwriting of Zheng Banqiao (1693-1765) is still
preserved in his little study in Xinghua. It was not accidental
that men of letters used to gather in northern Jiangsu after the
16th century, because the area had a booming economy at that
time.

The rise and decline of northern Jiangsu was closely linked
with the rise and decline of the Grand Canal and with the
navigability or the silting up of the Huanghe (Yellow) River.
The Grand Canal linking Beijing and Hangzhou, the longest
man-made waterway in the world, traverses the whole length of
northern Jiangsu from Xuzhou to Yangzhou. In Xuzhou is the
former course of the Huanghe River along which the mighty

river once flowed to the sea. And in Shanggang Township near Yancheng, a dyke to stop tidal waves was built between 1023 and 1030 by the famous politician and writer Fan Zhongyan (989-1052), after he was posted here as an official in charge of the salt trade. Now dubbed the Lord Fan Dyke, it serves as the roadbed of the Tongyu Highway. This is proof that the Grand Canal here was then less than 80 km. from the sea. The Grand Canal and the Huanghe River along with the waterways branching out from them once formed a web of canals resembling those seen south of the Changjiang today. The city of Yangzhou here was a foreign-trade port in the Tang Dynasty (618-907), and it later became an entrepot from which consumer items and table salt were carried to the vast population on the Central Plains. Its ideal geographical position made Yangzhou a prosperous city.

The prosperity of Xuzhou and Huaiyin areas was directly linked with the shipping business on the Grand Canal, a north-south lifeline. In the Yuan and Ming dynasties (1271-1644), the Huanghe River breached its dykes time and again to silt up the Grand Canal. But the central governments that had their capitals in Beijing always saw to it that this lifeline was dredged and open to shipping. Beginning from 1852, some 130 years ago, a part of the imperial grain shipment, which used to be carried along the canal to Beijing, was transported by sea. And in 1855, the Huanghe River shifted its course and flowed across Shandong Province to the sea. As a result the shipment of supplies from the south to the north on the Grand Canal was stopped.

The imperialist powers invaded China at this time, and the country was beset by internal troubles and external aggression. This, coupled with the opening of the Tianjin-Pukou Railway in 1911, made northern Jiangsu cease being an important communication link between the north and south. It slumped with each passing day in the wake of floods and famines brought about by the disrepair of the local dyke systems. In the nearly 100 years before 1949, the terrible plight of the people there had created in people's minds the notion that northern Jiangsu is backward and poor.

For geographical and historical reasons, northern Jiangsu in the early post-1949 years was still economically backward compared with southern Jiangsu. In the post-1949 period, the local people, under the guidance of the Party and government, embarked on a grandiose plan to construct water conservancy projects to harness the Huaihe River. This put an end to flooding and famines that occurred annually in the past. Over the past three decades or more, 17,200 million cubic metres of earth were excavated in the construction of a vast dyke and canal system, with the Grand Canal and the Main Irrigation Canal as its backbone for controlling floods and waterlogging and for irrigation and preventing tide incursion. This has brought a great change to northern Jiangsu's agriculture. The land along the banks of the Huaihe River, long known as a flood corridor, and the low-lying, waterlogged farmland in the Lixiahe area have been transformed into blooming fields producing two and even three crops a year. Implementation of the responsibility system after the Third Plenary Session of the Eleventh C.P.C. Central Committee in 1978 has added to the enthusiasm of the peasants, who for three or four years in the past had gathered a per-unit crop yield as big as or even larger than that reaped in the Suzhou area, banner rice producer in southern Jiangsu. Some localities in northern Jiangsu that were known as "flee-famine areas" have become "marketable grain" bases. Xinghua County, so low that it came to be known as the "bottom of the cauldron" on the Huaihai Plain, is annually producing over one million tons of grain — a record for the whole of Jiangsu Province. Being the former bed of the Huanghe River, the land lying between Xuzhou and Lianyungang used to be carpeted with wide expanses of white alkali salts. Leached with water now, the land sown to paddy yields good harvests. This area that used to get its grain supplies from the government now has a big surplus for delivery to the cotton areas in neighbouring Shandong Province.

Because it has an area larger in size than that of southern Jiangsu, northern Jiangsu produced more grain than southern Jiangsu in the early post-1949 years. But its per-capita share was lower. In 1975 it was 359 kilos in southern Jiangsu and 331 kilos in northern Jiangsu. With its 1983 grain output reaching 19.05 million tons, doubling that of 1978, the per capita share in northern Jiangsu came to 676 kilos — exceeding that of southern Jiangsu. As a result, the economic standing of northern Jiangsu has improved greatly in the whole province.

Northern Jiangsu's population, cropland, grain output, cotton production and oil-bearing crop are 60 per cent that of those in southern Jiangsu. The output value of its agricultural production makes up half of the provincial total, but the output value of its total industrial and agricultural production is only 30 per cent that of the entire Jiangsu Province. Northern Jiangsu's

MAIN ECONOMIC STATISTICS OF NORTHERN JIANGSU COMPARED WITH THE PROVINCIAL TOTAL

Item	Northern Jiangsu figure	Northern Jiangsu as % of the whole
Population	34.7 million	56.6
Cropland	2.99 million hectares	64.7
Grain output	19.05 million tons	62.4
Cotton output	402,000 tons	60.5
Oil-bearing crops	450,000 tons	61
Industrial and agricultural output value	29,300 million yuan	35.5
Of which:		
Agricultural output value	13,300 million yuan	51.9
Industrial output value	16,000 million yuan	28.2
Value of rural industrial output	4,200 million yuan	26
Financial receipts	1,700 million yuan	23.8

financial income and profit from rural industries constitutes only 20 per cent of Jiangsu's total.*

The figures above show that the absolute production of grain, cotton and oil-bearing crops and agricultural output value for the five municipalities in northern Jiangsu exceed those of southern Jiangsu. But northern Jiangsu's industrial-agricultural output value is far below that of southern Jiangsu due to the slow development of its industry, particularly rural industry.

Such is the basic economic situation in northern Jiangsu. In a word, northern Jiangsu's agriculture has made fast progress with improved irrigation facilities and the implementation of the responsibility system. This has, by and large, put an end to the backwardness and poverty that had stalked northern Jiangsu for a century or more. With the food and clothing problem for the population now solved, there are conditions for further growth. So it is improper to continue to regard northern Jiangsu as a poor, god-forsaken land. Its great potential and drive must be taken note of. The great advantages in its agriculture are already evident. Its coal mines supply the whole of Jiangsu Province with fuel. More and more rock crystal and other minerals are being discovered for the development of advanced technology. Glad tidings are coming from the Huaihai Oilfield where exploration drilling is in progress. In addition, there are large expanses of sandy flats waiting for the plough along its eastern coast. Hence there are bright prospects that northern Jiangsu's development may surpass that of southern Jiangsu.

II

Northern Jiangsu is not only geographically different from southern Jiangsu. The levels of socio-economic development in various localities within the area itself are also not the same.

---

* The figures quoted above are based on the assumption that the province is divided into two parts — northern Jiangsu, including the five municipalities of Xuzhou, Lianyungang, Yancheng, Huaiyin and Yangzhou; and southern Jiangsu embracing the six municipalities of Suzhou, Wuxi, Changzhou, Nantong, Nanjing and Zhenjiang.

The various localities have their own characteristics because of their varied natural and historical conditions. In our effort to find out the differences between these localities, we made a study of the small towns in northern Jiangsu. First, we found out from the map of Jiangsu Province (1:1,000,000), compiled by the provincial cartographic bureau, that a large number of the places in Xuzhou and Huaiyin municipalities go under the name of *ji* — "fair". In areas with more "fairs", there are few places with the name of *zhen* — "town". In areas such as the municipalities of Lianyungang, Yancheng and Yangzhou, where there are more "towns", there are fewer or no "fairs". If "fair" and "town" are a true indication of the different levels of economic development, they show that economic development is uneven in the whole of northern Jiangsu.

Fairs were probably places where people used to exchange commodities long, long ago. They really did exist in China in very ancient times. According to *Kang Xi Dictionary*, a fair is where "selling and buying takes place". It says a "fair" is held in the daytime and people from all around bring their commodities there. They trade before departing, with "each getting his due". The dictionary adds, "There is a fair within a distance of 25 km. . . . A noon fair is a big one attended mostly by ordinary people. A morning fair is attended mostly by merchants, and those going to an evening fair are mostly male and female pedlars."

These descriptions not only tell how commodities were marketed in ancient times but also give an account of fairs as we see them today.

Most of those going to a rural fair today are producers dwelling in villages. They bring some surplus farm produce or handicraft articles for sale, and with the proceeds buy whatever they need at the fair. This quite resembles bartering in primitive times. The bartering is done directly between the producers themselves, and banknotes are simply used as a medium of exchange.

In the morning, people go to a fair from their homes, to which they return in the evening. When people have to walk and carry loads with carrying poles, those going to the same fair live only in an area within a radius of 12.5 km. That is why the ancient books say, "There is a fair within a distance of 25 km." Those living farthest from the fair arrive at about noon, so the number of fair attendants is biggest in the middle of the day. People in northern Jiangsu call a townlet a "fair", because it is a place in which many people gather. According to the *Kang Xi Dictionary*, a "fair" means something of "a hotch-potch, . . . a gathering of people . . . a meeting place". A "noon fair" is attended mostly by producers who want to trade. Hence, the dictionary says "most of them are ordinary people".

Those who wait for customers at the fair in the early morning do not come from the villages. They are professional traders whom the ancient books call "merchants". At the fairs of today there are some traders who put up stalls on street sides very early in the morning on fair days, to wait for customers. When the peasants have not sold their wares by the time the sun is setting, they sell them at reduced prices at the fairs to save themselves the trouble of carrying them home. Then some people appear to buy up the goods, which they will offer at the next fair day or at another fair. These are the "male and female pedlars" described in the ancient books.

Such detailed descriptions of fairs in the ancient books are proof that fairs have existed in our country from time immemorial.

Fairs are not something new to me, who had lived in a village near the county seat of Chenggong, not far south of Kunming in Yunnan Province, during the War of Resistance Against Japan. Some 20 minutes' walk from the village where I lived was the Dragon Fair. There was only a temple and scores of houses there on ordinary days. But when a fair was held there every six days, some 10,000 people of all nationalities flocked to it from far and near to rub shoulders with one another and to create a bustling scene.

To further investigate fairs, we went to see two big ones: the Jing'an Fair in Peixian County and the Dali Fair in Suining County. They are much larger than the Dragon Fair in Yunnan

Province. Lining both sides of the streets were trading stores that were open every day, and the number of their clients swelled on fair days. There were innumerable temporary licensed stalls operated by private traders, offering cloth, garments and sundry items. The pavements were dotted with kiosks made of planks or corrugated sheets, in each of which squatted a shopkeeper. Most of the kiosk owners were repairers of wristwatches and radios. Some traditional barbers and blacksmiths engaged in repairing farm implements, did have their own shops, while others had only stalls. Different sections of the fair were marked out for different kinds of goods. On the side streets were "ordinary people" or peasants from villages offering basketfuls of eggs, sacks of rice and vegetables piled high on the ground. Most of the people at the fair were peasants bringing their own produce to sell. But the biggest sales returns were made by trading stores. It was estimated that the sales made directly by peasant producers in these big fairs we visited account for only one-third of the total sales.

These fairs differ from the Dragon Fair in Yunnan. In these fairs there are shops that do business every day, and there are stalls and peasants coming to buy and sell only on fair days. At the Dragon Fair there were no other trading activities with the exception of sales made by a few small shops to people dwelling on the street on the days when no fair was held.

Dali Fair, which we visited in northern Jiangsu, is a big, well-known one that can be found on school maps. Formerly known as a "small Nanjing", it is located on the boundary between Suining County and Anhui Province, from where people come to attend the fair. The fair has a population of 8,500, but on fair days some 20,000 to 30,000 people come to attend it. And on the day of the big Spring Fair as many as 100,000 people come, many from neighbouring Shandong and Henan provinces. At ordinary times, four fairs are held in every 10 days, with sales amounting to 200,000 to 400,000 yuan per fair. There are nine markets: hogs and sheep, oxen and horses, grain, timber, meat, eggs, sundry goods, vegetables and firewood. Offered at the stalls and shops are manufactured items from Shanghai and other cities in southern Jiangsu. There are no fewer than 10 barber shops, six inns and four public baths. But there are as yet no warehouses. Peddling, it seems, is done by a small number of private traders. The pedlars buy things at one fair and sell them at another. The profit thus made is, in fact, the remuneration they get for carrying goods from one place to another.

We have no idea how many such big fairs as Dali there are in northern Jiangsu. In the six counties of the Xuzhou Municipality, according to the data we have on hand, there are 286 fairs of all sizes. Twelve of them are attended by 20,000 people, 43 by 10,000 people, 65 by 5,000 people, and 166 by less than 5,000 people.

These fairs were very much held down during the "cultural revolution". But the peasants could not produce everything they needed, and nothing could stop them from exchanging commodities. Although sentries were posted on the streets to prevent them from coming to the fairs and to drive away pedlars, the fairs were held in other places. Such action taken against fairs had, of course, been very detrimental to the rural economy and the life of the peasantry.

Fairs such as these no longer exist in the three municipalities of Changzhou, Wuxi and Suzhou in southern Jiangsu. In southern Jiangsu today, peasants can be seen coming to towns to offer their produce directly to consumers at "rural trade marts", which have revived over the past few years. As a rule, there are only such marts in the morning before seven or eight o'clock. Although these marts play a part in supplying urban residents with grocery items, they do not play much of a role in the overall distribution of commodities. But the rural trade marts are open daily, whereas rural fairs are held once each several days.

It must be pointed out here that rural trade marts are not very common in northern Jiangsu. In our study of fairs in Yancheng and Huaiyin, we found that people go to fairs in the counties north of the Trunk Irrigation Canal, but although there are also fairs in counties south of the canal, they play only an insignificant role because of the existence of relatively large numbers of small towns whose shops, which are open every day, handle a large volume of rural trade.

As our survey of fairs in northern Jiangsu is still under way, what we have said above has yet to be verified. We have only given a rough account of the places that come under the name of "fair" in the map of the provincial cartographic bureau: 77 in the districts north of the Trunk Irrigation Canal and 15 south of the canal. There are more than 10 in either Suining or Huaiyin, where the concentration of fairs is the greatest, and more than five in Tongshan, Suqian, Muyang and Lianshui. The counties that have no "fairs" on the map are: Ganyu, Donghai and Guanyun in the Lianyungang Municipality, Sheyang, Jianhu, Dafeng and Dongtai counties in the Yancheng Municipality, Xuyi County in the Huaiyin Municipality, and Jiangdu, Xinghua, Taixian, Taixing and Jingjiang counties in the Yangzhou Municipality. This count does not fully reflect the distribution of fairs because some fairs are not marked on the map, and many places coming under the name of "fair" are probably not the venues of fairs any more. But the distribution of fairs on the map does to some extent tally with what the local cadres told us. Roughly speaking, there are more fairs north of the Trunk Irrigation Canal and fewer in the south, where the fairs are also smaller. However, the existence of fewer and smaller fairs does not mean that the flow of trade is small there. On the contrary, it shows that there are many more towns there with shops that do business on a regular basis to handle rural trade.

Fairs can be said to be the forerunners of towns. With the growth of commodity production in rural areas, fairs very likely grow gradually into towns. Buying and selling at fairs can be said to be trade at its initial stage of development in an underdeveloped rural economy with a big surplus of manpower. We saw tens of thousands of people jostling and making a lot of noise at the fairs. A man trudged scores of kilometres to bring a few dozen eggs or rice weighing 100 kilos or more to sell at a fair. For hours he squatted there to wait for customers, thus wasting a lot of time. If employment opportunities are available in the villages, who would bother himself to spend a whole day at a fair?

However, fairs are still a big attraction to peasants in the north of northern Jiangsu. There a folk-song says:

> *Fairs draw peasants like magnet,*
> *When men are ploughing,*
> *Their thoughts are with fairs,*
> *A lot of time he spends,*
> *Going from fair to fair,*
> *Buying here and selling there,*
> *Earning seven or eight yuan a day.*

People who have a dislike for pedlars may not like these few lines. But we have seen for ourselves the important role fairs play in commodity circulation and the peasants' desire to speed it up in the wake of the economic boom in the countryside. If marketing channels are clogged, a sizable part of the labour force will inevitably become individual pedlars. One problem meriting attention in our study is how to speed up the formation of towns to partially or wholly take the place of fairs.

The uneven distribution of fairs has heightened our interest in studying the uneven socio-economic development in northern Jiangsu. We have discovered that the numbers of fairs and towns vary in the northeastern and southwestern parts of northern Jiangsu. Then we observed that this difference is a reflection of the different ratio between industrial and agricultural production in a given area. Roughly speaking, the agricultural and industrial production ratio is:

7 to 3 in the counties of the Xuzhou Municipality;

6 to 4 in the counties of the Lianyungang Municipality, and in the counties north of the Trunk Irrigation Canal and in the Yancheng Municipality;

5.5 to 4.5 in the counties south of the canal in the Yancheng Municipality;

7 to 3 in the north of the Huaiyin Municipality; and

6 to 4 in the south of the Huaiyin Municipality.

The ratio for the counties of the Lixiahe area of the Yangzhou Municipality is the same as that for the counties in the
south of the Yancheng Municipality; in some localities industrial production exceeds agricultural production. But in the
counties south of the Nantong-Yangzhou Canal, the agricultural and industrial production ratio is 4 to 6 and the value
of industrial production exceeds agricultural output value and
is approaching the level of southern Jiangsu. The exact ratios
for all the counties have yet to be tabulated, but roughly speaking industrial production is lowest in northwestern part of
northern Jiangsu, and it goes up gradually in the southeastern
part. However, industrial production is lower than agricultural
production in localities north of the Trunk Irrigation Canal,
and in the Lixiahe area it is equal to or a little higher than
agricultural production. After crossing the Nantong-Yangzhou Canal we found that industrial output exceeds agricultural production.

Proceeding from these figures, we may divide northern
Jiangsu into two parts: the northwestern and southeastern
parts. The dividing line between the two cannot be drawn
concisely. Generally speaking, the northwestern part includes
the Xuzhou Municipality and the area north of the Trunk Irrigation Canal in the Huaiyin Municipality. The southeastern
part embraces the Lianyungang and Yancheng municipalities
along with the southern part of the Huaiyin Municipality and
the areas north of the Nantong-Yangzhou Canal in the Yangzhou Municipality. We are inclined to mark out a central
Jiangsu area by lumping together the Nanjing and Zhenjiang
municipalities with the area south of the Nantong-Yangzhou
Canal. In this way, Jiangsu Province would be divided into
three parts: northern Jiangsu, central Jiangsu and southern
Jiangsu, as we have dwelt upon before. Such a division, based
on general economic development trends at the present
moment, differs from ordinary accepted economic areas,
because it is based on some basic indexes of socio-economic development. The most important of these indexes is
the ratio between agricultural and industrial production in

a given area and the level of development of towns. To meet this requirement, we are compiling some comparable statistical indexes in preparation for conducting a general macro-economic survey of the whole of Jiangsu Province, with the help of inquiry forms. It must be pointed out here that the zonal differences deduced from statistics will never remain static for long. They will change with the growth rates achieved in different areas. Hence they are different from ordinary geographical economic areas. Our survey aims at helping to work out economic construction plans in the light of local conditions so as to avoid planning errors.

III

The route we took during the survey leads from Xuzhou to the interior of northern Jiangsu. Then, turning east to reach Lianyungang, it swings south to Yancheng, where it turns west to Huaiyin before moving south to Yangzhou. More time was spent in the north than in the south, and as a result our work was light at the beginning and intensive at the end, and there was little time left when we reached Yangzhou, where we had to spend a few days to conduct discussions. Hence we failed to go and tour the counties around Lake Hongze. That is why little or no mention of these counties is made in the summing up of our "way-probing" survey. This must be made good in the future.

In the account that follows, we would like to give an introduction to our tour and give a description of what we have seen and the problems we have come across. Some of the problems, which we noticed in a given locality, are likely to exist in other places too.

Xuzhou City was originally under the jurisdiction of Jiangsu Province. In the structural reform, six nearby counties were put under the jurisdiction of the city, and the Xuzhou Municipality is a part of the Huaihai Plain. The city itself is an important economic centre in the eastern part of this plain.

Although it is confronted by all sorts of restrictions brought about by administrative division, Xuzhou still maintains extensive economic ties with southern Shandong Province, northern Anhui Province and even with eastern Henan Province. Goods from Xuzhou were delivered to 44 counties in four provinces in early post-1949 days. Today, there are still over 20 counties in neighbouring provinces with a total of 20 million-plus population (population of the six counties in the Xuzhou Municipality is 6.9 million) that get their supplies from Xuzhou. The general economic feature in this area is that there are more fairs than towns, as is the case with a part of the Huanghe River and Huaihai Plain.

With a population of 780,000, Xuzhou is a medium-sized city endowed with good transport facilities and rich resources. The north-south Tianjin-Pukou Railway (opened in 1908-11) and the east-west Lanzhou-Lianyungang Railway (eastern section opened in 1921-25) crossed each other at Xuzhou. It is so rich in fossil fuel that the city is known as the "coal capital of Jiangsu Province". With coal has come electricity. The city's coal-fired power plant has a generating capacity of 800,000 kw. The 1980 output value of such industries as iron and steel, cement, machinery, chemicals and textiles established in the post-1949 years amounted to 2,000 million yuan.

Before we started out on the tour, we had hoped that Xuzhou would have done something to help promote industrial development in the village and towns in the six counties under its jurisdiction. But, to our surprise, we did not see a single factory chimney while driving for a long time along a road leading from the city to these counties. Some came into view after we had travelled 60 or 70 km. to reach a county seat. We inquired many times how many towns there were in this area, but the replies we got were always: "Only one town in a county, and that is the county seat."

The towns in Xuzhou Municipality put on a new look after 1978, and they have made some headway in rural industrialization. For instance, the production of either the fur-factory machinery plant at Fengxian County, the woollen mill at

Peixian County or the textile mill at Suining scaled to three million yuan last year. But with the exception of some lime or brick and tile works, we seldom caught sight of factory buildings along the road outside the county seat. That is why the industrial output value in each of the counties only accounts for 30 per cent of the total output value of its industrial and agricultural production. (It accounts for 61.8 per cent when the industrial output value of Xuzhou is added to it.) More than half the industrial output value (30 per cent) is generated by the food-stuff industry, 14 per cent by the farm-produce processing industry and 7.8 per cent by the building-material industry. These figures made us disappointed at the insignificant role played by the "coal capital" in promoting rural industrialization. Why is it that this city, endowed with rich energy resources and good communications, has not spread industry to the neighbouring rural districts in the way it has been done by cities in southern Jiangsu?

In "Restudy of Small Towns" I have stressed the part Shanghai and other medium-sized cities around it play in rural industrialization. But this is not the case with Xuzhou. Why? Through discussion with local officials, we came to understand that industry in this "coal capital" consists mainly of mining, which is labour-intensive. The manufacturing industry in the city was started late in the post-1949 years after the founding of the People's Republic.

Xuzhou's industrial production amounted to only 40 million yuan in 1949. In the post-1949 years, coal-mining in Xuzhou grew by leaps and bounds because fuel was in great demand in southern Jiangsu, where industry was developing apace. Its yearly coal output was doubled within five years in the early 1960s. Twelve million tons are now mined annually. But its mining technique still remains labour-intensive. The work force in the city has jumped from 50,000 in 1949 to the present total of 390,000, including those employed in newly established industries. But the bulk of the work force is employed in the mines. This shows that the nature of the industry in Xuzhou is quite different from that of Shanghai and neighbouring cities.

A large part of Xuzhou's industry consists of coal-hewing. Raw coal is mined but not processed. Such an industry can in no way help industrialize nearby rural districts.

For a long time, crop-growing has been the mainstay of the rural economy in the Xuzhou area. There are no cottage industries. Influenced for years by the idea of "taking grain production as the leading factor", there has been no industrial development in the villages. Rural industry has just been started.

The responsibility system instituted in the countryside after 1978 had added immensely to the enthusiasm of the peasantry. As a result, agricultural production has doubled within five years in the Xuzhou area, with grain output jumping from 1.7 million tons in 1978 to 3.65 million tons in 1983, and cotton soaring from 28,000 tons to 73,000 tons. The per-hectare yield of ginned cotton reached 1.06 tons — the highest in Jiangsu Province.

Hence the changes in the villages have been brought about by agricultural growth, and the biggest change is that the basic needs of the peasants have been met. Dried sweet-potato chips were eaten formerly; now it is rice and wheat flour. The eat-and-wear problem has been solved, but the 1983 per capita income was only 250 yuan. The people, in general, are not well-to-do. Such is the situation in the northwestern part of northern Jiangsu.

No longer "eating from the big pot", following the implementation of the responsibility system, peasant households in northern Jiangsu, like their counterparts in southern Jiangsu, have surplus labour that can be used to augment their income. But how to utilize it and what employment is to be created are determined by the geographical and historical conditions in each locality. As a rule relatively few peasants in either northern or southern Jiangsu go in for small industries. Most of them take up sidelines or such agriculture-related occupations as rice-milling and distillation of liquor, and the making of bricks and tiles for use in villages. Over the past year or two, there have emerged in various localities in northern

Jiangsu some small manufacturing enterprises resembling those in southern Jiangsu. But they have not occupied a dominant position.

I would like to dwell here on the export of labour services, a phenomenon we saw in Fengxian County of the Xuzhou Municipality. This is something that is new and growing very fast in the whole of Jiangsu Province. In the Xuzhou Municipality, 13,000 people have been organized to undertake construction work under contract in other places. They set out to work in the spring and return to their homes in the winter. An ordinary worker can bring home more than 1,000 yuan in wages, and a skilled worker, 2,000 to 3,000 yuan. Their earnings total tens of millions of yuan per year. No wonder the export of labour services has been locally dubbed "smokeless industry making good money".

The export of labour is not confined to Xuzhou or northern Jiangsu. It is learned that a million construction workers left Jiangsu Province last year to work in all parts of China — Shenzhen in the south, the Daqing Oilfield in the north, and in such faraway places as Karamay in Xinjiang and Ngari in Tibet. They are welcome everywhere for their good workmanship, speed and low-cost construction and for their abstention from stealing public property. I heard of the export of labour when conducting my field study in Nantong and Shazhou last year. I was informed that construction workers in the Nantong Municipality brought back a total of over 100 million yuan annually. This is a big sum that not only helps improve the livelihood of the villagers but also provides funds for developing rural economy. This is primitive accumulation — a source of capital investment for building industry in the villages and townships.

During the current tour we met a man in Fengxian County who was the first to organize a construction corps in the Xuzhou area to work elsewhere. A cadre member with the prefectural Party committee, he was assigned to work in Fengxian, his home county, during the "cultural revolution". There he was put in charge of a construction corps. At that time the two factions in the locality were warring with each other, and as a result the construction corps was not able to carry on its work any longer. Pulling out of the place, the corps went to the Liaohe Oilfield in northeast China to build construction projects for the government. The organizing abilities and talent of the corps leader and the capacity of the northern Jiangsu peasants for hard work soon won a name for the corps. Numbering only a few hundred at the start, the ranks of the corps swelled to several thousand in a few years' time. Now it has 100,000 peasant builders. Although its founder had left to take a ranking post in the municipal Party committee, the corps is still growing in strength.

The villagers in northern Jiangsu have a tradition of leaving their native places to find employment elsewhere. This is why Xuzhou and many other localities have taken so readily to exporting labour. With its water conservancy facilities falling into disrepair, northern Jiangsu was plagued by floods and famines in the past. People fled to places south of the Changjiang River to find food almost every year. Before the coming of floods, peasant families sealed the doors of their houses with mud and then fled their homes. In some localities like the Lixiahe area, whole villages were deserted during the flood seasons. Those who fled would never return again if they found employment and got established in other places. During my childhood, I had seen refugees from northern Jiangsu growing crops on newly formed land around Lake Taihu. When the water in the lake rose and submerged their crops, the refugees could only flee to cities to become coolies or beggars. In the pre-1949 years, the most backbreaking and lowest-paid jobs in Shanghai were done by northern Jiangsu refugees. Fleeced to the bone, many died. Others, who managed to get themselves established, became the lowest stratum of urban society. It is estimated that the ancestors of one million out of the 10 million population of Shanghai today came from the Yancheng-Funing area. They used to live in the slums of Yangshupu and Zhabei. Almost all the barbers, manicurists and cooks in Shanghai were people from Yangzhou, who still carry on these trades not only in other parts of China but also in places abroad where overseas Chinese live in compact communities.

The present-day export of labour is essentially different from the exodus of peasants in the wake of floods and famines in the past. The construction corps are well organized and led, and they are made up of trained people working in the service of the people. They render a useful service to other areas, particularly to frontier regions. Theirs is a new phenomenon under socialism, in fact, they aid the frontier areas with technical know-how and labour. The planned export of labour is a good measure to reduce population pressure in populous Jiangsu Province, although those who have left still have their residence registered in their home province.

In an article titled "Play a Lively Population Chess Game" I wrote two years ago, I said that two moves should be taken with regard to China's population. One is to develop small towns to serve as population reservoirs. The other is to send people to open up rich natural resources in sparsely populated areas. After witnessing the "export of labour" during the current survey, I realize the importance of combining the two moves in the chess game.

The labour corps, whose members do not register their residence in the places to which they go, are welcomed by people in the minority nationality regions. At present, they do only construction work, but they would gradually take up other undertakings in the years ahead. Now they stay away from home for only short periods. They will do so for longer periods in the future. When their ranks have grown, they will help in bringing about a more even distribution of population. When a new thing emerges, it will certainly grow and thrive if it really meets objective needs.

IV

Heading east from Xuzhou we reached Lianyungang, which has under its jurisdiction three counties, each of which with many towns, not just a single one. The county seat of Donghai

County is Niushan Town (pop. 15,000), to the west is Taolin Town (pop. 10,000). The county seat of Ganyu County is Qingkou Town (pop. 22,000), to the east is Haitou Town (pop. 10,000) and to the south is Shahe Town (pop. 11,000). The county seat of Guanyun County is at Yishan Town (pop. 36,000), to the north is Banpu Town (pop. 12,000) and to the east are the towns of Xuwei and Yangji (pop. 7,000). The offices of the Lianyungang Municipal Government are located near Xinhaiqu (pop. 230,000), to the north is Houzui Town and to the south is Nancheng Town (pop. 6,000).

With the exception of the county seats, all the aforementioned towns have not yet set up township governments, thus, according to local officials, they enjoy preferential tax rates. (Such rates for village-and-township industry have now been cancelled.) They have, in fact, been generally recognized as "towns". On our map (1:1,000,000) many of the places have the word "town" behind them. We have asterisked the places which are not marked "town" in the map but are identified as "towns" in materials supplied us by the local authorities.

Unlike Xuzhou Municipality, there are towns but no "fairs" in every county in the Lianyungang Municipality. Such a difference should be taken note of, but the difference is by no means very large, in fact. When dwelling on "fairs", I have said that there are shops that open daily in the bigger fairs and that goods are sold at the front of many shops while paddy is grown at the back. People are engaged in farming as well as in trade, and it is difficult to make a count of the non-agricultural population. On a fair day, a large number of people dwelling in a fair and in villages around it put up stalls on both sides of the street to offer wares procured from wholesalers. They are casual traders. Many peasants also come, bringing eggs, vegetables and other items they produce themselves, to be sold at the fair. With the proceeds, they buy back whatever they need. They cannot be defined as "traders", but are people who barter at the fair. Most of those attending fairs in the Xuzhou area are casual traders and peasants. There are fewer permanent shops. It is probably for this reason that they are called "fairs" instead of "towns".

There are more shops and factories doing business on ordinary days in Donghai County's Taolin Town and in Ganyu County's Shahe Town in the Lianyungang Municipality. In Taolin are 20-odd enterprises, including three well-known breweries and 40-odd shops. In Shahe are a knitwear mill, a flour mill and many small and big shops. And on fair days, traders and people flock to these towns from far and near. The number of people attending a fair exceeds 20,000, and in the Spring Festival or temple fair their numbers swell to as many as 50,000. There is not much difference between these towns and the Dali Fair in Suining County. But on a fair day, the bustle and hustle in Dali Fair is not as big as in the towns of Taolin and Shahe. Hence the difference between "fairs" and "towns" in northern Jiangsu is, in the main, indicated by intermittent fair activities and continuous trade, irregular business and regular business, and stalls and shops. With many shops doing business every day, places like Taolin and Shahe are called "towns". In northern Jiangsu places that go under the name of "town" are, in general, the venues of fairs attended by lots of people from neighbouring localities. There may be large numbers of people, but the barter trade carried on between the producers themselves is relatively small. Such trade increases proportionately in some small fairs which have few shops and stalls and are attended by several thousand people at a time. They are locally called "vegetable" or "straw sandal" fairs. It can be seen here that fairs should be classified into big and small ones of different dimensions. As trade handled by shops and stalls mounts, fairs eventually grow larger and become towns.

When we were touring northern Jiangsu, leading officials at the municipal and county levels gathered at a meeting to hear reports on the Party Central Committee's No. 1 and No. 4 documents of 1984, both of which stressed the strategy of developing towns and promoting commodity production in the countryside. To all was driven home this idea: "No stability without agriculture, no prosperity without industry, no vitality without commerce, no progress without knowledge." Hence the question then was not whether to develop rural industry and towns, but to establish what types of industry and determine how to found towns.

It seems that some people there still toss with the idea that a town can be founded by just setting up administrative offices and putting up some sort of a signboard in a fair. It is really not that simple. So we have to dwell here again on the difference between a fair and a town. I am convinced that a real town could only come into existence when rural commodity production has attained quite a high level of development, which cannot be easily achieved by expanding agricultural production alone. Industry must be established on the village-township level.

The fact that there are towns but no fairs in southern Jiangsu, is probably due to the fact that commodities were produced there by rural handicraft industries in very early times. And the growth of rural industry over the past few years has brought a boom to the towns.

In northern Jiangsu, where traditional rural industries are backward, fairs alone can handle commodity circulation in localities that produce only farm produce. As a result, towns cannot be established there easily. Industrial commodity production differs from agricultural commodity production. The former not only requires markets for its products, but also raw materials before the goods are made, and various types of service during the manufacturing process. Rural industry relies to a great extent on towns that are economic centres in the rural districts. This means that the establishment of towns in rural northern Jiangsu can only come after the establishment of industry on the village-township level and the further growth of agricultural commodity production. That is to say, the establishment of towns takes in the development of rural industry.

Peasants in northern Jiangsu have just solved their eat-and-wear problem, and only a small number of them are becoming well-to-do. Their eat-and-wear problem has been solved by increasing farm production, and to become well-off they have to undertake sidelines and industrial production.

Northern Jiangsu lags far behind southern Jiangsu in rural industrial development. As I have said before, the ratio between industrial and agricultural output value in the suburbs of Xuzhou and in the six counties of the Xuzhou Municipality is 3 to 7, according to an estimate by local officials. That in the Lianyungang Municipality is a little higher — about 4 to 6. These estimates are about the same as the data we collected in several towns we visited in Donghai and Ganyu.

Xuzhou was originally a city under the jurisdiction of Jiangsu Province. Its statistics can be easily separated from those of the counties under its jurisdiction. But it is different to do so with the city proper of Lianyungang, which was formed by the merger of three towns that have not been physically joined together yet. This makes it difficult to classify which industrial enterprises fall into the rural-industry category. If viewed only from the ownership angle, there are a total of 1,002 collectively-owned enterprises (accounting for 80 per cent of all the enterprises), but their production amounts to only 380 million yuan or 28 per cent of total industrial output value in the city. We know that well-run collectively-owned enterprises were made into publicly-owned ones at one time. So a classification made on the basis of ownership alone cannot give a true ratio of rural industrial production. Further research has to be made to solve that problem.

From what data we have on hand, it can be seen that there is little industry in northern Jiangsu. It is only in the Yangzhou Municipality that industrial production amounted to 2,000 million yuan in 1983 (most of which should be redrawn into the central Jiangsu area). That for the other municipalities is below 1,000 million yuan. It is 790 million in Yancheng; 430 million in Huaiyin and 530 million in Xuzhou. That in Lianyungang is the lowest — 280 million, but this municipality embracing only three counties is the smallest — about one-fourth the size of the Huaiyin Municipality. Generally speaking, the production value of rural industry in a municipality of northern Jiangsu is equal to only that of one county in southern Jiangsu, because northern Jiangsu's rural industry was started late. As a rule, industry was given little attention in the development programme prior to the promulgation of the Party Central Committee's No. 1 and No. 4 documents of 1984.

As northern Jiangsu's rural industry was started late, its collectively-owned enterprises have a weak foundation. When the peasants in northern Jiangsu were getting enough to eat and wear and wanted to be well-off, the government policy was one of encouraging the setting up of specialized households following the institution of the family responsibility system. The situation is quite different in southern Jiangsu, where rural industry was established earlier under the commune system. As collective units, the communes and production brigades and teams under them set up industrial enterprises with funds they accumulated themselves. The enterprises were managed by the collectives, which distributed the income to commune members. After a period of five to six years, most of the collectives were consolidated and had grown in size.

In northern Jiangsu, where rural industry was started much later, and the responsibility system was instituted earlier, the number of specialized households grew rapidly. Because of this, we wanted to find out what role specialized households were playing in rural industrialization. In southern Jiangsu, industrial enterprises were set up at an earlier date by collective. Are industrial enterprises in northern Jiangsu to be started by individual specialized households or by amalgamations of these households? If so, how would they in the future develop into regional collective enterprises or inter-regional amalgamated concerns? These problems will be studied at a later stage.

The data collected in Ganyu County shows there were nearly 60,000 specialized households and 1,087 amalgamations of households in the county in 1983. The number kept increasing very fast. *One Hundred Households Rich Through Hard*

114 SMALL TOWNS IN CHINA

Work, published by the county Party committee in March 1984, carries the success stories of 109 specialized households and amalgamations. Forty-two of these are engaged in industry (mechanical repairing, making farm implements, raw-material processing, production of building materials and mining), 10 in transport, 28 in the raising of poultry, fish and animals and 27 in fruit growing. It can be seen here that most of the specialized households are engaged in sidelines. Those who are expert at raising pigs and poultry and at growing vegetables and fruit are also engaged in growing the grain they consume themselves. Each of these families makes almost 10,000 yuan a year. One of them of a collective nature is a household specialized in poultry-raising. While raising chickens on its own, this household has hooked up with 47 other families to which it supplies chicks and technical instruction. Another example cited is of four households jointly operating a small fishing craft. They fish in the sea and the proceeds from the sales are shared out to each according to the amount of work done.

The rural enterprises are operated in various ways. Most are run by individual households, some of which also operate, under contract, brick kilns, repair shops or wooden bucket-making workshops, etc. One of the enterprises cited is a farm machinery repair workshop contracted from a collective by nine persons. The collective which supplies them with the building and tools receives in return a fixed profit annually. Some enterprises, such as workshops producing fire-proof materials, plastic goods, wicker baskets, phosphate fertilizer and foundry products, are run by individual owners who employ workers and pay them wages. The largest number hired by a workshop is 15. What we have seen in Ganyu County shows that it will take some time for specialized households to merge into collective enterprises.

In the county we saw a department store jointly operated by individual households. Each of the employees or salesclerks puts in a share before they came to work in the store. They receive wages and a share of the profits earned. We were told that such an arrangement was readily accepted by peasants because funds could be raised quickly and employment made available for young people. People we met said the peasants who had cash in their pockets now were glad to spend money to get jobs for their children. Such amalgamations of individual households are growing in numbers. We learned that there were 375 amalgamations involving 2,000 persons and a total investment of 270 million yuan operating in Ganyu County today.

Here is an example of a collectively-run concern that came into existence with the merger of individually-run enterprises in Fengxian County of the Xuzhou Municipality: In the county's Xumiao Village is a workshop run by the Dong brothers, making mirror frames, which find a ready market in the cities of Beijing, Tianjin and Nanjing as well as in the provinces of Shandong and Henan. Each of the 32 worker-owners, on the average, makes 2,000 yuan annually. The workshop in 1984 merged with the county supply and marketing co-operative which makes available to it factory premises and a sales outlet in the county seat while supplying it with 30,000 yuan and raw materials. The co-operative detailed bookkeepers and salesclerks to help. The profits earned are shared between the workshop and co-operative according to terms stipulated in their agreement.

Northern Jiangsu's peasants have cash in their hands in the wake of good harvests, and the export of labour earns tens of millions of yuan that flow into the villages annually. Seeing that funds were needed for rural industrialization, we tried to find out how this money, which found its way into innumerable homes, was spent. In southern Jiangsu, rural industries were collectively-run concerns, and the profit accumulated was used first for expanding production, and then distributed to peasants in the form of wages. The first thing the peasants did with the money was to improve their living. They bought food and clothing first and then built housing. The houses erected were one-storey at first. Later two-storey houses were built everywhere, in a housing boom that has been sweeping rural southern Jiangsu for several years.

In northern Jiangsu, where the eat-and-wear problem has just been solved, old houses are being replaced by new ones, as thatched mud cottages are pulled down to give way to break-and-tile dwellings. But this is not done very fast, and old thatched cottages still account for half of the housing in some localities. And atop some houses, only the fringes of the straw roofs are lined with tiles. Where has the money of the peasants gone?

What impressed us most when we were in Ganyu County were the many hand tractors, each drawing a trailer, that we saw running on the highways. We were told that these machines were bought by the peasants this year. A total of two to three million yuan was spent by the peasants in the county after January 1984 in the purchase of 50 motor vehicles, 300 small boats and 850 tractors. This is indicative of the zeal with which the peasants invest in production. They are eager to go into transport. A few households, which undertook the transport of goods with trucks they bought themselves, had become rich, with the annual income of each household shooting up to 10,000 yuan. People wanted to buy trucks everywhere, but the supply of transport vehicles lagged far behind rural economic expansion.

We should take note here of the accumulation and use of funds in rural economic development. For the past five years or more, southern Jiangsu has on the whole become self-supporting in capital investment in the developing rural economy. Loans are no longer obtained from the government now. On the contrary, some funds accumulated in the countryside are being invested in the urban areas. This is an important new trend. Rural southern Jiangsu has attained such a high level of development because the communes and their production brigades have, in addition to agricultural primitive accumulation, put in funds to establish industries. After setting aside a part to be shared out among commune members, which the peasants use to fund agricultural production, to erect public buildings or to be put into public reserve funds, the profits accumulated by rural industry are channelled back to industrial production. This is an effective means of fund accumulation by the collectives.

As it has been mentioned above, investment in northern Jiangsu's rural development over the past few years came mainly from the accumulation made by individual peasants, specialized households, amalgamations of specialized households and the export of labour services, and this accumulation is scattered in innumerable households. What are the methods to be employed to collect such scattered funds for industrial investment? Bank savings are no doubt a good method, but how much money can those absorb? Some people have estimated it never exceeds half the amount of money in the hands of the peasantry that could be used as investment funds. What about the remaining money? We have written above that there are peasants getting jobs in factories by buying shares in the factories. Such a method has in fact the essence of stock certificates, except that they are not transferable. Are there any other places where more flexible measures are being tried out to create a new type of stock enterprise? We are looking forward to seeing some, someday.

V

Going south from Lianyungang we reached the Yancheng Municipality, which was formed by silt brought down over the centuries by the Huaihe and Huanghe rivers. With its eastern coastline washed by the sea, it is an area that has been noted for its salt production from time immemorial. A salt official was first posted here way back in the Han Dynasty (206 B.C.-220 A.D.). Yancheng (Salt City) has under its jurisdiction seven counties, three of which — Funing, Xiangshui and Binhai — are situated north of the Trunk Irrigation Canal. These three counties and Guannan and Lianshui counties in the Huaiyin Municipality have long been regarded as the poorest in northern Jiangsu. The situation there began to take a turn for the better following the completion of the Trunk Irrigation Canal. Working like Trojans for the past three decades and more, the peasants there have built irrigation facilities on an immense scale. The land was cultivated more scientifically. All this, coupled with the sound policies implemented after 1978, has given these once impoverished counties a new lease on life.

That part of the Yancheng Municipality south of the Trunk Irrigation Canal is divided into two — the eastern and western parts. Land formed earlier in the western part. It is said that Fan Zhongyan (989-1052), who was serving as an official here in the second decade of the 11th century, had built a tide-prevention wall called the Lord Fan Dyke that now forms the roadbed of the Tongyu Highway. It is also said that Shanggang (Upper Mound) Town on the road was formerly a sandy mound to which people flocked to escape from tidal waves. Around Yancheng there are many places that still bear the name *gang* (mound), as Big Mound, Middle Mound and Dragon Mound. This is proof that the land east of the highway was formed only some 1,000 years ago, during which a stretch of land measuring 50 km. across was formed along the coast east of the Tongyu Highway. The silt carried down to the East China Sea by the Huanghe and Changjiang rivers is still creating land along the Jiangsu coast. As a result, there are extensive tracts of sandy flats which become a boundless expanse of land at low tide. The well-known Dongsha (East Sand) is 50-60 km. off the shore. It is estimated that over half a million hectares of land along the Jiangsu coast alone could be won from the sea for crops if dykes are thrown up to keep off the waves.

To begin with, I will give an account of the area east of Yancheng, where salt has been produced since very ancient times. As salt is an important ingredient in the human diets, the feudal dynasties of bygone days monopolized the salt trade. All the salt produced by the local people was handed over to the government at a minimal price. Then salt officials entrusted salt merchants with the duty of selling it all over China. Hence it was called "official salt".

Yancheng was a salt collecting centre, and Yangzhou was

a port to which salt merchants brought their salt for delivery to different parts of the country. Men of wealth went to wine and dine in Yangzhou. But the workers who toiled and sweated to produce salt on the coast were terribly exploited and led a miserable life. The localities where they lived were economically extremely backward.

In the later part of the Qing Dynasty (1644-1911), an entrepreneur by the name of Zhang Jian made his appearance in Nantong where he planned to establish factories in his native place to "save China through industrialization". He imported machinery and set up textile mills in Nantong. To get raw materials for the mills, he grew cotton on sandy land stretching along the coast between Nantong and Yancheng. The salt fields were ploughed under to make way for the cotton plant.

During World War I, the imperialist powers were busily fighting among themselves, thus loosening their grip on China and other parts of eastern Asia. As a result, a modern textile industry came into existence in Wuxi, Changzhou and Nantong in southern Jiangsu Province. This laid the cornerstone for a national industry operated by Chinese capitalists on the Changjiang Delta. The cotton that went to feed the mills was, for the most part, grown on the northern Jiangsu seaboard — the biggest cotton-growing area in the northern part of the province.

The rise or fall of this cotton area was closely linked with the prosperity or slump of the textile industry run by national capitalists on the Changjiang Delta. The cotton-growing area prospered when the textile industry began to pick up in the early 1930s. It slumped after the outbreak of the War of Resistance Against Japan in 1937 during which northern Jiangsu became a theatre in which our New Fourth Army fought see-saw battles with the Japanese invaders, who brought ruin to many towns and villages. This brought a sharp downturn in the economy.

In the post-1949 years, the economy in the cotton region began to improve, but its growth was later arrested by the implementation of "Leftist" policies. A turn for the better came after 1978.

Beginning from 1979, settlers were brought from the interior to reclaim land for crop cultivation in the Xindong Township, not far from Jianggang Town. The population there grew to 8,100 within five years. This is indicative of the great interest people have in opening up the sandy flats here.

With a population of 7,149,000, the Yancheng Municipality has only 614,000 hectares of cultivated land and each of the agricultural population has a share of only 0.093 hectare. But in this populous area with little land there are over 13,300 hectares of sandy beaches that can be opened up for crop cultivation in Dongtai County, situated near Jianggang Town. To date only 3,670 hectares have been put under the plough in Xindong Township, giving each inhabitant nearly half a hectare. The per capita income there was 309 yuan in 1981. It was 347 yuan and 475 yuan in 1982 and 1983 respectively — exceeding the levels in other counties of the Yancheng Municipality.

This survey in Jianggang dwells on the prospects of bringing in settlers to open up wasteland. There are still some 10,000 hectares of such land in Dongtai County. Some 20,000 settlers can be sent there. It is estimated that there are over 530,000 hectares of wasteland along the 400 to 500 km. coastline of northern Jiangsu. If the government puts an investment (4,500 yuan per hectare) into building infrastructural facilities on the wasteland with local labour, at least 1.5 million settlers can come to put the land under crops.

The population of Jiangsu Province is 60 million, and it is expected to increase by another six million or more by the year 2000. This is a problem that merits attention. If efforts are made to encourage settlers to come in the next 15 years, the opened land would absorb an agricultural population of 1,000,000. And if townlets with 5,000 people were to be established at intervals of 15 km., there would be some 30 townlets with a total population of 150,000 in the reclaimed areas. This would play an important part in reducing the population pressure in Jiangsu Province in the coming 15 years. If each settler were given 0.133 hectare of land to enable him to attain a standard of living like those in other parts of the province, the population of the reclaimed areas would increase by 150 per cent to 3,000,000 — half again the population in the province, in the coming 15 years.

The land reclamation effort we dwelt on here does not include the Dongsha (East Sand), a vast expanse of sandy flats off the northern Jiangsu coast. The map shows that it stretches for 20 km. from north to south and 40 km. from east to west and that it emerges from the sea at low tide. It can be reclaimed only with government investment in the construction of a massive dyke system around the Dongsha sandy flats. Its opening up would provide employment for Jiangsu Province's growing population.

To send settlers to reclaim wasteland constitutes a safety valve for the province's population pressure. Another important outlet is the establishment of rural industry and towns on the coast, which would enable local governments to obtain financial resources to provide facilities that settlers must have for production and for living. In Jianggang, where people are engaged in fishing, we have seen that a foodstuff industry has been established. This has made peasants in the nearby villages take up sidelines, thus augmenting their income. A small town with industry is able to accumulate funds for use on road improvement as well as in erecting theatres and other cultural facilities. In the wake of rural industry come shops, then post offices and telephone services to make life convenient for all. Working part-time on the farm and part-time in industry, settlers on the reclaimed land would live quite decently. As a result more and more people in the villages from which the original settlers came would arrive to turn more sandy flats into blooming fields.

Our survey in this respect has just begun. The pioneering work that has been done in Jianggang and other places must be summed up for use in opening up more wasteland. Problems awaiting solution must not be left unnoticed in the course of land reclamation.

VI

That portion of the Yancheng Municipality south of the Trunk Irrigation Canal is divided by the Tongyu Highway into the eastern and western parts. Cotton is grown in the eastern part and food grain in the western part situated in the Lixiahe area, which also embraces the western part of Dongtai, Funing and Jianhu of the Yancheng Municipality and most of the suburban districts of Yancheng City, Gaoyou, Xinghua, Baoying and Jiangdu of the Yangzhou Municipality, the northern part of Taizhou and the southern part of Huai'an. The Lixiahe area is northern Jiangsu's lowest depression with Xinghua located at the "bottom of the cauldron".

The Lixiahe area spreads over several municipalities. The western boundary of the area forms a dividing line, on one side of which cotton grows and on the other side food grain is cultivated. As a result of the exchange of cotton and grain that has been going on here for a long time, a string of towns have come into existence along this line. The most famous ones from north to south are Fucheng in Funing County, Shanggang in Jianhu, Wuyou in suburban Yancheng, Liuzhuang and Baiju in Dafeng County and Dongtai, Anfeng and Fu'an in Dongtai County. Dotting the dividing line are 22 towns or 12 per cent of the total within the Yancheng Municipality. These towns used to be entrepots for farm produce and locally produced salt. Most of them originated as villages. Hence the majority of their population are peasants. Agricultural population accounts for 80 per cent of the total in many of the towns in Jianhu and that of the towns in Dongtai County numbers 125,000, accounting for 60 per cent of the total population of 210,000 of the towns. If the current administrative standards for towns are used as a yardstick, they are not qualified to be towns. In the post-1949 period, commune or township administrative set-ups were established in some of these towns. As a result they became political centres and grew somewhat in size. As rural industry was established in some of the towns over the past few years, they are no longer just trading and political centres. Industry has attained quite a high status in the towns' economic structures, and some of the towns are almost as well developed as those in southern Jiangsu.

Generally speaking, there was little industry in these towns prior to the 1970s. In 1966, there were in the Yancheng Municipality only some 280 rural industrial enterprises, most of which engaged in food and cotton processing and the making and repairing of iron or wooden farm implements. Industry was started in some of the towns during the mid-70s, and experienced quite rapid growth after 1978. According to 1983 statistics, there are 5,603 rural industrial enterprises with a work force of more than 240,000 in the Yancheng Municipality. Their total production amounted to 790 million yuan that year. High-rise buildings made their appearance for the first time in some of these towns, where cultural centres have been built, roads paved and underground sewers laid out. The towns are taking on a new look and experiencing an economic boom.

Our trip to Dagang Town in the suburbs of Yancheng has changed our notion that there are no well-developed towns in northern Jiangsu. It is true there are not many towns like Dagang in this part. But what has taken place there shows that with the advent of rural industry, towns would prosper. What Dagang has done can be achieved by other towns in northern Jiangsu, which have all the conditions for establishing rural industry like that of southern Jiangsu.

Situated on the southwestern fringe of the Yancheng Municipality, Dagang lies at a place where the boundaries of Dafeng and Xinghua counties and the former Yancheng County meet. With a population of 5,500, it has for long been one of the well-known large towns in the Yancheng Municipality as well as one of the most ancient towns in the Yancheng-Funing area. It was made a town more than 400 years ago in the Ming Dynasty. There were then 100 households, and its population by the 1930s reached 6,000 to 7,000, exceeding that of the present day. The town is located in a fertile area criss-crossed by canals and rivers, known as a land of rice and fish in northern

Jiangsu. Peasants come from far and wide on boats to trade in the town that has become a centre for the exchange of farm produce and sideline products.

The town was booming before the outbreak of the War of Resistance Against Japan in 1937; there were then no fewer than 700 shops, eating houses and other stores in town. Scores of rice shops dotted the streets and long lines of grain-laiden boats constantly coming and going presented a majestic scene. At that time, there were dozens of old-style schools with a total enrolment of 50,000-60,000.

Occupied by the Japanese army during the war, Dagang began to decline. Prosperity returned somewhat in the early post-1949 period. But in the 1950s the government monopolized the purchase and marketing of grain and banned privately-owned rice shops. This brought a recession to the town, whose prosperity had been built on the rice trade. The population was reduced on three occasions: in 1954 more than 300 people were sent to other places with the reorganization of the trading network in town; a total of 600 people were resettled in the villages during the three harsh years of the early 1960s; and another 300 were mobilized to go live in the countryside after 1970. Though it has been increasing over the past few years, the population has not yet reached its peak of the past.

Things began to improve in Dagang in the 1970s when the town started to industrialize by recruiting factory workers from southern Jiangsu, where factories "stopped production to make revolution" and workers were sent to the rural districts. Industry in town grew by leaps and bounds after 1978, and its production, which totalled only 8.49 million yuan in 1978, jumped to 20 million yuan in 1983 — taking first place among the towns in the Yancheng Municipality. The per capita income of the town dwellers shot up from 70-80 yuan in the 1960s to 300 yuan in 1983.

The implementation of sound policies is the most important factor that brings prosperity to Dagang, and the method employed to achieve it is industrialization. When the town was in a slump and its people were faced with a shortage of food and clothing, the county government had to extend a loan of some 10,000 yuan every year to help the needy families. With the rapid growth of industry in the 1970s, the town's economy has been improving year by year, and now Dagang boasts 16 state-owned enterprises, seven collectively-run concerns and another 28 operated by communes and township administration. The 1983 output value of agricultural-industrial production in the township amounted to 50 million yuan, 36 per cent of which was accounted for by commune-run industries, and 17 per cent by enterprises set up by production brigades. Added together, the two amounted to 53 per cent of the total. The industrial output value of the township is already a little larger than that of agricultural and sideline production.

Dagang's industry has absorbed a lot of surplus manpower from the countryside. With a large population and little land, the township has only 0.08 hectares of cropland for each inhabitant. People used to leave the villages to find jobs elsewhere, and now 3,000 to 4,000 of them are still working in Yancheng City proper, adding to the population pressure there. Today some 2,000 people dwelling in the surrounding villages are profitably employed in rural industries established in Dagang. They come to work in the morning and return to their homes in the villages in the evening. They no longer go to find employment in cities. Rural industry has relieved the population pressure in the urban centres.

After developing its own industry, Dagang began to help spread industry to the surrounding countryside. With the assistance of the three knit-wear mills in town, 30 production brigades have set up in the villages a loose agglomeration of branch mills that keep their own accounts and are responsible for their own profits or losses. The knit-wear mills do the procurement of raw materials and the marketing of products for the small mills. This provides an example of a large factory successfully assisting smaller ones.

Dagang has also set a good example for northern Jiangsu in the absorption of technical and trained people as well as in spreading industry to the villages by setting up industrial amalgamations. It has started quite early in adopting a new way to recruit technicians, one of whom was a man once wrongly branded as a counter-revolutionary. When this man came to Dagang, he was not discriminated against but encouraged to bring his talents into play to help speed the town's industrialization. Technical people who came could keep their minds on their work because they were taken good care of. More skilled people have been recruited from other places, and there are now 73 of them. They have already helped train 120 local technicians, while the local factories have sent 260 people to get training in other places. Seven of every 10 workers in 14 of the commune-run factories have received such training. Placing emphasis on making contact with other areas, Dagang's factories have established business ties with 74 enterprises elsewhere, and are co-operating with another 36. The town has 97 people serving on five purchasing and marketing teams stationed in cities and has also set up 12 economic information centres in various large and medium-sized cities. As a result, Dagang's industry has built up connections with Shanghai and Tianjin. This has helped the town develop its industry.

Except for municipal cities and county seats, few places in northern Jiangsu have developed rural industry as successfully as Dagang. I give an account of Dagang here with a view of showing that northern Jiangsu has the conditions for rural industrialization. It also shows that the influence of such cities as Shanghai and Tianjin is not confined to localities close to them, because the spread of techniques and knowledge, which is done mainly by man, can overcome great distances. Remoteness and proximity, of course, play a part here, but it does not mean that the spread can only be effected between places that are closely linked together. An example is provided by Dagang, which absorbs technical information from Shanghai and Tianjin and co-operates with them. Although northern Jiangsu is far away from industrial cities and has poor communications, it can be influenced economically by large cities provided efforts are made to create the ways and means to do so. It is our hope that more Dagangs will emerge in northern Jiangsu.

After moving across the fringe of the Lixiahe area, we came to the counties of Gaoyou and Xinghua. Time was running short and we did not tour the villages. But we visited Gaoyou and Zhaoyang towns, seats of the administrations of the two counties.

The Lixiahe area has been transformed into a paddy land with a web of canals and rivers resembling those south of the Changjiang River, thanks to water conservancy projects built after the founding of the People's Republic. On the low-lying land here only a single crop of rice could be grown in a year. There was waterlogging every two out of three years, and the yield averaged only 2.5 to 3 tons per hectare. The result was that large numbers of people fled their homes to find food in areas south of the Changjiang. For some time the government shipped in relief grain, after 1949. A total of 600 tons was delivered to Xinghua County alone between 1951 and 1952, and another 40 tons arrived in 1955 when agricultural co-operatives were being formed in the county. In 1954, most of the 200 blacksmiths there had fled to find a living in other places. The situation began to improve after the harsh years of the early 1960s, but soon came the ten disastrous years of the "cultural revolution", during which the average per capita income of the peasants remained below 100 yuan per year. Things began to pick up in 1978 and today the Lixiahe area has become a big producer of marketable grain in China. With an average per-hectare rice yield of around 11.25 tons, Xinghua has become the banner paddy county in the whole of Jiangsu Province. Such an achievement within five years is truly a miracle.

The distribution of towns in the Lixiahe area is similar to that in the land of canals and rivers around Lake Taihu in southern Jiangsu. A small town in which farm produce is traded is usually located at a place criss-crossed with canals that make transport easy. For instance, in Gaoyou County, there are 46 small and large towns, evenly distributed at intervals of five to ten km. On the average there is a town for every 27 sq. km. of land. The large ones have a population of 7,000 to 8,000 each, and the smaller ones have a population of nearly 1,000. The three largest towns are Linze, Sanduo and Jieshou, each with 9,000 inhabitants. They are situated near the boundaries of neighbouring counties quite far from county seats. The same is true with the biggest towns of Shagou, Anfeng and Dainan in Xinghua County. These towns are the venues of inter-county trade, but most of them have not shaken off the trappings of fairs which are held there at five-day intervals throughout each month. These big fairs have been growing in size and are being held at shorter intervals since 1978. And in Gaoyou County's Baqiao Town, where a fair is held in every five days, fish, meat and vegetables are for sale every day and there are 40-odd stalls offering grocery items daily.

Formerly a fair was held every five days in the town of Shanggang in Jianhu County of the Yancheng Muncipality. Today, fairs there are not held on fixed dates, and 20,000 people come to town daily to trade farm produce and handicraft products. Such is the process by which fairs are becoming towns. It can be seen here that a gradual transformation is taking place in the large and small towns and fairs in the Lixiahe area, where an increasing number of economic, political and cultural centres are emerging in the countryside.

In the large towns, the non-agricultural population is increasing. In this low-lying area where flooding had been very frequent in the past, people chose to build their houses on high ground. This gave birth to villages of enormous size, some of which have several thousand households each. These villages were, and still are, the venues of fairs. Hence the agricultural population of these fairs is large, proportionately. The non-farm population is increasing with the growth of industry and commerce. As a result, the agricultural population now accounts for only 34.3 per cent of the total population in the 46 towns of Gaoyou County. Those who farm and work in industry account for 24.6 per cent, students 13.3 per cent, and non-farm population 27.8 per cent. The agricultural population has dropped from 50 per cent to 34.3 per cent because many peasants have gone into industry in the past few years. This is a sign that towns are emerging.

It can be seen that the peasants in some of these villages are supplying what the others need at what are called "vegetable fairs", each of which is usually attended by 400 to 500 people at a time. These fairs are located within a radius of 5 to 7 km. In localities with good communications, some of these fairs are held in places where communes have their offices. Each of the large ones attracts several thousand people at a time. Offered for sale are thermos flasks and other manufactured items. There are four to six big fairs, each attended by 10,000 people or more, in a county, and the venues of the biggest ones are usually at the county seats. At big fairs, each serving three to five communes, most of the trade is handled by shops, some of which have in stock such more expensive items as wall clocks, radios, TVs and bicycles.

As a rule, towns have been founded in the county seats of northern Jiangsu, and none has emerged in localities with many big fairs. It appears that the big fairs are in the process of becoming towns. As local rural industry has only just been started, these fairs mainly serve as centres for the collection and distribution of farm produce and for the sale of manufactured goods brought in from big cities.

The rural industrial enterprises in the Lixiahe area were, for the most part, set up in the early 1970s. Although industry has developed on quite a big scale in some large towns there, the value of industrial production in the Lixiahe area still lags behind that of farm production.

Here let me cite Xinghua County as an example. It has long been known for its iron wares. What industry Xinghua had before the founding of the People's Republic in 1949 consisted of a few iron workshops in the county seat. But factories turning out machinery, electronic products, chemicals and other products have been mushrooming since the early 1970s. More than half the factories, whose 1983 output amounted to almost 400 million yuan, are located in the county seat of Zhaoyang.

The same is true of Gaoyou Town in the county with the same name. Formerly the town had three or four iron workshops whose production came to some one million yuan per year. Today, there are 100-plus factories, and their 1983 output value totalled 176 million yuan. The townlet of Baqiao in the county, which started to embark on an industrialization programme in the early 1970s, now boasts a dozen or so factories, with output value amounting to 6.17 million yuan, to account for 50 per cent of the total agricultural-industrial output value in the township. It came second among all the townships in the county. And in the tiny town of Nanchacun, the Red Star Leather Products Factory jointly operated by 100-odd households turned out goods worth 4.8 million yuan in 1983. The factory has surfaced a 2-km.-long road and built a public bath in town with its accumulations. It seems that the peasants in this part are coming to understand that in the wake of the growth of farm production, they have to go in for industry in order to become well-to-do.

In a word, farm production has seen rapid expansion within five years in the Lixiahe and other areas referred to above. The expansion is most conspicuous in the Lixiahe area previously plagued by flood and famine. This area, where people used to "flee from famines", has become a granary. In Xinghua's Dainan Town, the per capita income of the farm population jumped from 131 yuan in 1978 to 422 yuan in 1983, a more than three-fold increase in five years' time. Statistics show that the per capita income of the non-farm population in the town is not as great as that of the agricultural population. This has made some people believe that the "difference between town and country" has been smoothed out. But actually it means only that industry here is underdeveloped and lags behind agricultural growth. The difference between town and country cannot be solved with such a formula.

The major problem in this part of northern Jiangsu today is still how to accelerate rural industrialization to catch up with other areas economically. The growth of farm production has indeed solved the food and clothing problem, but new problems are surfacing. After eating their fill and delivering their shares of public grain to the government, the peasants still have lots of grain left. What are they going to do with the surplus? As we have seen at the fairs, there is a scarcity of consumer and grocery items. But there is plenty of food grain that cannot be sold out because there are few buyers. This is the case with other farm produce. Garlic fetched a good price last year. As a result, the acreage sown to this crop was expanded in 1984, but few traders came from outside to purchase garlic. This resulted in a glut of garlic and there were no facilities to preserve it. The garlic growers were making a hue and cry at the time of our visit. This shows that both storage facilities and marketing channels cannot keep pace with agricultural expansion. It is certain that a marketing problem would emerge if food processing failed to keep pace with the growth of farm production.

The way out for northern Jiangsu peasants is to undertake poultry raising and stock breeding, which have been expanding very fast lately. In a previous article on small towns, I wrote about large quantities of meat chickens being shipped to the south. I suggested that with grain production going up, there is in northern Jiangsu a surplus that can be used as feed for chickens, pigs, rabbits and other farm animals. But the poultry and animals raised have to be marketed. At present they are transported live in a primitive way to southern Jiangsu and large numbers of them die on the way. This compels northern Jiangsu peasants to establish a meat packing industry. Plans are under study to erect warehousing and cold storage facilities in some towns to store meat and then send it out of northern Jiangsu.

While in Xinghua County we saw a processing factory that dehydrates and packs vegetables grown in a township for distant markets. This is a typical processing factory in the service of agriculture. So are workshops turning out ready-to-eat, sauced chickens, preserved eggs and other foods. What northern Jiangsu urgently needs is a food processing industry, the establishment of which will speed up the increase of specialized households and the feed industry. This will cause a cyclic agriculture-industry system to emerge directly from bumper farm harvests.

It should be pointed out here that this will not hamper the setting up of other manufacturing industries, not even such an advanced sector as the quartz rock crystal-based laser industry. To begin with, food processing, a much simpler industry, can be established now to make the peasants more well-to-do and to bring consecutive good harvests. This will lead to the accumulation of funds and pave the way for the building up of advanced industries and special manufacturing industries.

The question for northern Jiangsu now is how to industrialize and what industries are to be set up. I cannot offer specific suggestions without an in-depth study. What I would like to point out here is that northern Jiangsu has started its rural industrialization late, and its further development relies much on good agricultural harvests. Hence the road it takes cannot be the same as the one traversed by southern Jiangsu. A solution to this problem should be made from a practical, down-to-earth approach.

During this "way-probing" tour we did not go to the localities around Lake Hongze which are under the jurisdiction of Huaiyin City, or those west of the Grand Canal, because time was running short. Members of our advance party are now conducting a survey of these localities, and I hope to join them one day. An account of these areas will be written later. We did not visit central Jiangsu, which embraces the Nanjing and Zhenjiang municipalities and the counties of the Yangzhou Municipality that are situated south of the Tongyang Canal. A survey of these areas, too, will be made later.

First draft written in Nanjing on June 7, 1984.
Rewritten in Beijing on July 18, 1984.

SMALL TOWNS IN CENTRAL JIANGSU

Fei Hsiao Tung

The long, narrow triangular area linking the cities of Nan-jing, Zhenjiang and Yangzhou is called the silver triangle, on the lower reaches of the Changjiang (Yangtze) River. I visited this area on two occasions in the mid-summer and early winter of 1984.

Owing to the limited duration of my first visit in mid-June, I went only to two counties on the outskirts of Nanjing and listened to briefings about Nanjing and Zhenjiang. Prior to my second visit, I drew up an outline and specified my intentions so as to make up the deficiencies in my first visit. I arrived in Zhenjiang on October 24 and stayed for six days at Yang-zhong County, an island county in the Changjiang, to make detailed inquiries about its rural collective enterprises and the co-operative and individual industries run by rural households. Then I went to Taizhou and Taixing, to the north of the Chang-jiang, and returned to Nanjing on November 6. The whole investigation took 14 days.

My two trips were separated by less than six months, but the situation there had developed very rapidly. This pace prompts us to envisage things in the light of development and explore and understand the objective laws from what we have observed. Three years ago, when I first put forward the project of studying small towns, the rural production responsibility system had just been adopted in southern Jiangsu, and many rural enterprises were still undecided about what they would do. In the last few years, my study followed what the people had done and I travelled from southern Jiangsu to northern Jiangsu and then to the Nanjing-Zhenjiang-Yangzhou area.

My trip to the silver triangle took place immediately after the publication of the decision of the Third Plenary Session of the Twelfth C.P.C. Central Committee. All the urban and rural cadres, workers and staff of rural enterprises and members of rural households I contacted were considering the question of how to adapt to the new situation in the nation's urban economic reforms. In my talks with them I learned many new things and was strongly affected by the atmosphere. Taking this as the main line, I will try to describe and analyse the features of the triangle area's economic and social development and its future trends.

I have seen the prospects of close unity between rural areas, small towns, and big and medium-sized cities and of the inter-connections between rural economy, rural industries and urban economy. These broad prospects present higher demands on our study of small towns, so it is necessary for us to widen our field of vision and imagine new possibilities, in this study.

I

After my investigation in southern and northern Jiangsu, I noticed one area in which I had not made any contact, the Nanjing-Zhenjiang-Yangzhou area, generally embracing the entire Zhenjiang and Nanjing municipalities, the southern part of Yangzhou municipality, and some of the area's neighbouring places in Anhui Province. Geographically, its southwestern part is hilly and its northeastern part consists of plains. Extending along both banks of the Changjiang, it borders both southern and northern Jiangsu. Therefore, when I first went to Zhenjiang I asked people of experience whether we could call this area "central Jiangsu", as far as economic development is concerned.

Of course, there must be effective standards in dividing economic areas so as to show their positions in entirety. In my article, "Small Towns in Northern Jiangsu Province", I used the ratio between industry and agriculture in a county's total output value to divide different areas. At that time, the ratio was generally 7:3 in the Suzhou, Wuxi, Changzhou and Nanjing municipalities, with the output value of industry exceeding that of agriculture. However, the ratio was 3:7 in the northern part of northern Jiangsu. The industrial portion gradually increased from north to south and generally reaches one half in Yangzhou municipality. As I had not worked out this ratio for Nanjing, Zhenjiang and Yangzhou municipalities, I asked for comments on my idea of calling these areas "central Jiangsu", in an economic sense.

To determine the economic position of Nanjing, Zhenjiang and Yangzhou municipalities in the province, I calculated the 1983 ratios between the industrial and agricultural output value of the four dependent counties of Zhenjiang Municipality in my recent survey (see Table I). Moreover, on the basis of 1983 industrial statistics I also calculated the average industrial output value of all the dependent counties of Jiangsu's various municipalities and used it as a supplementary standard to examine the effects of the industry-agriculture ratio standard (see Table II).

Table I

INDUSTRIAL OUTPUT VALUE AND ITS PROPORTION IN THE FOUR COUNTIES OF ZHENJIANG MUNICIPALITY

(Unit: 100 million yuan)

County	Total industrial and agricultural output value	Industrial output value	Industry as % of the total
Dantu	3.96	2.57	65
Danyang	11.31	8.50	75
Jurong	4.09	2.10	51
Yangzhong	3.60	2.84	79

Note: The industrial output value in the table includes that of the county, the townships and the villages.

Table II

AVERAGE COUNTY INDUSTRIAL OUTPUT VALUE OF JIANGSU'S VARIOUS MUNICIPALITIES (1983)

(Unit: 100 million yuan)

Municipality	No. of Counties	Average county Industrial output value	Highest county industrial output value
Nanjing	5	1.63	2.45
Wuxi	3	10.67	13.58
Xuzhou	6	1.85	2.87
Changzhou	3	5.73	11.34
Suzhou	6	8.17	13.49
Nantong	6	5.76	9.59
Lianyungang	3	1.38	1.69
Huaiyin	11	1.49	2.88
Yancheng	7	2.48	4.80
Yangzhou	10	4.30	7.68
Zhenjiang	4	3.02	6.83

Table I shows that the ratios between industrial and agricultural output value of the four counties under Zhenjiang are higher than those of northern Jiangsu and close to those of southern Jiangsu. As shown by Table II, there are four municipalities in Jiangsu — Suzhou, Wuxi, Changzhou and Nantong — whose average county industrial output value each exceeds 500 million yuan. The same figures for Xuzhou, Lianyungang, Huaiyin municipalities and the five counties of Nanjing Municipality are between 100 million and 200 million yuan, and those for Yancheng, Yangzhou and Zhenjiang municipalities stand between 200 million and 500 million yuan. These figures basically conform with the output value ratios between industry and agriculture. The figures and ratios demonstrate the economic positions of these cities in Jiangsu.*

---

* The average county output value in Table II eliminates to a large extent the biases arising from the sizes and numbers of population in different counties and generally indicates the average per capita level.

Obviously, the economic levels in most of the silver triangle area are close to those of southern Jiangsu and higher than those of northern Jiangsu.

However, Table II also reveals an exception, that is, the average industrial output value of the five counties in Nanjing Municipality is about or less than one half of that of Yangzhou or Zhenjiang Municipality and still remains at the general level of northern Jiangsu. I noticed this fact in my first visit to two of these counties, but it was not so clear as the figures indicate. According to what I learned from my southern Jiangsu survey, rural industrial development is inseparable from the role played by the central city in an area. Therefore, the big and medium-sized city system, including Nanjing, Zhenjiang and Yangzhou, should exercise a relatively strong influence over the rural industry in its area, just like the Shanghai-Suzhou-Wuxi-Changzhou-Nantong urban system. As two galaxies, the two systems should light their respective outer space by radiation. But the facts do not tally with our expectations, so I tried to find the reasons.

First of all, I looked into the history of Nanjing, Zhenjiang and Yangzhou. The three cities control the throat of the lower reaches of the Changjiang and their advantageous geographical position has made them famous historical places in military strategy. From the Kingdom of Wu in the third century to the Taiping Army in the last century, they all built defence works in these cities. The city wall of Nanjing was capable of providing shelter for tens of thousands of soldiers and there are still gun platforms in the eastern suburbs of Zhenjiang. Therefore, the primary function of the three cities has long been military defence. Being capitals of several dynasties and the Kuomintang (KMT) government, Nanjing and Yangzhou have tended to be closed in their city formation and structure.

Then I compared the industrial output value and its structure of the three cities with those of Suzhou, Wuxi, Changzhou and Nantong (see Table III).

Table III

THE 1983 OUTPUT VALUE OF HEAVY AND LIGHT INDUSTRIES IN SEVEN CITIES OF JIANGSU

(Unit: 100 million yuan)

City	Total industrial output value	Output value of heavy industry	Output value of light industry	Light industry as % of the total
Nanjing	85.4	52.8	32.6	38
Zhenjiang	28.2	13.2	15.0	53
Yangzhou	54.4	21.2	33.4	61·
Suzhou	86.8	28.3	58.5	67
Wuxi	86.9	36.9	50.0	58
Changzhou	60.5	25.2	35.3	58
Nantong	60.1	16.6	43.5	72

As shown by Table III, among the seven cities Zhenjiang and Yangzhou are relatively weak in industry and Nanjing stands third in total industrial output value. Judged by the light industrial proportion in the total industrial output value, Nanjing is one-third, Zhenjiang is one half and the rest are about two-thirds. This proves that Nanjing and Zhenjiang are cities with dominant heavy industry. Moreover, a large proportion of Nanjing's heavy industry consists of military industry. Thus I think the closed historical background, weak industrial strength and the dominant heavy industry are the main reasons for the above-mentioned exception.

Then people may ask: As Zhenjiang has a weak industrial foundation dominated by heavy industry, how can the industrial level of its four counties be close to that of southern Jiangsu? We conducted a survey on this question. An analysis of the 46 units which have business relations with 42 townships and town enterprises in Danyang, a county whose industrial output value leads the other counties in Zhenjiang Municipality, reveals that only one is in Zhenjiang. In Yangzhong County, which has the highest industrial proportion of total industrial and agricultural output value of Zhenjiang's four counties, there is a township plant making parts for instruments and meters in the chemical industry. In recent years it has maintained close or loose connections with 180 units in design, production, marketing and materials supply. None of them is in Zhenjiang, six, or 3 per cent, are in Nanjing, and most of the rest are in Shanghai, Beijing and other big and medium-sized cities. To avoid a one-sided conclusion based on individual cases, we conducted a random sample survey of 3 per cent of the plant directors, purchasing and marketing staff and technicians of the township and town enterprises in the four counties, and asked them to name the most important city in which they have kept contacts in regard to funds, raw and semi-finished materials, equipment, technology, products and market information. The highest proportion of such contacts, according to their answers, is with Shanghai, one-fifth plus with Nanjing and one-sixth with Zhenjiang.

Table IV

MAJOR OUTSIDE CONTACTS KEPT BY TOWNSHIP AND
TOWN INDUSTRIES IN THE FOUR COUNTIES
OF ZHENJIANG MUNICIPALITY

City	Number of contacts	% of the total
Shanghai	408	37
Nanjing	234	21
Suzhou, Wuxi, Changzhou and Nantong	215	19
Zhenjiang	185	17
Beijing and other places	71	6

From the above analysis I realized that the three cities — Nanjing, Zhenjiang and Yangzhou, especially the first two, have not fully played their central roles of leading the whole regional economy in co-ordinated development and there are huge potentialities in this respect. Most rural areas in this region are expanding their township and town industries by primarily seeking the co-operation of long-distance cities, which has enabled the region to follow closely the progress in southern Jiangsu. If I call the role of an economic centre in a local region "short-distance extension", then the same role played by faraway cities may be called "long-distance radiation".

I heard during my survey that to strengthen short-distance extension, Nanjing was adopting measures in 1984 asking enterprises in the urban districts to help several township and town enterprises in its dependent counties. The success of establishing this type of economic link through administrative methods still needs to be seen, but it shows the attention being paid to the city's closed character in the regional economy and relative weakness in short-distance extension. Generally speaking, the Nanjing-Zhenjiang-Yangzhou region stands at the middle level in its economic development and is changing its closed character into an open one. It has tremendous potentialities and promising prospects. That is why I used the term "silver triangle" at the beginning of this article.

II

When a city transforms its closed character into an open one, it marks the coming of a new period in which the urban and rural economies in a region will achieve co-ordinated development. We need to study many new problems in regional economic development from both urban and rural aspects. I will explain how I understand the linking type of economic entities and the relationship between planned economy and market economy, based mainly on what I saw in Yangzhong County.

Yangzhong is composed of three sandy islands in the Changjiang River and covers an area of 228 square kilometres. Most of its territory is on the central island, the Taiping Shoal. This alluvial oasis was historically a place where the people on the north and south banks of the Changjiang went to flee the disasters of war and passing ships cast anchor to escape storms. Hence the name Taiping (Peace). There is no confirmed date of the earliest settlers, but it was in 1912 that Yangzhong first became a county.

I chose this young county of islands as the main subject of my survey because I heard its township and town industry ranks second in Zhenjiang Municipality and its per capita industrial output value is very close to that of Danyang, the leading county in this regard. (The latter's per capita industrial output value was 1,112 yuan in 1983 while that of Yangzhong was 1,092 yuan.) Yangzhong's small industries at the levels below the village have been booming, too. The rise and growth of rural township and town enterprises is generally found in places with good transport facilities. But the central island of Yangzhong has only one ferry for motor vehicles. On our way to Yangzhong, a breakdown of our car delayed us for 20 minutes on the ferry and trucks formed long lines on both banks. I learned that a sixth- or seventh-force wind can cut Yangzhong off from the outside world. How can a county with such unfavourable transport conditions have developed its township and town industries?

On the second day of my arrival at Yangzhong, the young county Party secretary and county head told me that the county asks these industries to develop the "scattering type of economy". At first I didn't understand this strange term, but later explanations helped me learn its meaning. "These industries cannot follow the method of operating with closed door," they explained. "They must have their outstanding products and become key township and town enterprises. Only in this way can they extend to the lower levels and raise the economic results of the whole county." In other words, the township and town enterprises should extend the industry to the villages or even to rural households like scattering sand, thus bringing benefits to residents of whole townships and towns. I summed up the idea with the sentence: Let every household get rich.

Letting every household get rich is not only the goal of developing industry in Yangzhong but also what its people are doing now. There are now six levels of industry in the county. First, the county enterprises which include the county's state and collective enterprises and the joint enterprises with outside partners at the county level. Second, enterprises at the township and town level. Third, enterprises at the village level, including those collectively owned by the village and jointly run by several villages. Fourth, enterprises at the group level, including those collectively owned by one group or jointly operated by several groups. Fifth, joint household enterprises. Sixth, household industrial enterprises. The enterprises at the first four levels belong respectively to the previous county, commune, production brigade and production team enterprises. The joint household enterprises are run by the households that made an investment.

According to statistics supplied by Yangzhong, in 1983 there were 121 collective enterprises at the county and town levels, 131 township enterprises and 212 village enterprises. No statistics were available at the group and lower levels. In Xinba Township alone, however, there were 117 enterprises run by groups and 187 run by individual households or jointly run by households. This indicates that the number of enterprises at the six levels increases from the higher to the lower levels and they constitute a pyramid-shaped rural industrial system.

To get an idea of how this industrial system enables the individual households to get rich and what its internal relations are, I will describe a few typical cases.

Old Man Du had been an accountant in a co-operative in Xinba Township and his family has become a household specializing in the making of copper locks for refrigerators and ovens. From my interview with him, I learned that there are seven persons in his traditional Chinese family: Du and his wife, a daughter, two sons and two daughters-in-law. In 1981 they spent 400 yuan for a drilling machine and one son prepared a small lathe by himself at a cost of 150 yuan. With such simple equipment they started their household plant. Their raw material is the copper scrap they buy from other plants and the processes of smelting, mould-making, casting and machining are all done by themselves. There is a clear division of work among the family members: Old Man Du, the family head, is the ex officio plant "director" and takes care of purchasing, marketing and some bench work. One son operates the lathe and another makes the mould. The two daughters-in-law and daughter work as assistants. The old man's wife is in charge of household work.

Three years after the start of the plant, the Dus built a row of six rooms to replace the original four simple rooms. After paying the product processing tax (5 per cent) and industrial and commercial management fee (1 per cent), they bought equipment to the tune of more than 5,000 yuan and accumulated a circulating fund of 5,000 yuan. One half of their products are sold to rural enterprises that supply auxiliary parts for refrigerators. The incomes are distributed according to the principle of piece-work payment agreed upon by the family members. For their food, Old Man Du thinks the reliable method is to cultivate their three *mu* of ration land by themselves. As they have meat every day, the harvest (600 kilogrammes of grain) is enough for their annual food grain.

From this interview, I got a vivid illustration of what I heard a few years ago: you cannot get rich without industry. Household plants like the one run by the Du family have exceeded 600 in Yangzhong County.

Then I read a material about joint household enterprises. There are 45 households in the No. 7 Heping Village of Youfang Township, of which 22 have skilled carpenters. In the early 1960s the production team set up a factory to make wooden brush handles. Owing to equalitarian ways of distributing incomes, its highest annual earning was some 1,000 yuan. Beginning in 1980, they first adopted the method of contracting out jobs by the team and then formed eight combinations with investment by the joining households. By the end of 1983, these combinations had altogether 44 shares and 156 workers (102 of them came from other villages or townships because the village has only 91 able-bodied persons).

After deducting the cost of materials, taxes and other expenses from their annual output value of 450,000 yuan, they had a 30 per cent net income or 130,000 yuan. Of this sum, 110,000 yuan were paid for wages and 20,000 yuan for dividends. This village now has 14 joint household combinations making wooden brush handles. From January to September 1984, their output totalled 733,000 yuan and the products were sold to eight provinces and more than 30 printing houses.

The factory run by the production team in the village was in a sense shattered by joint household enterprises. This reminds me of what I heard from a cadre member in my native Wujiang County, prior to this survey. He told me that as the growth of individual and joint household enterprises made a powerful impact on the rural collective enterprises, they had to adopt measures to restrict the former. I don't think this is a correct attitude. This shows a lack of proper understanding.

When the township and town enterprises were rising several years ago, some people said they undermined and made an impact on the urban enterprises. Now the joint household and individual enterprises are rising, and the township and town enterprises should not forget what their position was in the past and complain about the former's impact. Why the two successive impacts are so similar needs to be explored. Instead of imposing restrictions, we had better sum up and examine the problems in the collective enterprises.

One of the problems to be solved by the Decision on Reform of the Economic Structure adopted by the Third Plenary Session of Twelfth C.P.C. Central Committee is that state enterprises eat from the "same big pot" of the state and pay no attention to economic results, and that workers and staff members eat from the "same big pot" of enterprises and lack the same enthusiasm for production that masters of the enterprises have. This state of affairs was even more serious a few years ago compared with the present time. That was why township and town enterprises — collective enterprises responsible for their own profits and losses — were full of vitality at that time. But we must recognize that a considerable part of the township and town enterprises have not completely got free of eating from the "same big pot". If they do not readjust the relations among responsibility, power and benefit within the enterprises, township and town enterprises will eat from the "same small pot" while state enterprises eat from the "same big pot". The pot supporting state enterprises is not easy to see. But the pot of a township or town enterprise is easily visible and when there is not much rice in it, the enterprise has to make extra efforts.

To consolidate their positions and make further development, the township and town enterprises must face up to their problems and carry out economic reforms simultaneously with the urban enterprises. I was told during my visits at the grass roots units that some measures of reform were already adopted. They have scored remarkable results in consolidating and expanding the township and town industries.

In addition to introducing reforms in township and town enterprises, Yangzhong County also suggested practising "scope returns", that is, these enterprises should assist small ones at different levels and become the core force in developing the small-area economies. This is a far-sighted arrangement. It will organically link up the township and town enterprises with those at the lower levels and develop industrial and economic activities in small areas around the former's outstanding products. At the same time, spurred by the small enterprises, the township and town enterprises should renew their products, adopt better techniques and institute scientific management and operation. Thus, the township and town enterprises can also raise themselves.

The Xinglong Township Plastics Plant in Yangzhong has played its role in helping small factories. It successively assisted eight village factories by entrusting them to produce semi-finished materials and process parts. As a result, the factories have consolidated their productive capacity and the plant also expanded its output. Together they produced close to 10 million yuan worth of plastic goods in 1983, making up one half of the township's industrial output value in the year. People say: "When one plant helps eight, the whole township becomes rich."

I visited the Confectionery Factory of Hongsheng Village, Lianhe Township. It has transferred its paper box-making and kernel extracting to production groups or households, and concentrated its efforts on turning out new products. The output of its 27 varieties surpasses 1,000 tons a year and is sold to 16 provinces and municipalities.

There are many township and town enterprises like the two mentioned in Yangzhong. This has brought about the general situation of mutual promotion between township and town enterprises and small enterprises in the county. It was estimated that, in the first nine months of 1984, the total output of Yangzhong's village, group, joint household and individual enterprises could exceed 20 million yuan. At the same time, the township and town enterprises would also grow at a rate of 30 per cent.

The practice of "scope returns" in Yangzhong reminds me of what I heard about a state plant in the Tingxi area, Gansu Province, prior to National Day (October 1) 1984. It is an enterprise directly under a ministry and most of its managerial staff, technical personnel and workers and staff members come from other places. Except for getting food supplies from the locality, it seems to be isolated from the outside world. The local people only see the incoming of raw materials, the outgoing of products and the smoke belching from its stacks. The plant definitely belongs to a model different from the township and town enterprises in Yangzhong. If the enterprises which perform the central role of economic activities in small areas can be classified under those of the open type, the Gansu plant falls under the category of inverted type. This type of enterprises only absorbs the things they need from the surrounding areas and exercises no influence on the local economy. If a city has a large proportion of such enterprises, it must tend to be a closed one. Otherwise, it will belong to the open type and exercise its influence on its surrounding areas.

Then I raised the question in my mind whether the reform of our urban enterprises should follow the pattern of the open-type township and town enterprises and take the road of concerted urban and rural economic development. The material I collected from Yangzhong indicates that the county has established close or loose links with quite a number of urban enterprises, and many other urban enterprises have voluntarily come to forge economic connections. The two-way links, one from above and another from below, integrate the big and medium urban enterprises, county enterprises and those at or below the township and town level, to form an urban-rural economic entity. This entity aims at achieving the concerted development of a regional economy and enabling every household to become rich.

The C.P.C. Central Committee issued several documents in recent years to affirm the position and role of the township and town enterprises and the Decision on the Reform of Economic Structure, in particular, clearly elaborates the meaning of socialist planned economy. The decision completely shattered all the obstacles for the township and town enterprises which basically engage in market economic activities. Some leaders of these enterprises told me that they cast away their doubts and worries and would no longer be afraid of the market economy. Their feelings are understandable. But I think we should make great efforts to study the relations between planned economy and market economy and gradually reach a unified understanding on a scientific basis. Otherwise, both the township and town enterprises and the urban enterprises which are in the process of reform will meet all sorts of obstacles in their economic activities.

I have considered for a long time the relations between planned and market economy. Owing to my insufficient study of economics, however, I could not reach a clear conclusion. I was very glad to read the committee's decision because it explains what I wanted to say but was unable to state clearly.

Why have the comrades engaging in township and town enterprises not been so active and bold in the past few years?

It was because some comrades always liked to be confined by concepts and pitted market economy against planned economy. As people know that planned economy is a major feature of socialist society, the nature of its opposite — the market economy — needs no explanation. In order to avoid being linked with capitalism, the township and town entrepreneurs did all they could to link up and co-operate with urban state enterprises and to establish direct or indirect connections with enterprises within the planned economy. The big efforts made by township and town enterprises to link up with urban enterprises gradually formed the previously mentioned urban-rural economic entities. The significance of such an outcome goes far beyond the original intention.

Actually, only a small number of enterprises and products succeeded in establishing direct and indirect links with enterprises within the planning system, and most of the township and town enterprises are still subject to market regulation. In Yangzhong County, the former make up about 10 per cent of the total output value of township and town enterprises, while the latter account for the remaining 90 per cent.

Then how do the vast majority of township and town enterprises conduct their economic activities in the market? The Yangzhong examples fall into three methods:

First, supplying urban needs in small quantities. Of the large varieties of industrial products needed by cities, some are small batches with particular specifications; such orders are not easily accepted by urban producers. So the township and town enterprises take over such production jobs. One copperware factory in Yangzhong mainly turns out auxiliary parts for state textile mills and machine-building plants and its smallest orders amount to only several hundred yuan each.

Second, providing what the big industries do not make. In the words of township and town entrepreneurs, they "fill in the blanks". The confectionery factory mentioned above fills in the blank of children's confectionery that city factories have neglected to manufacture. And it is doing an excellent business.

Third, making small but easily marketable articles. The township and town enterprises always pay attention to the city's needs for small articles. Taking advantage of their ability to change products rapidly, they turn out thousands of small articles for daily use in the cities. A large number of enterprises in Yangzhong belong to this category.

In solving the supply of raw and semi-finished materials, the township and town enterprises resort to comprehensive use and other methods like joint investment and compensatory trade.

Thus, the market economic activities undertaken by the township and town enterprises are mainly for satisfying urban and rural needs in production and living in accordance with objective economic laws. If we examine the below-to-above planning system, the planned economy and the market economy are supplementary in our socialist society. In actual economic activities, therefore, the genuine planned economy is not opposed to the market economy and the two can be unified and harmonious. It is precisely because of this unity that a completely new situation of concerted urban and rural development can appear in Jiangsu Province.

III

Along with the transformation of big and medium-sized cities from closed to open character, the rural areas of Jiangsu also began to discard their closed state of half self-sufficiency. On the basis of concerted expansion of regional economies, the township and town industries constitute the new links connecting the city and countryside. These links are managed by different kinds of talented people in the enterprises that have emerged in the rural areas. Their training, progress and change vividly show the process by which the rural social system has transformed from closed into open character.

The growth of township and town industries generally follows the three stages of initial establishment, expansion and gradual maturity. Many rural people are proud to describe the growth of such enterprises. For instance, one township had only an agricultural machine station in the 1950s and the station helped set up a hand-operated loom factory with some added equipment. In the course of development, the factory diverted part of its resources to assist in establishing a plant of modern textile machines. This kind of magical division makes many enterprises "close relatives". From the relations within many groups of enterprises, we can perceive a general view of the three generations of enterprises corresponding to the three stages of development. In most of the townships, each started with one, two or three first-generation enterprises and then branched out to set up the second-generation enterprises. In turn, many third-generation enterprises were created later.

The first generation of township and town enterprises were mostly set up towards the end of the 1950s by pooling the handicrafts of rural and market town households. These units were mainly engaged in producing farm tools and boats and simple machine parts, pressing oil, milling rice and building. They appeared under the names of joint iron, wooden and bamboo handicraft co-operatives or agricultural machine stations. With out-dated equipment and simple technical processes, they turned out crude products which yielded little profit or even failed to cover the cost. This means the initial township and town enterprises stayed in the labour-intensive, shop stage, based on mixed handicraft and mechanical production.

The simple first-generation enterprises laid the foundation for the later generations. Therefore I always asked about the founders, in my surveys. They consisted of both enthusiasts and skilled handicraftsmen. The former were the leaders and organizers of the first-generation enterprises who became cadres during the land reform in the early post-1949 years. Although they did not have much schooling, they had a strong sense of responsibility to change the poor and backward state in their native places.

The upsurge of establishing factories in 1958 was followed by the general dissolution two years later. In spite of this twist, these enthusiasts did not dissolve all they had set up. They kept some of the industrial units to turn out farm tools, things indispensable for the local peasants, and thus served agricultural growth. Now most of the workers, who were handicraftsmen of the first-generation enterprises, have retired and the former enthusiasts have mainly switched to other posts. But their initial arduous efforts should be recorded in the history of township and town enterprises.

The initial stage of these enterprises lasted for a long time and generally they entered the period of development in the early 1970s. This was true in both Zhenjiang and Yangzhou municipalities and southern Jiangsu. During the development period, there are two phases with the convention of the Third Plenary Session of the Eleventh C.P.C. Central Committee as the demarcation: The first phase was undercurrent growth and the second is one of liberated development.

Those who made the biggest contribution to the enterprises in the development period are the enthusiasts, the skilled people and the new workers who have just put down their hoes. I met an enthusiast and a skilled man at a plant making parts for instruments and meters of the chemical industry, in Changwang Township, Yangzhong County. The plant's Party secretary is a man on the young side of 50 with a primary school education. He had been head of an agricultural producers' mutual-aid group, teacher of adult literacy classes, accountant in a farm co-operative and Party branch secretary of a production brigade after the founding of the People's Republic, before he became in 1968 the Party branch secretary of the Changwang Township Farm Tool Factory, the predecessor of the present plant. At that time the factory was in a bad condition. He looked for skilled people and found a worker in the county who had passed his apprenticeship in Shanghai and been a lathe turner for ten years.

Then the plant bought two small lathes and this master worker trained four apprentices, including the present plant director, in the first year. Eight additional apprentices were trained in the second year. When I asked him how many of the plant's 500 workers were his apprentices or his apprentices' apprentices, he smiled but gave no answer. Someone replied for him: practically every one. The plant now has 11 work-shops and six functional departments. Its output reached 3.87 million yuan in the first ten months of 1984 and earned 1.1 million yuan in before-tax profit. An undertaking of such a scale has been built by an enthusiast — the Party branch secre-tary — a master worker and its workers recruited from peasants.

In the last two years I met and heard of quite a number of enthusiasts and skilled people. The former are interested in developing industry because they feel the sharp contradiction between population and land; the latter possess skills because most of them are workers and cadre members who have stayed in the rural areas for a period of time or have retired, and urban and rural educated youngsters. In the ten years of turmoil during the "cultural revolution", the two groups of people got a chance to integrate city with countryside and knowledge with skill. I elaborated this point in my article, "Small Towns, Great Significance".

Here I want to talk about their courage and resourcefulness. Despite heavy political pressure at that time, they had the mettle to develop industries and the methods to face the situa-tion. The above-mentioned plant making parts for instruments and meters in the chemical industry still has the placard bearing the name of farm tool factory. They are now two separate units, but the placard served as a talisman at that time. There-fore, the growth of township and town industries could be only an undercurrent before the Third Plenary Session of the Eleventh C.P.C. Central Committee.

Precisely because of political pressure, the links established by the township and town industries with big and medium-sized cities were accidental in the undercurrent period and based on production experience rather than science and technology. The skilled people usually have an education below the senior middle school level. By combining themselves with the labour and funds of the rural areas, they did not put any new or richer elements into the factors of productive forces. They only promoted the combination of existing potential factors for industrial productive forces in the rural areas and formed an elementary industrial productivity. That is why the township and town industries turned out whatever the techniques of the skilled people could make and took up any products whose industrial raw materials they could get or whose demand they learned of. This was essentially a forced blind development.

The political pressure was taken away after the Third Plenary Session of the Eleventh C.P.C. Central Committee and the township and town enterprises began realizing fully the energy accumulated in the undercurrent phase. For a time they showed spectacular growth. But not all of them can keep on growing and enter the stage of active development with clear aims. This is because what awaits them is a more severe test — their competition with urban enterprises and competition among themselves. To survive or to be eliminated depends on whether the enthusiasts and skilled people of these enterprises can smoothly transform themselves into various specialized persons and overcome the series of difficulties in funds, raw materials, equipment, technology, management and operation, and marketing.

In the township and town enterprises that have stood the test, the change of skilled people into specialized personnel was completed in the first phase of the development period. Management personnel of the enterprises at that time learned the art from the enthusiasts and were promoted from the first-generation of accountants, people responsible for supply and marketing or educated skilled workers. Young and with a junior or senior middle school education, they made up the first batch of specialized management people. We may say the first-generation enterprises were like shops, but they represented the beginning of a transformation into mass industrial production.

This batch of managers generally has foresight, resourcefulness, courage and energy. At the time when their enterprises were basically not included in the planning system, it was completely up to them to decide what to produce on the basis of existing conditions and information. Moreover, the production funds depended partly on accumulation and partly (mostly, in some cases) on the workers and staff. The management personnel set for themselves the goal of "only success, no failure" and generally learned through painful tempering how to forge ahead successfully. Their foresight means the ability to recognize products that are easily marketable and have broad prospects for development. Resourcefulness means their initiative to create the needed conditions and not take the conventional way of waiting. Courage means the big strides they dare to make. For instance, three months after an electric appliance and material plant had broken ground, it was able to turn out more than 100,000 yuan worth of products when I visited there. Energy means their arduous efforts to learn what they do not understand.

To the management personnel of township and town enterprises, the demands of the economic activities of industrial production are truly severe. They must know both production and operation, arrange schedules for workers, keep good contacts with other factories or stores, take care of production progress and watch market changes. Many plant directors told me that they never left the plants before 10 p.m. or slept before midnight. A large number of plant directors managed to use every bit of time to study related college courses and acquired a lot of specialized knowledge. In the course of practical work, they have generally trained themselves into new entrepreneurs of relatively profound knowledge. Their achievements do not come from their unusual talent but from the economic activities undertaken under pressure and general competition among enterprises and products.

The present generation of enterprises have really made a long stride forward towards modernization and are capable of turning out chemical fibre fabrics, machine tools, chemicals and parts for instruments and meters. The industrial techniques disseminated by urban people have blossomed. The mature growth of township and town enterprises, however, increases their dependence on cities for specialized personnel, technology, raw materials and marketing. But this dependence is different from that characterized by blind connections in the first phase of the development period. Thus, these industries have broken the restrictions of such unfavourable factors as administrative divisions and geographical locations and established links with big urban industries. There are all sorts of organic combinations, gradually becoming stabilized and closely knit. An increasing proportion of them are technical connections and co-operation.

There are tremendous gaps between China's urban and rural areas in science and technology. In Yangzhong County, for example, its 190 industrial technicians make up only 0.16 per cent of the total industrial workers and staff, and there is not even one technician with a professional title in all its township and town enterprises. In this situation economic activities inevitably require the movement of science and technology and technical personnel from the city to the countryside. This movement is closely connected with industrial economic activities and has nourished a large group of educated rural youngsters to become industrial technicians.

The flow of science and technology to the rural areas goes through two channels. One is the flow of urban technicians to the countryside, which takes two forms — permanent and temporary. The permanent form means transferring urban technicians to work in the township and town enterprises. Again take Yangzhong County for example. It received 18 technicians in this way in 1984. One of its plants issued a public announcement to recruit technicians and has established contacts with more than 600 outside applicants. Sixty-four of them will be transferred to work in the plant. The temporary form means inviting advisers, part-time technicians or technical personnel for short-time work and signing technical contracts. In 1983, Yangzhong County formally invited 201 engineers and technicians for short-period work and many others for solving technical problems.

Another channel is dispatching local technicians to study in cities. In the first half of 1984, the township and town enterprises of Yangzhong sent 45 technicians to study or receive training in colleges and research institutes, 24 to study in secondary technical schools, 205 to provincial training classes and 1,260 to receive training in enterprises of other places. Apart from learning scientific knowledge and technology in the cities, they widened their understanding, kept in touch with modern industrial society, became familiar with modern equipment, and got acquainted with intellectuals.

In conducting surveys at the grass roots, I saw how the township and town enterprises urgently looked for technical personnel. As county governments have realized the importance of training technicians, many training classes like those of enterprise management and of technical, secondary technical and college courses have been set up at the county, township, village and enterprise levels. By the end of 1983, Yangzhong County had trained 6,000 elementary and intermediate technicians.

In the townships and towns where enterprises developed at an early date, their major ones have entered the third or matured period. They now have the necessary conditions in funds, technology, personnel, equipment, information and market, their scale is large enough, their economic and technical strength is strong and their products can face competition. They continuously renew their products and move towards advanced and serial production. Capable of making high-grade woollen fabrics, precision machines, chemicals and electronic products, they are gradually becoming technology-intensive industries. With modern and scientific management, they are going in for specialization.

If we compare the third-generation enterprises to galloping horses, their leaders must be the riders. Most of them have at least a junior middle school education and many are senior middle school graduates. Of Yangzhong's 83 county enterprises, 33 directors are senior middle school graduates and a number of them have taken college courses. They know production, basic scientific knowledge and modern management and carry out systematic production and operation. These re-

sourceful directors are adept at making wise decisions and
working out good plans, understand the importance of and
know how to make use of information and are acquainted
with the four links of production (production, marketing,
distribution and consumption) and such economic knowledge as
marketing and the law of value. Led by these leaders, the township and town enterprises are not afraid of strong market competition and rely on their fine-quality products, better service
and good reputation. Five Yangzhong products received first-
class scientific and technical or fine-product awards issued by
the state, province (municipality) and county. The township
and town enterprises of Yangzhong now produce over 2,000
varieties of products and 20 of them are sold in world markets.

Through different channels the matured enterprises have
trained and formed a contingent of technical personnel, and
they have their own ranks of design and trial manufacturing.
Possessing sufficient ability to absorb science and technology,
they can trial manufacture the products which are the results
of studies by research institutes and colleges, and quickly start
batch production. Besides the movement of technical people,
the increasing flow of science and technology to the countryside
is effected by the transfer of scientific and technical material
and information. This reinforces the rural science and
technology.

The supply and marketing people of township and town enterprises have always been extremely active and shoulder many
heavy tasks in production and operation. First, they are
responsible for the supply of raw materials and the marketing
of products. It is not an easy job to ensure the adequate supply
of a plant's raw materials under the market economy. It is even
more difficult to realize the timely sales of all products and
rapidly receive payment under the conditions of keen competition on the market, incomplete stipulations in the contract, and
the long payment delay among township and town enterprises
and between commercial and industrial enterprises. Second,
they should be able to explain the merits and demerits and uses
of their products, make comparisons with the same kinds of

products turned out by other plants, and persuade the consumers to understand and accept their own products. At the same time, they are charged with collecting scientific and technical information and transmitting other useful information, and play the major role in establishing connections with other enterprises. Finally, they help install and repair their products and equipment. One supply and marketing staff member told me: "We cannot learn all we need from the book and neither have our experiences had been put in publications; but I think we have gained some genuine knowledge."

IV

In the concerted development of regional economies, the new urban-rural links are also reflected in the rapid speed and growing variety of information communication and continuous feedback. During the surveys I got a strong impression of the unprecedented stress on information laid by leaders of township and town enterprises. They consciously regard the feedback ability as an important condition for developing township and town industries and a prerequisite for raising their enterprises' competitiveness and capacity to face changes. In selecting and using cadre members, they put the ability to handle information on an equal footing with that of management and techniques. Quick response becomes one of the most important qualifications in selecting cadres. They set up departments staffed with specialized personnel to collect and transmit information. Many county and township industrial corporations have information or development sections to acquire and handle information and analyse and make use of it.

As far as the development of township and town enterprises is concerned, they mainly need market and technical information. The market information includes the amount of demand for specific products and changes in variety and their future prospects obtained from markets, meetings to order major goods, exhibition sales, trade fairs and government commercial departments. The technical information consists mainly of the latest technical developments and their impact on production and market. According to the experience of Yangzhong County, the two kinds of information play the role of promoting exchanges, guiding operation, broadening circulation, transmitting science and technology, and facing competition. As the production, supply and marketing of the products of township and town enterprises are mainly subject to market regulating, the enterprises depend to a large extent on information. We may therefore say that the exchange and feedback of information are the necessary conditions for the survival and development of township and town industries.

In all the places we visited, the township and town enterprises have created through their experience in the market economy many methods of collecting information. First, the collection by supply and marketing staff members. In Danyang County the number of people dispatched to collect information in different parts of the nation by the township and town enterprises exceeds 12 per cent of their total workers and staff. The usually followed method is continuous extension. For example, the plant in Changwang Township, Yangzhong County making parts for chemical industry's instruments and meters first got some information about products from the relative of a young local man, who worked in a Shanghai refinery. Then the young man extended his contact to other plants. In this way the plant snowballed its sources of supply and marketing and at the same time established its information network. Now it has formed links with 160 units under 11 ministries in 25 provinces, municipalities and autonomous regions, and signed agreements with them for getting new information, new techniques and new products.

Second, setting up information stations and technical and product windows in the Shenzhen and Xiamen special economic zones and industrially developed cities like Shanghai, Beijing and Tianjin. Yangzhong County opened five windows in Shenzhen and other places, and Danyang County established a special counter for its products in the Zhuhai Special Economic Zone. Here the windows refer to stores selling the county's fine or famous-brand products or windows and counters in exhibition centres showing these products. The purposes are to attract customers at home and abroad, observe market changes and collect commodity information, and then to use the collected knowledge in deciding whether or not to start making new products and getting technical information.

Third, collecting information through establishing links with colleges, scientific research institutes and state industrial enterprises and by appointing advisers. All the enterprises which keep their vitality and continuously renew their products generally have their "backers". In the last five years, the above-mentioned Yangzhong plant making parts for chemical industry's instruments and meters developed two kinds of parts in 10 series, 200 varieties and 2,000 specifications, and some of them filled the blanks in China. The products are sold in 16 countries and regions. A major reason for its success is the continuous flow of information about products received from its connecting units. The township and town enterprises invite many advisers — experts, scholars, managers of big stores and heads of wholesale organizations — to transmit to them news about the latest products; they also get information about the renewal and improved quality of products from scientific researchers; and they learn the amount and direction of the flow of their products from people working in related departments.

Fourth, collecting information from annual conferences and meetings to order major products, and from academic symposia. At first, township and town enterprises were not qualified to attend these meetings. But their staff members voluntarily went to the meeting places. If they could not attend the conferences, they took the chance to meet the participants, tell them about their enterprises and sincerely ask for their suggestions and assistance. As a result they made a lot of friends and gathered large amounts of information. In this way some enterprises acquired or maintained their outstanding products and have gradually stood in the front ranks of their industries, thereby becoming qualified to attend specialized conferences themselves.

Fifth, collecting information through scientific and technical commissions and associations, local committees of the Chinese People's Political Consultative Conference (CPPCC), county statistical bureaus and other organizations. In the counties I visited, their scientific and technical commissions have set up development sections, and their township and town enterprise bureaus have established consultation service corporations. These organizations are in charge of collecting information about new products and technical problems. The county scientific and technical associations keep contacts with local intellectuals and local people working in other places, and ask them to supply the new developments in their specialized fields. The democrats in the local CPPCC committees also gather information for the township and town industries by means of their widespread social contacts. The county statistical bureaus also use their data to analyse the production conditions, consumption of materials and economic efficiency level in the local places, the province or the nation, and pass on their findings to the township and town enterprises.

Therefore, the first feature of collecting and using information by township and town enterprises is the large number of channels. The methods mentioned above are a summary of the results of our surveys and there are far more channels than these in the actual flow of information to the countryside.

The second feature is adeptness at catching what they want. The people in these enterprises created the new terms of "direct information" and "indirect information". The former refers to information obtained from the data about marketability, output, demand and economic efficiency of products. This is easy to observe and get. Because it reflects the past or present economic activities, production plans worked out under its guidance may be passive, to a certain extent. Indirect information refers to that derived from one's own analysis. The director of the Xichang Township Rubber Factory in Shazhou County, whom I mentioned previously, is good at using indirect information. Deng Xiaoping once said: "Football training should start from childhood." When the director heard of it, he turned his mind to making children's footballs, which have been popular on the market.

Township and town entrepreneurs are racking their brains to analyse information. Apart from meeting the people's needs by collecting information from the markets, they vigorously analyse people's tastes and interests and create new products satisfactory to the consumers, and thus enrich and guide people's demand. A supply and marketing staff member of a town enterprise in Danyang County noticed in Shanghai that many people liked to use knitted undergarments as outer clothes. After making an investigation, he designed a new-style knitted woollen jersey. His mill quickly developed this new product. When the sample jerseys were sent to Shanghai two weeks later, they were immediately sold out.

Besides observing production trends in their own industry, the entrepreneurs also pay close attention to the development of other industries related to their own in the socialized mass production, thus forecasting the prospects of their own products. An emery wheel plant in Yangzhong County, for example, closely watches the new products of machine-building industry. When a new machine appears, it will try to design and turn out a suitable grinding tool.

The third feature of collecting and using information by township and town enterprises is rapid transmission and quick results. It generally takes a short period of time from acquiring a piece of information to using it and producing economic results. The entrepreneurs of these enterprises usually travel by airplane and rely heavily on telegraph and telephone for communication. The received information soon produces returns. After confirming the reliability and feasibility of a piece of information through careful analysis, these enterprises will immediately adjust their production and operation accordingly. For example, foreign businessmen showed great interest in Danyang County's silk fabrics in the wake of establishing a counter of Danyang products in Zhuhai. Staff members of Danyang learned from these businessmen that if silk fabrics are made into clothes of the popular foreign style, there will be a big potential market and a chance to make huge profits. Feedback of this information enabled the county to take action and the new silks sent to Zhuhai were sold out in a few days. The whole process of information transmission and feedback took less than 40 days.

The fourth feature of collecting and using information by township and town enterprises is the high rate of utilization and big economic returns. During my surveys, I heard of many cases in which a piece of information saved an enterprise from being eliminated, led to big sales or opened a market. The Bashan Production Brigade Auxiliary Lamp Parts Factory in Jiepai Township, Danyang County, for instance, originally produced integrated circuits. Owing to the poor quality of products, it suffered losses for several years and was on the verge of closing down. Then it learned the news of an increasing demand for street lamps arising from widened urban streets. The factory borrowed 30,000 yuan to turn to making auxiliary lamp parts. By renewing its products, the factory became profitable and its output shot up from 630,000 yuan in 1980 to 2,010,000 yuan in 1983. Its volume of business with Harbin, Changchun, Beijing, Tianjin and Wuhan reached 4.4 million yuan in 1984.

During the whole process of my surveys, I learned that the township and town enterprises' demand for information varied in their different periods of development. In the initial period, their channels to get information and the amount of information received were both limited. Once they acquired some information, it would take a long time to make necessary adjustments. Moreover, what they got was only direct information. When their growth reached a certain stage, their information channels gradually diversified, the amount of information increased, the time needed to make use of information was gradually shortened, and the proportion of indirect information also steadily went up. In the matured period, there is plenty of information from diversified channels, its transmission is accelerated by modern means of communication, and the time to make use of it is drastically reduced. A factory in

Changwang Township, Yangzhong County is renewing a variety or product in every five days.

Continuous feedback and transmission not only quicken the growth of township and town enterprises, but bring big changes in rural society. Like a strong current, it breaks through the sluice gates between city and countryside, thereby forming the urban-rural information circuit and promoting the concerted development of urban-rural regional economies.

We may reach the same conclusion from actual observation or theoretical analysis. A high-efficiency social system must be an open-type one because it continuously needs the exchange of materials, energy and information to ensure its steady development, adapt to the outside environment well, and influence efficiently its surrounding environment with defined aims. A closed system cannot influence its outside world. Only by continuous feedback and transmission of information can a system gradually transform itself from a closed to an open type. Information is precisely a major factor in the growth of rural society and township and town enterprises.

The matured township and town enterprises should be an open social system. As mentioned previously, they need to get large amounts of specialized personnel and information from the cities; on the other hand, they will move out products to market and realize the value of products through exchange. To be successful in a market economy, the township and town enterprises need such outside resources as talented people and information, but the key factor lies in their rational internal structure — effective, flexible and scientific management.

The township and town enterprises have their own features of management and operation. First of all, there are considerable flexibilities in operation. The principle guiding their operation is: "All is oriented to the market, all for the consumers." Faced with an ever-changing market and the steadily increasing and new demands of consumers, they can rapidly adapt to the changed situation and flexibly regulate their operation and service.

Some enterprises have placards bearing different names, i.e., a township electrical materials factory in Yangzhong County is at the same time a water meter factory and a steel and wood furniture factory. When water meter sales are slack, it concentrates on making easily marketable electrical materials and furniture. According to the fluctuations of demand, it turns out the three major products alternately and thus stabilizes production. Moreover, a vast number of small township and town enterprises are capable of switching products rapidly. In Yangzhong County, 62 enterprises, or 15 per cent of the total, switched products in 1983. My investigation in Yangzhong showed that 60 village enterprises at Yongsheng and Xinglong townships renewed their varieties of products 175 times since their establishment, averaging three per enterprise.

The flexible character of township and town enterprises is also manifested in the forms of their service to consumers — visiting the consumers to provide service, offering consultation service, training operators for the consumers, etc. Their flexibility is vividly expressed in the words popular among township and town enterprises: "We have what the others do not have; when the others make the same products, ours are better; when the others turn out better products, ours are cheaper; when the others also offer cheaper products, we switch to producing different ones."

The township and town enterprises are able to adopt flexible and diversified operations mainly because they enjoy considerable autonomy. The local county or township governments manage them through guidance rather than mandate. This guidance management is accomplished through economic levers like taxation, credit, price, profit and interest rates and the provision of information and other services. The production process is completely decided by the enterprises as independent commodity producers. They decide their switch to producing other products, expansion, addition of new projects, ways to use their accumulation funds and enlargement of investment. All this basically guarantees their flexibility.

The third feature of these enterprises' management and operation lies in the contracted responsibility system at all levels. By clearly defining the responsibility, power and benefits and carrying out clearly stipulated rewards and punishments, the system mobilizes the enthusiasm of workers and staff members. The key enterprises I visited during my surveys generally adopt strict responsibility systems. In a month every worker must fulfil a fixed amount of output value and the requirements for cost, the number of working hours used, and quality. Strict cost accounting is adopted for each production process or workshop. Workers of a production process have the power to refuse the sub-standard products sent by the previous production process, which proves an effective method to ensure quality. Moreover, the production progress and quality of work are known to everybody. The director of the Lianhe Township Emery Wheel Plant in Yangzhong County, an advanced county unit in enterprise management, told me: "Its contracted responsibility system links a person's rewards with his contributions and completed tasks and with the plant's production and economic results, which overcomes equalitarianism between individuals and between workshops and fully mobilizes the enthusiasm of workers and staff members. If anyone gets less bonus, he will not quarrel with the leadership. But he will check the cost or quality targets and take proper measures."

The fourth feature of management and operation by township and town enterprises is their adoption of scientific management. Some advanced enterprises have applied such modern methods as goal management, total quality control, value engineering and linear programming. After deciding their goals of operation in the light of market conditions, some plants in Yangzhong and Danyang counties follow the method of dividing each overall goal into many small ones for every production link and level, and establishing around planned management other management in production, techniques, quality, equipment, labour, finance and materials so as to ensure the fufilment of the overall goal.

From the first to the third generation, the township and town enterprises experienced tremendous changes in management. Passive decision-making in operation has changed into an active one with many choices; extensive guidance in operation, paying little attention to economic results, has been transformed into an intensive one stressing economic efficiency; centralized and small-shop type management has been replaced by one of decentralization and clear responsibility at different levels; single-line management has become systematic management; and the basis of management has switched from experience to science.

V

After my surveys in Yangzhong, I visited Taizhou City and Taixing County. In Taizhou I learned of a new problem worth our notice and study — non-adaptability between administrative and economic divisions under the system of placing counties under municipalities. Specifically, Yangzhou cannot "pull" the county-status city of Taizhou; people call this "a small horse pulls a big cart". After Taizhou became a county-level city and was placed under Yangzhou, it has been on an equal status with surrounding counties that had been under its economic influence and their economic ties have been more or less restricted by administrative division. Taizhou is unable to play fully its central role in regional development and its own economic development also suffers from lack of rear support.

Historically speaking, Yangzhou and Taizhou have been neighbouring twins on the north bank of the Changjiang River, each playing the role of a commodity-circulating centre in its surrounding area. Both made outstanding advances in the last few decades. It was said that they possessed similar economic strength. For historical reasons, Yangzhou is more widely known than Taizhou. They were both under the Yangzhou Prefecture and on an equal footing after liberation. When Jiangsu Province eliminated the prefectural administrative level and adopted the new system of placing counties under municipalities in 1982, Yangzhou became a municipality under the province with jurisdiction over the former Yangzhou Prefecture, while Taizhou became a county-level city under Yangzhou. The original fraternal relation has become one of superior and subordinate. However, a city's economic links with the area under its influence have been formed over a long historical period based on an inevitable law — a law that cannot be artificially altered. Hence the above-mentioned problems.

Generally speaking, the system of placing counties under municipalities in Jiangsu is beneficial in breaking administrative divisions, realizing rational links in regional economies and accelerating economic development, and has gained practical results. But, owing to the short preparatory period for adopting the new system, it is impossible to make detailed studies on regional economic development. New problems like those of Taizhou are inevitable.

From my surveys in northern and southern Jiangsu, I discovered the relatively weak and slow development of township and town enterprises and small towns in northern Jiangsu. This is mainly because of the lack of medium cities with relatively strong economic strength like Suzhou, Wuxi, Changzhou and Nantong. Therefore, when some of the counties in northern Jiangsu are promoted to municipalities, the phenomenon of "a small horse pulling a big cart" becomes fully clear.

In southern Jiangsu the result is different — some cities or towns with their own features and laws of development lose the areas under their influence. For example, Tingshu Town under Yixing County, a historically famous town for pottery making, is unable to exercise its influence owing to its status under a county. And Changshu, now a county-level city under Suzhou, for another example, the limit of its administrative status also hampers its further growth.

The problem manifests itself differently in northern and southern Jiangsu, but it finds a concentrated expression in the relations between Taizhou and Yangzhou. We must realize that, as it appears in the stage of regional social and economic development, the solution calls for study of this development. Now a group of experts and scholars are making penetrating investigations in Taizhou, and I believe that their study and the efforts of the departments concerned will find proper methods to solve the problem and provide useful experience for our study of the regional economic development of small towns. I also want to suggest that Jiangsu Province will further undertake the study of strategies for regional social and economic development and properly adjust the existing administrative divisions on the basis of actual conditions.

My surveys in Nanjing, Zhenjiang and Yangzhou stressed the study of township and town enterprises and urban-rural regional development. Although this study still remains at the exploratory stage, it is a new field in the study of small towns. Township and town enterprises, I think, have generally passed the initial and development periods and are steadily maturing. A major indication of the maturing period is the tendency towards becoming knowledge- and technology-intensive enterprises. An old problem — the surplus of labour power — will rise for the second time in the third period of the development of township and town enterprises. The enterprises arose from the first surplus of labour power, and their development brought about the recovery and prosperity of small towns and touched off a series of changes in urban and rural productive forces and social relations. Then what does the second surplus of labour power mean? I don't think it will simply repeat what happened before. The tertiary industry emerging in the places of developed township and town enterprises is a signal and it might be the overture to a comprehensive merger of urban and rural areas based on solid economic links.

Therefore, the development process of township and town enterprises and the exploration of its social and economic consequences should be the theme of study in the new stage of small towns. The questions to be studied may include the significance of township and town enterprises in urban social and economic reforms, their universal and peculiar characters, and the relations between these enterprises and the urban-rural system of social values. During our inquiries about new questions, we will also strengthen and deepen the analysis of small town communities so as to lead the study of small towns forward.

Nanjing, Nov. 5, 1984

THE SHIFT OF SURPLUS AGRICULTURAL LABOUR FORCE AT DIFFERENT LEVELS

— A Survey of Four Administrative Villages in Wujiang County

Zhang Yulin

The idea of "shifting agricultural labour force" is defined in the following two ways: first, with the diversified development of agriculture, some labourers originally engaged in crop planting have been transferred to engage in occupations such as forestry, animal husbandry and fishery; secondly, some agricultural labourers have moved into such non-agricultural sectors as industry, handicraft industry, transport, construction, commerce, catering trade and cultural and educational work. The former move represents a deepening of division of labour within the agricultural sector, and the latter a development of the division of labour between the agricultural and other sectors of the economy, this being known as "the shift of the surplus agricultural labour force".

In the course of achieving their industrialization and modernization, all the developed countries in the world without exception underwent the process of shifting a sizable portion of their agricultural labour force to non-agricultural sectors of the economy. But the forms adopted and the changes of social relations caused by this process have varied significantly in different countries, depending on the nature of their social system. In the early stages of the industrialization of capitalist countries, the farmers who entered the cities after going bankrupt joined the ranks of urban workers and the urban poor.

As for how this shift takes place in China, what forms it adopts and the impact it has had on our social structure and city-countryside relationship will be discussed in the following essay.

As the basis for our study, we investigated the conditions in Wujiang County, Jiangsu Province. The findings of our investigation suggested that the shift in the labour force was completed section by section. One section was transferred to industrial and commercial undertakings within the village; another section to nearby township towns or the county towns; a small section to small towns or small cities further away, and only a very small section to medium-sized or big cities. We define such a phenomenon as "the shift of surplus agricultural labour force at different levels".

To make a detailed analysis of this shift, we investigated the redistribution of the labour force in Waiyi Village, as a fairly typical case, and compared it with that in three other villages in the same area but with different natural conditions.

I. The New Situation in the Development of Commodity Production in the Country

Wujiang County is situated on the shores of Lake Taihu in the southeastern part of Jiangsu Province, bordering the suburbs of Shanghai on the east and adjoining the Hang(zhou)-Jia(xing)-Hu(zhou) plain area of Zhejiang Province on the south. Zhenze Township is situated in the southeastern part of the county near Zhejiang Province. Zhenze, a town directly under county jurisdiction, is an industrial and commercial centre in the southwestern part of Wujiang County as well as the seat of the township government and the commune administration. The town of Nanhu is located 9 km. west of Zhenze and is under the administration of Huzhou Municipality, Zhejiang Province. Waiyi Village, the one we chose to investigate, is situated between these two towns and the Ditang River, which runs through Jiangsu and Zhejiang provinces, passes Zhenze and Nanhu and skirts the village on the north. Parallel to the north bank of the river runs the Shanghai-Huzhou Highway. Travelling to either of the two towns from the village is an hour's trip by motorboat or a 40 minutes' ride by bike. The village is an industrial and commercial focal point where quite a few branch shops of the local village-run factories and supply and marketing co-operatives are located. The above-mentioned factors were helpful to our research of the shift of agricultural labour force to the industrial and commercial undertakings in the village and to the nearby cities and towns, so we chose Waiyi Village as the target of our investigation. The three villages we used for comparison are Nanpubang Village, which is situated close to Zhenze; Zhonganqiao Village, situated along the highway 2.5 km. from Zhenze; and out-of-way Meijiabang Village, also 2.5 km. from Zhenze.

Comparing these three villages permits us to study the effect which different locations and transport conditions have on labour transfer.

Waiyi Village has a population of 1,321, which is divided into 322 households. It has 137 ha. of cultivated land or less than 0.5 ha. per capita; of which 108 ha. is paddy fields or 0.33 ha. per capita, and 29.1 ha. is non-irrigable land or less than 0.1 ha. per capita. The amount of cultivated land per capita is moderate on nationwide scale, but its other production conditions are far superior to most places in the country. The village is situated in the monsoon area of the subtropic zone. Its warm, humid and rainy climate, fertile land, location near a large lake, and good water conservancy are all favourable to the development of diversified agriculture. In addition, its location near a large city offers many conveniences for the development of rural industry.

For a rather long period in the past, under the influence of the "Left" deviation, peasants were confined to engaging in single-crop collective farming and grain production, and a lot of economic forms suitable to the present production level and a variety of production items were restricted. In the 1970s, some commune-run or production brigade-run industries were set up, but restrictions in the other areas still persisted, so the general situation did not improve much. The Third Plenary Session of the Eleventh Party Central Committee corrected these "Left" mistakes. In the last few years a contract responsibility system linking remuneration with output has gradually been implemented. A household-based contract system was adopted at the end of 1982, and the restrictions on rural handicraft industry, transport, commerce and the mobility of labour have all been relaxed. The unclogging of commodity circulation channels has opened up new avenues for developing commodity production, thus bringing about gratifying changes in the economy. They are primarily as follows:

(1)   Along with the continued growth of grain production, there has also been considerable development in diversified agriculture. The village's annual crop production in 1982 increased 13.3 per cent as compared with 1978 while its silkworm cocoon production nearly doubled, increasing by 86 per cent in the space of these four years. Domestic animal and poultry breeding (chiefly chicken, duck and rabbit) has also developed fast.

(2)   Industries run by commune have witnessed rapid development. Not only has the number of factories increased, but their size has also expanded, and new products have been put into production.   (The original ones consisted of a used pail renovation plant, a feed-processing plant, a vegetable-processing plant.   With the establishment of a water-proof building materials factory, there are now four factories in all.)   Not long ago, the village got in touch with a factory in the suburbs of Shanghai and with the help of Shanghai technicians they succeeded in turning out a new type of building material — pitch, thereby opening up a new vista for industry in the area.   The 1982 industrial output value increased 2.25 times over that of 1978, and profits have risen by 96 per cent.

(3)   Handicraftsmen no longer just go out to work and hand over their earnings to the production team in exchange for work points. Rather now, with the approval of the collective, they take the initiative to produce and market goods on their

own and only hand over a certain amount of their earnings to the production team as public funds. Some blacksmiths, carpenters and bamboo carpenters have taken on apprentices and started up handicraft workshops. Some of the products go to Shanghai and other cities, where demand for them is strong.

(4) With the development of diversified agriculture, industry, handicraft industry and construction, rural transport has emerged. The villagers equipped 10-15 ton plastered boat with a 12-horse power diesel engine and used it to ship steel, cement, timber, limestone, sand and other building materials and heavy goods to the village's factories, enterprises and to its peasant families who wish to build new houses. In 1982 it had about 10 such boats, their number increasing to 22 in the first half of 1983. Of these, 11 were under contract to collective units, and the other 11 privately managed.

The above changes boosted the output value of collective agriculture, industry and sideline occupations to 929,000 yuan in 1982, an 82 per cent increase over 1978, giving the villagers a per capita output value of 703 yuan. In the total output, farming took up 37 per cent; forestry, animal husbandry, sideline and fishery (including transport) 27 per cent; industry 35 per cent; others about 1 per cent. The average per capita net income was 387.56 yuan with 257.56 yuan (66 per cent) coming from collective enterprises and 130 yuan (34 per cent) from household sideline production (including private handicraft industry and transport). The commodity ratio of agriculture and sideline products, taken as the ratio of income from production team-sold products to the total income, is 61 per cent.

The trend of economic development in the three other villages is more or less the same as that of Waiyi Village, only one of the villages has not started village-run industry yet (Meijiabang Village) and one of the villages has progressed further with it (Zhonganqiao Village), while the other one (Nanpubang Village), which is located near Zhenze, has more labour force flowing into it. The above is the economic basis for shift of the labour force at different levels.

II. New Structure of the Labour Force

The alteration of economic structure and the development of commodity production are one side of the coin, while the deepening of social division of labour is the other. Having had a look at the changes in comprehensive management and commodity production in Waiyi Village, we will now turn our attention to examining the social division of labour among its labour force and households.

First we will examine the structure of its labour force. In counting labourers during our investigation, we did not follow the usual practice of basing our computations on a certain standard representing an able-bodied labourer, but rather took each natural labourer as one unit in our calculation. The reason for this is that in some production activities, a male labourer is not abler than a female one, and an able-bodied one is not more productive than a semi-able-bodied one. For instance, in silkworm raising, the female is the main force; and in rice-transplanting, a young girl is more efficient than a strong man. Our calculation and analysis should reflect as accurately as possible the fact that peasants are used to arranging labourers, male, female, able-bodied and semi-able-bodied, in mixed groups in production. In addition, after the adoption of the household contract system, rural households began to undertake comprehensive management of farming, mulberry planting and sericulture, domestic animal and poultry raising and other family sidelines, thereby blurring the clear-cut division among labourers engaged in different occupations. Therefore we have decided to regard all the labourers involved in these production activities as being engaged in agriculture, with the exception of those hands engaged in such diversified lines as duck and chicken raising, whom we have placed in a separate category. Cadres are administrative personnel and most of them take part directly in agriculture, industry and other productive activities. They could have been grouped into different trades they participate in, but to show management is also a kind of social division of labour, we have made it a separate category. The following table shows the division of labour in different trades, based on the method of calculation explained above.

The structure of the labour force in the three other villages is roughly the same as that of Waiyi Village, the main differences lying in the proportion of labourers engaged in certain specific trades as a percentage of the total work force. In Meijiabang Village, which is 2.5 km. away from town, far away from the highway and without village-run industry, farming takes up 66.38 per cent of the total labour force and industry, handicraft industry and transport take up only 26.7 per cent. In

Table I

COMPOSITIVE PRODUCTION ACTIVITIES OF PEASANT HOUSEHOLDS IN WAIYI VILLAGE

	Labourers	As % of the total
TOTAL	798	100
Agriculture	472	59.15
Of which:		
Farming	471	
Engaged mainly in domestic animal and poultry breeding and fishery	1	
Industry and transport	257	32.2
Of which:		
Industry	191	
Handicraft industry	24	
Transport	42	
Education and public health	12	1.5
Of which:		
Teachers	9	
Doctors	3	
Cadres (including those in township government, commune-village co-ops and enterprises)	46	5.8
Others	11*	1.4

* Including 9 labourers sent out by the commune to set up farms on the eastern part of Lake Taihu and 2 working at other places by their own.

Nanpubang Village which is very close to town, farming takes up 47.4 per cent of the labour force and the other three trades take up 45 per cent. In Zhonganqiao Village, which is situated along the highway, 2.5 km. from town and has very sound village-run industries, farming only accounts for 31.79 per cent of the total labour force, the other three trades making up 61.46 per cent, the exact reversal of the figures for Meijiabang Village. Besides this, with the exception of Waiyi Village, the other three villages all have a few people who are engaged in commercial business.

It is worth noting that the shift of labour force is a complicated social economic process. The above figures only provide us with a general picture of the structure of the present rural labour force but are not sufficient to reflect the whole situation. A further examination of the process reveals that there are two outstanding features in the labour shift from agriculture to other sectors of the economy at present: (1) Only a small proportion of people are engaged in work totally separate from agriculture, the bulk of labourers being concurrently engaged in agriculture and other occupations. In Waiyi Village, the focal point of our investigation, there were only 37 people engaged in occupations totally separate from agriculture, representing 12.3 per cent of the total labourers in trades other than agriculture, and the remaining 87.7 per cent devoted 20 to 30 per cent of their work hours to agriculture. In comparison, Meijiabang Village, which has no village-run industry, the industry-engaged people have to go to the seat of the commune administration or towns to work, thus leaving less time for agriculture. The situation is exactly reversed in Zhonganqiao Village, which has a prosperous village-run industry. There, quite a number of people work in factories but each person devotes only 5-6 hours per day to factory work, the rest of their work hours being devoted to agriculture. (2) As far as the quality of the labour force is concerned, there is no balanced distribution between those remaining in agriculture and those switched to other trades. Table II illustrates it.

Analysis of the table shows able male labourers and those with some education have mostly switched to other trades. For example, among the 101 male labourers under the age of 25, 75 have made the switch, constituting 74.3 per cent; of those under 35, 66.4 per cent or 164 out of 247 have switched; and of those with education above junior middle school, 62.3 per cent or 124 out of 199 switched. Among those able hands with some education who still remain in agriculture, most are farm machinery operators, technicians, managerial personnel of the irrigation network and women who can't leave due to housework and other reasons. In No. 6 Production Team, there are four capable labourers with education above junior middle school and still working in agriculture. One is the brigade's irrigation network guard, one a tractor driver, one has a baby too young to be left alone and the other is a girl about to get married. This goes to show that quite a number of young educated labourers have switched to other trades, but most of them are still partially involved in agriculture. This is of great significance both in theory and in practice. The later parts of this essay will devote to this point.

III. The Development of Division of Labour Among Peasant Households

Now let's have a look at how peasant households divide their labour.

Since the adoption of the contract responsibility system linking remuneration with output, the rural economy has been divided into two administrative levels. One is unified management at the collective level, the other is decentralized management of the level of the peasant households. Accordingly, the division of labour and co-operation are also double-layered. At the collective level the division of labour and co-operation involved decisions concerning who will be a tractor driver, who will take charge of water network and who will work in industrial enterprises. In principle, the collective makes these decisions. The division of labour and co-operation at the level of the peasant households include specialized households and those engaged in more than one occupation concurrently. A household is a production unit, consumption unit and a living unit combined in one. Household management, at present, is both a key yardstick for measuring the depth of social division of labour, while at the same time conditioning its development. This issue should be studied separately. Table III shows how labour is divided among the households of Waiyi Village.

The situation in household management in the three comparison villages is quite similar to that in Waiyi Village, but there are some differences in the proportion of the families engaged in different trades. Table IV spells it out.

From the two tables we can see that households engaged concurrently in agriculture and industry (or other trades) hold a prominent position. The more and the nearer they are to town, the more numerous such households will be. Facts in the foregoing section have shown that in an area with a well-developed rural economy like the area where we conducted our investigation, quite a lot of labourers are involved in both agriculture and industry. The facts in this section reinforce the conclusion that about half of the rural households no longer belong to pure farming households but are now doubly engaged. Like the labourers who have become entirely separated from agriculture mentioned in the previous section, some households have similarly began to leave agriculture as well, but their number is still small. In a word, an enormous number of labourers and households are switching to non-agricultural or other sectors while still remaining involved in agriculture but only a few labourers and households have made a complete switch. That this has brought remarkable changes in the social and economical structure of the rural community is an irrefutable fact. The question is: how did this happen?

Table III

THE DIVISION OF LABOUR AMONG THE HOUSEHOLDS OF WAIYI VILLAGE

	Households	As % of the total
TOTAL	322	100
Peasant households	102	31.7
Purely agriculture-engaged households	96	
Specialized ones*	6	
Households engaged in agriculture and industry or other trades concurrently	190	**59**
Those in agriculture and industry concurrently	127	
Those in agriculture and handicraft industry	14	
Those in agriculture and transport	24	
Those in agriculture, industry and handicraft industry	8	
Those in agriculture, industry and transport	8	
Those in agriculture, handicraft industry and transport	—	
Those with some members doing teaching and medical work	9	
Others	—	
Non-agricultural households growing grain for their own consumption**	13	**4**
Industry-engaged households	11	
Handicraft industry-engaged ones	1	
Teachers	1	
Small merchants	—	
Households entirely separated from agriculture***	5	1.6
Labourless households	12	3.7

* According to Wujiang County government, households which hand in more than 2,500 kg. of grain are considered to be "specialized in grain cultivation", but actually they should only be regarded as "specializing in grain cultivation" or "big grain producers".

** "Non-agricultural households growing grain for their own consumption" refers to those whose labourers have switched to other trades but due to limitations in the state's grain production, are not supplied with commodity grain and therefore have to grow their own.

*** "Households entirely separated from agriculture" refers to those that do not need to grow any grain, even for their own consumption. They are assigned land to grow grain for their own consumption, but leave it to the care of their relatives who provide grain for them, or else they buy grain on markets at a negotiable price.

Table IV

HOUSEHOLD LABOUR DIVISION OF THE THREE COMPARISON VILLAGES

	Meijiabang (without industry)		Nanpubang (near town)		Zhonganqiao (with best village-run industry)	
Households total	174	100.00%	265	100.00%	221	100.00%
Farming households	87	50.00%	29	10.94%	33	14.9 %
Households concurrently engaged in agriculture and industry or other trades	77	44.3 %	172	64.91%	154	69.7 %
Non-agricultural ones but growing grain for their own consumption	6	3.4 %	28	10.56%	22	10 %
Those entirely separated from agriculture	2	1.15%	21	7.92%	5	2.3%
Labourless households	2	1.15%	15	5.66%	7	3.2%

IV. The Reasons Behind the Emergence of Doubly Engaged Labourers and Households and Their Prospects

The emergence of so many doubly engaged labourers and households is attributable to the following reasons:

The first is the nature of agricultural production itself.

One of the outstanding characteristics of agricultural production is its seasonality, which forms the natural basis for the integration of agriculture with rural industry and handicraft industry. Historically, the integration of small agriculture with household handicraft industry served as the cornerstone of our rural economy.

This economic form formerly flourished in the area we surveyed. Xiang Zhisheng, a local old hand in silk work, described the former processing of silkworm cocoons in his memoirs: "The sound 'yi-ya' (the sound of a wooden machine creaking) used to echo throughout the village all the year round. The whole family, old and young, took part in the process. Farming was not neglected while housework was also attended to. . . . In the area around Zhenze, the annual output of raw silk amounted to 10 tons which brought the peasants an income amounting to more than 1,000,000 silver yuan." The twenties and thirties witnessed the dumping of Japanese rayon on the Chinese market and the rise of the domestic capitalist mechanical textile industry, which dealt a heavy blow to rural silk production and processing, thus accelerating the impoverishment of the peasants. The household silk production was destroyed by the heavy pressure exerted by imperialism and bureaucrat capitalism.

Now, having broken away from such pressure for more than 30 years and after the development of the rural collective economy and state-owned industry, the peasants are quite capable, through their collective effort, of running industries at village and town levels. On the other hand, while state-owned urban industry is concentrating on manufacturing products of high-grade, precision and sophistication, the production of intermediate products needs to be carried out in the countryside. So, from a macroscopic point of view, urban industry and rural industry can help each other, subject to the regulation of the state plan, by supplementing each other's deficiencies. For instance, the countryside needs to obtain equipment and technology from the city, while the city needs to utilize the countryside for its own development. Under the new conditions, it is only natural for agriculture and industry to become more closely integrated with each other. Take the area we investigated for example. In a year, it has seven months' busy season (two rice harvests and four silkworm raisings), among which three months are the busiest. During this period, labourers are in great demand but when it is over, the households only leave a semi-able-bodied labourer to look after the fields. The doubly engaged hands are very much involved in farming during the busy farming season, and devote themselves entirely to industry during the slack season. The industrial products, like the intermediate products of emulsified pitch manufactured by Waiyi Village, sewing machine frames produced by Zhonganqiao

Village and the intermediate products of dyestuff produced by Nanpubang Village, are all needed by urban industries. Such a combination of agriculture and industry is indeed beneficial to bringing into full play the latent potentialities of both the urban and the rural areas and especially that of rural labour force.

Secondly, the practice of the doubly engaged peasant households is quite sensible from the point of view of consolidating and developing the rural collective economy. Even after the adoption of the household contract system, the bulk of the rural economy is still organized on a collective basis. It is only by bringing into full play the initiative of all peasants can the collective economy be continuously strengthened and developed.

At present, peasants engaged in industrial work earn more than those engaged in agriculture. When redistributing labour power, those in charge of organizing the collective economy should see to it that in each family there is someone engaged in industry, so that those who remain in agriculture can keep their minds on their work.

Of course, there are other ways to redistribute income, such as using industrial profit to aid agriculture, or distributing income on the basis of the amount of grain each rural household hands in, and when circumstances permit it, the state can also use price policy to intervene. But even if a rough balance of income between agriculture and industry is achieved, farming is still much more toilsome than industrial production because the working conditions are different. Farmers are exposed to all kinds of weather and they must work extraordinarily hard during the agricultural busy season. Furthermore, this state of affairs stands to remain unchanged for a rather long period of time. So when distributing the labour force, the organizer should also consider the issue from this point of view, and ensure that each household has a hand in industry. What we saw during our investigation of the four villages is in keeping with our statements above.

Another factor that necessitates the integration of agriculture with industry is that rural industry needs to be further stabilized and agriculture is still effected by natural disasters, so this integration promises to promote the steady growth of rural economy.

All the above have combined to account for another factor of the mass emergence of doubly engaged labourers and households.

Thirdly, from the household's view, the combination is inevitable. A household is a unit of both economic life and human reproduction. It has both the function of economic production and consumption and also the duty of upbringing young and looking after the old. In the final analysis, family structure is determined by the level of development of the forces of social production and the nature of the relations of production. The former in which the young and old are taken care of is also determined by the forces and relations of production. As soon as this form comes into being it has a kind of stability, which, in return, produces an impact on economic life.

Now let us take a look at Waiyi's family structure:

Table V

FAMILY SIZES IN WAIYI VILLAGE

	Household	As % of the total
Families total	327	100
Families with 1-3 members	98	30
One member	26	
Two members	29	
Three members	43	
Families with 4-5 members	159	48.6
Four members	83	
Five members	76	
Families with 6-11 members	70	21.4
Six members	46	
Seven members	18	
Eight members	4	
Nine members	1	
Ten members	—	
Eleven members	1	

If we designate a family consisting of a couple and their unmarried children as being a "nuclear family", one containing a couple, their unmarried children, parents and unmarried brothers and sisters as being an "extended nuclear family", one with two married couples of the same generation as being a "joint family" and one without a couple as being an "incomplete family" then the composition of Waiyi's family structure is basically as follows:

Table VI

FAMILY STRUCTURE OF WAIYI VILLAGE (1)

	Household	As % of the total
Families total	327	100
Nuclear ones	99	30.3
Extended nuclear ones	171	52.3
Joint ones	4	1.2
Incomplete ones	53	16.2

Note: The statistics for the above two tables come from 1982 census. There were five more families than there are now.

Table VII

FAMILY STRUCTURE OF WAIYI VILLAGE (2)

	Household	As % of the total
Households total	327	100
Those with old and young	136	41.6
Those with old but without young	59	18
Those with young but without old	71	21.7
Those with neither	41	12.6
Those made up by old only	20	6.1

For the purpose of discussing how the young and old are taken care of, we define males over 55 and females over 50 as "the old" (because they need to live with their children who can share the heavy physical labour and housework) and children under 15 as "the young" (because those below the age of 15 are still in school, and need to be taken care of by others while only those above 16 are considered labourers). Table VII shows the distribution of the elderly and young among the families in Waiyi Village.

The above three tables suggest that the primary form of rural family is the "extended nuclear family", containing both old and young members, with an average size of four to six people. The able-bodied labourers in such families cannot all switch to other trades, since some must remain at home to look after the old and young.

Industriousness has long been one of the outstanding qualities of our peasants — whoever is able to work will go out and do some. The elderly can raise pigs and chickens, and children after school can cut grass to feed the pigs and sheep. So the main form of our rural economic and social life still consists of able-bodied labourers co-ordinating their activities with the old and young working together with them in engaging in agricultural and sideline production, in doing house chores and in organizing family life. Especially at present, since most rural industries have not yet stabilized, the income from comprehensive management of farming, sericulture and household sidelines, though not very large, still pays for most of the peasants' living expenses. So successfully arranging its agricultural and sideline production and housework is a prerequisite which a rural household must fulfil before it can shift its surplus labour to other trades. This is also one major reason why most households cannot switch all of their able-bodied members to other trades, and why they must still concurrently engage in agriculture and industry.

Large-scale socialized production is the direction in which the whole social economy is developing. Therefore we encourage specialization among labourers and peasant households. But socialization cannot be realized by itself alone. Specialized production must be coupled with pre- and post-production services and housework socialization. This requires raising the level of the social forces of production and takes a long time. As far as the area we investigated is concerned, specialization in agriculture will come first. Households specialized in poultry and fish breeding are likely to develop first. Then, as the management of land is increasingly concentrated in the hands of a smaller number of people, some key grain-growing households will also emerge. As for the shift of the surplus agricultural labourers to non-agricultural sectors, at present, most such labourers have to divide their efforts between several different trades concurrently, with only a few totally switching over to trades other than agriculture. But the number of specialized households will gradually increase with the rise of the level of production management in industry and other trades. Enterprises above the township level will see a more rapid development of specialization. But even then, so long as the three above-mentioned causes underlying the emergence of doubly engaged labourers still exist, it is inevitable that their number will remain large.

V. The Shift of Surplus Agricultural Labour Force and the Setting Up of Urban-Rural Integration Towns at Different Levels

Understanding the inevitability of a large number of labourers and households being doubly engaged and only a few being specialized makes it easier to study the forms that the shift of rural surplus labour takes at different levels.

We collected cadres' and commune members' opinions concerning the shift through holding individual interviews and informal discussions and have summarized them below. The points they made tally with the actual situation and touch upon the work which they are currently engaged in.

(1) The collective should first ensure that there are enough hands in agriculture and their quality is passable. Agriculture is the basis of national economy, so it should never be weakened. Educated young peasants are indispensable to the reali-

zation of agricultural modernization, and so they require cautious treatment. While attending to both industry and agriculture, the latter should be given due attention. Only the extra hands in agriculture should be shifted. The disposition of extra hands should be made on a family basis, so that as many as possible families will have some members engaged in industry or other trades. The families whose members are totally shifted should be among those with fewer members.

(2) Generally speaking, in a family of four, five or six, including old and young members, there must be a male and a female labourer to attend farming, sericulture and poultry and livestock breeding, and to take care of the aged and the young. If one of the two is to be transferred, it should be to a place nearby, such as a village-run factory or commercial centre. He will go to work early and come back late (meaning to work in the fields for some time every day both before and after going to work in the factory), at least do so during the seven months of busy season in farming, enabling him to devote a certain amount of time to farming, sericulture, sideline production and various housework.

(3) When farming, sericulture and sideline production and housework have been well-arranged and consideration has been given to factors mentioned in (2), if there are still extra hands, they can be shifted to towns farther away to take part in industry, commerce and service trades. Nevertheless, most of them will still be needed to lend a helping hand during the busy season, so they cannot go too far away.

(4) Only those that are not needed even during the busiest season can be totally separated from agriculture and be transferred to places farther away, according to need.

(5) Only a small number of households with few members (those with only one labourer or which consist of only an ablebodied young couple who can both do jobs other than agriculture) can withdraw from agriculture as a household.

At present, the surplus agricultural force is shifted to trades other than agriculture in accordance with the above-mentioned patterns. This is what we meant by the shift of surplus labour force at different levels.

A door-to-door survey reveals the situation in Waiyi Village. (See Table VIII.)

Analysis of the above figures shows that under present production conditions, solely agriculturally-engaged labourers take up 62.16 per cent of the total. Among them, women are in the majority. Women labourers engaged in agriculture account for 83.6 per cent of the total, while men account for 46.5 per cent. If the surplus is balanced against the shortage, the present need for solely agriculturally-engaged hands is only 53.5 per cent of the total, accounting for 38 per cent of the total men labourers and 77 per cent of the total women labourers. In other words, if we only consider labourers engaged solely in agriculture, 46.5 per cent of the total labourers in Waiyi Village are surplus, with 62 per cent of the total male labourers and 23 per cent of the total female labourers being surplus respectively. The surplus agricultural labour force has not totally shifted to other trades, so there should be more shifting in the future.

Table VIII indicates the shift of surplus agricultural labour force which has taken place at different levels. The first level shows the local shift. In Waiyi Village, labourers who shifted locally constitute 50 per cent of the total shifted force. The second level shows the shift to nearby towns. This group is proportionately 37.7 per cent of the total. The third shows the shift to towns far away which makes up 12.3 per cent of the total. Following is a detailed account of the workers at the third level. These are labourers employed as peasant workers by the state-run Zhoupu Paint Factory in the town of Zhoupu in the suburbs of Shanghai. Among them, some work in the factory. Others go to Beijing, Shanghai, Guangzhou and other big cities with the factory's technicians to do construction work as members of the factory's construction team. This is in fact a provisional export of labour to distant places.

There is some difference in quality among the shifted labourers of different levels. At the lower level, that is labourers

Table VIII

LABOUR DISTRIBUTION OF WAIYI VILLAGE

	Total	Subtotal	Male	Female
Households	322			
Population	1,321			
Labourers	798		462	336
Present labour power distribution pattern				
Engaged entirely in agriculture[1]	496		215	281
Engaged in agriculture and other trades concurrently[2]	265			
Switched but still in the same brigade		151	125	26
Switched to towns nearby		114	91	23
Separated from agriculture	37		31	6
Present surplus[3]	85			
Might be engaged in agriculture while doing other jobs		76		
Switched in the brigade			39	30
Switched to towns nearby			5	2
Might separate from agriculture		9	6	3
Labour shortage[4]	16			
Shortage of solely agriculturally-engaged labourers		6	1	5
Shortage of labourers engaged in agriculture and other trades concurrently		10	4	6

1. "Engaged entirely in agriculture" refers to those engaged in farming, sericulture, livestock and poultry breeding and sideline production.
2. "Engaged in agriculture and other trades concurrently" refers to those that not entirely separate from agriculture while engaging in industry, transport, commerce and other production activities, some mainly in agriculture and others mainly in other trades.
3. "Present surplus labour force" refers to labourers who can shift.
4. "Shortage" refers to households which are short of hands. The real surplus can be determined by subtracting "shortage" from "present surplus labour force".

shifted to towns at different administrative levels with in the county, there doesn't seem to be much difference if only a few labourers are counted. But if more are counted, and the situation is viewed as a whole, difference shows up.

The following table compares the ages and educational levels of the shifted labourers who stayed in the same village shifting chiefly to the village-run industrial and commercial undertakings and those who shifted to Zhenze Town (including commune-run enterprises as they are also in town).

Table IX

AGE STRUCTURE AND EDUCATIONAL LEVELS OF SHIFTED AGRICULTURAL LABOURERS AT DIFFERENT LEVELS

	Inner village shift		Shift to Zhenze Town	
	Person	As % of the total	Person	As % of the total
Age groups				
25 years old	133	30.15	171	47.5
26-35 years old	143	32.43	108	30
36-45 years old	90	20.4	38	10.56
46-55 years old	63	14.3	30	8.33
56-65 years old	12	2.72	13	3.61
TOTAL	441	100	360	100
Educational levels				
Illiterate and semi-illiterate	246	55.78	78	21.67
Primary school	75	17	97	26.94
Junior middle school	99	22.45	147	40.83
Senior middle school	21	4.77	38	10.56
TOTAL	441	100	360	100

The above statistics reveal that those who shifted to Zhenze were comparatively younger and better educated than those who shifted within the village. Differences in education surpass those in age.

In the four villages, only few college and secondary technical school graduates and some ex-servicemen were assigned jobs in cities. Apart from them, among the workers in the high level, there are only ten Waiyi people who are employed by the construction team of Zhoupu Paint Factory in the suburbs of Shanghai. These ten are all young junior middle school graduates. This suggests that the quality of the shifted labour at the high level is far better than that at the lower level.

The shift of the labour force at different levels has great impact on the labourers' work and life-style. Generally speaking, the higher the level, the more involved in industry, and subsequently, the less involved in agriculture, e.g. people employed in enterprises in Waiyi Village work seven hours a day and during agricultural busy season they spend four hours daily in agriculture; people employed in enterprises in Zhonganqiao Village work five to six hours a day and during busy farm season spend half of their time in agriculture; people employed in commune-run enterprises and enterprises in Zhenze work eight hours a day and during busy farm season they can only spend two to three hours on agriculture; those working in far away towns or cities are totally separate from agriculture and devote all their time to industry, commerce and other trades. From this, one can see the manner in which industrially-engaged labour is becoming specialized. Although there are a few solely industrially-engaged labourers at the low level, they are administrative and technical personnel and their number is small. In correspondence to this, the industrial productive forces vary at each level. According to the Sept. 1983 Zhenze Township statistics, the fixed assets per capita for the workers on the commune-run factories were 1,931 yuan, while those of village-run factories were only 592.9 yuan. The two foundries in Zhonganqiao Village and the used pail renovation plant in Waiyi Village are poorly equipped. As a result, their workers can readily put aside their tools and return to farming. But workers in commune-run textile factory must work in succession, one shift after another. That is to say, the level of the industrial means of production with which the workers are integrated determines the changes which are brought about in their work and life-styles. If they advance along this ladder step by step, more and more peasants become workers.

The nature of socialist labour is characterized by unity which is realized at different levels. The shift of surplus agricultural labour force at different levels is chiefly the unity of the labour forces at different levels. (The word "chiefly" here suggests that there are also some secondary economic forms.) Village-run industry and commerce are collective industry and supply and marketing undertakings serving agriculture and industry and people's life, managed through the joint efforts of village's labourers; commune-run industry and commerce, therefore, are enterprises which are jointly run by the commune members. In towns like Zhenze there are already some state-run industrial and commercial enterprises or undertakings. By taking part in the work in those units, labourers join the unity of the whole society.

The shift of surplus agricultural labour force at different levels to different places, to engage in joint ventures at various levels, initiating industrial and commercial undertakings at various scales and of different scopes, naturally leads to the establishment of industrial and commercial centres at different levels. That's what people mean by little towns at different levels which can be grouped as follows: At the first level is the industrial and commercial network in the village; at the second level are the industrial and commercial centres, each having a service radius of several villages and can be called village towns; at the third are centres whose scope embraces an entire township, and can be called township towns. As far as ownership is concerned, the industrial and commercial undertakings at the above three levels are all collectively-owned enterprises of differing scopes. Furthermore, at the fourth level are towns with the administrative level of county jurisdiction where there are state-run enterprises, service trades and cultural and educational facilities of a fairly high level, making them economic and cultural centres of a larger scope. They have closer ties with big and medium-sized cities, and can be called county towns. Our cities are thus linked up with the countryside by the above-mentioned little towns at different levels. Using small towns at different levels to link the countryside with big and medium-sized cities is an important feature in the process of building up our countryside, and should be the way towards its urbanization.

PEASANT WORKERS IN COUNTY TOWNS

— A Survey of Wujiang County

Zhang Yulin

During our investigation on towns directly under county jurisdiction (called county towns) in Wujiang County, Jiangsu Province, we encountered a great number of labourers whose residence is in the countryside and who maintain their membership in a rural people's commune, their grain rations* supplied by production teams, but who have been admitted to work in the nearby county towns. Among them, most are permanent workers. Part of their wages are deducted by their production teams for use as public funds. People call them "peasant workers".

Under the existing system, county towns are considered "cities" at the lowest level. In the past, workers were employed from the countryside only when there were heavy or seasonal tasks, and none were engaged on a permanent basis. But with the changes which have taken place since 1978, the above-mentioned peasant workers are increasing. Many of them now work in one enterprise for year after year, and are no longer "seasonal workers". They are even included in the annual statistical report of the county labour department, with a footnote explaining that they are "from the countryside". According

---

* Since the introduction of the contracted responsibility system based on households, a new method of land distribution based on grain rations has been adopted.

to the 1982 Labour Department Statistics of Wujiang County, among the 67,266 staff members of the state-owned and collective enterprises, there were 10,123 peasant workers, accounting for 15 per cent of the total. This poses a question to us: Is this an inevitable trend of economical and social development, with such a large number of peasant workers entering county towns? What effect would it have on the construction of small towns and the countryside?

I

Let us start with an analysis of the trend of economic and social development of Wujiang County.

Wujiang is a county under the jurisdiction of Suzhou Municipality, Jiangsu Province. Bordered by Lake Taihu to the west, Suzhou to the north, the Shanghai suburb of Qingpu County to the east and the fertile Hang(zhou)-Jia(xing)-Hu(zhou) plain on the south, it is an area with well-developed economy. With lakes scattered all over and criss-crossed by rivers, Wujiang County presents ideal conditions for farming, sericulture, fish and animal husbandry. Besides, being situated close to big cities, it can take advantages of both city and countryside to develop its industry.

In the past few years and especially after 1978, great progress has been made in the county's agriculture, sideline production and industry. According to the county's Statistics Bureau in 1982, its industrial and agricultural output value totalled 1,155 million yuan, an 82.6 per cent increase over 1978, representing 1,578 yuan per capita; industrial output value (excluding that of brigade-run enterprises) amounted to 669.96 million yuan, a 70.4 per cent increase over 1978 and accounting for 58 per cent of the total output value of industry and agriculture. This represents a per capita income of 334.33 yuan with 241.85 yuan from collective distribution and 92.48 yuan from household sidelines and is 23.8 per cent larger than the average national per capita income of 270 yuan.

There are seven county towns almost evenly scattered over the county, functioning as the political, economic, cultural and transport hubs. Most of the state-owned and collective enterprises and state-owned commerce are concentrated in these towns. With the development of the county's agriculture, sideline occupations and industry, the last few years have witnessed the flourishing of these towns. In 1982, the industrial output value of the seven county towns reached 505.67 million yuan, accounting for 75.5 per cent of that of the whole county and representing an increase of 52.4 per cent over 1978, and more than 10 times as compared with that of 1952, shortly after the founding of the People's Republic. The turnover from commodity retail trade in the seven towns was 12,316.31 million yuan, 60 per cent of the county's total and more than twice that of 1952. Such a remarkable development of production in county industries, whose equipment was originally sub-standard, naturally boosted the demand for labourers. But the point is, in 1982 the registered residents of the seven towns were 812 fewer as compared with 1952, the proportion of the town people in the county's total declining by 5.7 per cent. On the one hand, the full employment of the towns' labourers still couldn't meet the needs of their economic development, and on the other hand, there was a sizable contingent of surplus rural labourers

Table I

TOWN POPULATION FLUCTUATIONS OF WUJIANG COUNTY

	Town population	Proportion in the country's total
1949	79,043	16.9
1952	82,217	16.7
1957	79,051	14.8
1965	68,581	11.7
1975	63,532	9.2
1978	65,210	9.4
1982	81,405	11.2

seeking jobs. Under these circumstances, a flow of rural labourers into county towns occurred.

A town is the core of the countryside and the vast countryside is its extension, so its development is chiefly the result of rural economic and social development, while its own development plays a certain part, but not the major one. It is only natural, in the course of its development, the town depends on the rural forces, admitting labourers from the countryside and setting up rural services. In this sense, it was an objective requirement of their economic and social development that the county towns in Wujiang recruited a lot of peasant workers.

II

Just making a sweeping analysis of Wujiang County is insufficient to elucidate the matter of peasant workers, so we made a systematic study of Zhenze, one of the seven county towns.

Historically, Zhenze has long played a role in collecting and distributing commodities in the southwestern part of the county. With the rapid development of its industry, Zhenze has now grown into an industrial and commercial town specialized in industry. In 1982, industrial output value totalled over 55 million yuan, an 81.6 per cent increase over 1978 and a 420 per cent increase over that of 1970. It's worth noting that while the town's economy has grown by leaps and bounds, there was no corresponding increase in the size of its population. Rather due to the full employment of the town's labour force, it absorbed a lot of peasant workers. Some commune- and brigade-run enterprises have emerged in the area near the town and all of their workers are practically those similar to peasant workers. They are chiefly engaged in industry but concurrently also keep a hand in agriculture. Their output value and labour force are not yet counted in the town's totals. Thus a town can be defined in two ways: one is as an administrative unit, which would give Zhenze population of 8,226 registered residents, according to 1982 census. The other is as a community formed by social life, so that its population would then include not only its registered residents, but also peasant workers working in town, employees of the nearby commune- and brigade-run enterprises, resident students of middle schools and the mobile population staying in hotels. According to the second definition, Zhenze has a population of 13,017, which is 4,791 more people than are registered, and accounting for 58.2 per cent of those who are registered. That is to say, population has grown a lot in the areas surrounding the town. It is merely owing to the restrictions on issuing town residency permits that its residency structure has been altered. This article does not intend to discuss the residency restrictions in big or medium-sized cities, which involve many factors. However, as far as small towns are concerned, the main purpose of these restrictions is to avoid increasing the issue of commodity grain.

Here is a detailed account of the peasant workers:

In March 1983, we made a unit-by-unit survey together with the town's Labour Recruitment Service, and found that the total staff in town (including that of state-run industry, county- and town-run collective industry and commerce, service trades and Party and administrative units) amounts to 5,621, of which, 4,474 are town residents, accounting for 79.6 per cent of the total. The remaining 20.4 per cent are peasant workers amounting to 1,147 people.

The peasant workers can be subdivided into four categories: (1) "Workers whose land has been taken over", e.g. when the land of a nearby production brigade or team is taken over for use by a certain enterprise or institution, the production brigade or team concerned, now that their amount of land per capita has decreased, becomes more sensitive to the pressure of surplus labour force. To solve this problem, the enterprise or institution which has taken over the land arranges to accept a certain number of peasants from the brigade or team to work in the enterprise or institution. These peasants keep their status as rural residents as well as their grain rations supplied by the brigade or team. There are 118 peasant workers of this type, accounting for 10.28 per cent of the total peasant workers. (2) "Temporary workers within the plan." The enterprise or institution cannot officially recruit workers from the countryside, but is permitted to recruit "temporary workers". However, they are only nominally temporary, in reality, they become permanent workers of the enterprise or institution. There are 643 peasant workers of this kind, making up 56.06 per cent of the total. (3) "Expense-paid workers". The wages of these workers are not included in the total wage account, but paid by the enterprise directly from the production expenses. They can enter the towns to work without the approval of the county labour department. Zhenze has 235 peasant workers of this type, accounting for 20.49 per cent of the total. (4) "Contracted workers", e.g. the enterprise or institution enters into a contract with a production brigade for a project, pays the brigade a total sum of contract fees, and the wages of the peasant workers are paid by the brigade. Like other peasant workers, they come and work in the factory, the management of production being the responsibility of the factory itself. There are 151 peasant workers of this type, making up 13.16 per cent of the total. The above facts show that the enterprises at the county level and below have tried various ways of getting more workers so as to meet the needs of production development. This is the real reason why there are so many kinds of peasant workers.

At present there are peasant workers in all the trades in Zhenze except for banking. As a result, they have entered almost every sphere of social and economic life. The banking system gives priority to the vertical administrative relationship so the local banks do not have the flexibility to recruit labourers. They can meet their requirements for staff since they are given top priority in the town recruitment of labour. They do not have to employ peasant workers on the whole, but as far as the banking system is concerned, the credit co-ops under the agricultural banks are resuming the nature of the collective economic organization for peasants. In the future, the commune credit co-ops set up in towns will also recruit rural residents. Then the situation in which the banking system does not have peasant workers will be changed. Now the distribution of the peasant workers in all trades of Zhenze is as follows: There are 429 peasant workers in the state-owned factories, accounting for 30.5 per cent of the total staff; 501 peasant workers in the collectively-owned factories, 20.5 per cent of the total staff; 20 in communication, post and telecommunication sectors, 12.4 per cent of the total; 119 in public sectors of capital construction and environmental protection, 34.4 per cent of the total; 77 in commercial and foreign trade sectors, 7.7 per cent of the total; 1 in township government and mass organization, 2 per cent of the total. In addition, some individual labourers also employ assistants from among the rural residents.

What merits particular attention is that the proportion of peasant workers in those big and developing factories, which are in great need of labourers, is in excess of the average figure of 20.5 per cent for the whole town. For instance, in the Zhenfeng State-Owned Silk Factory, peasant workers account for 33.3 per cent of the total staff; in Wujiang State-Owned Winery Mill, they constitute 42.3 per cent of the total staff, in the collectively-owned Dongfeng Chemical Plant, they make up 26.2 per cent of the total staff. And in Wujiang Wool Dye Factory, which is jointly run by the town and the commune, peasant workers account for as much as 71.4 per cent of the total staff. One of the major reasons that the factory is called "jointly-run" is that this facilitates the recruitment of more peasant workers.

Who are the peasant workers who entered the town? With the help of the management departments of all of the industries, we conducted a survey on the peasant workers of the whole town on a one-by-one basis from the end of June to early July, 1983. The findings are as follows:

(1) Proportion of sexes: male 573, female 752. The female workers are in the majority due to the flourishing of Zhenze's silk-reeling and textile industries which has created greater demand for women workers than for men.

(2) The age structure of Zhenze's peasant workers is as follows:

Table II

AGE STRUCTURE OF ZHENGZE'S PEASANT WORKERS

Age group	Number of people	As % of the total
below 20-30	860	65.9
below 20	429	32.9
21-25	206	15.8
26-30	225	17.2
31-45	302	23.1
31-35	153	11.7
36-40	87	6.7
41-45	62	4.8
46 and above	144	11.0
46-50	46	3.5
51-55	33	2.5
56-60	32	2.5
60-	33	2.5
Unknown*	20	

* People of unknown age were not calculated in the percentage. This applies to the following statistics too.

The persons listed in the above table are mostly young and able-bodied peasant workers. The marriage age in rural areas is 25 for men and 23 for women. Thus, almost half of the peasant workers are unmarried.

(3) Comparative educational levels of peasant workers and workers with town residence are shown in Table III on the next page which demonstrates the educational level of the peasant workers is lower than that of the staff who are town residents but much higher than that of rural labourers.

(4) The time of recruitment of peasant workers is demonstrated in Table IV.

Table III

COMPARATIVE EDUCATIONAL LEVELS OF PEASANT WORKERS AND WORKERS OF TOWN RESIDENCE

Educational levels*	Number of people	As % of the total	Comparison with workers of town residents (%)	Comparison with rural labour (%)
Senior middle school	106	8.3	—19	+ 2.5
Junior middle school	490	38.2	—9.2	+20.6
Primary school	517	40.3	+10.8	+29.7
Illiterate and semi-illiterate	170	13.2	+13.2	—52.8
Unknown	42			

* The educational level of the rural labour force is based on our investigation in Waiyi Village, Zhenze Township, 4 km. from Zhenze Town.

Table IV

TIME OF RECRUITMENT OF PEASANT WORKERS

Beginning year	Number of people	As % of the total
1969-1974	41	3.1
1969	1	
1970	—	
1971	2	
1972	5	
1973	10	
1974	23	
1975-1978	215	16.3
1975	55	
1976	69	
1977	33	
1978	58	
1979-1983	1,060	80.5
1979	105	
1980	206	
1981	225	
1982	226	
1983	298	
Unknown	9	

The year when they entered the factories reflects their length of service. This table reveals that quite a number of peasant workers have become veterans in their enterprises.

As was mentioned earlier, peasant workers were admitted into factories as temporaries, a status which originally referred to workers in odd and auxiliary jobs. But among these peasant workers, only a small proportion hold such jobs. The majority are engaged in operating machines, and some even become technical backbones. Statistics show: among the 757 peasant workers in nine important factories, such as the Zhenfeng Reeling Mill, the Wujiang Winery, the Dongfeng Chemical Plant, the Wujiang Rubber Factory and the Zhenze Silk Mill, there are only 65 peasant workers not working in workshops, including cooks, gardeners and 38 odd jobbers, accounting for 8.6 per cent of the total. The remaining 91.4 per cent are machine operators. Among the 263 peasant workers in the Zhenfeng Reeling Mill, there are 233 reelers and 11 rewinders. According to regulations before the "cultural revolution", a qualified reeler is a grade-5 worker and a qualified rewinder, a grade-4 one, ranking only below technical workers, such as turners, fitters, planers and maintenance workers. Some of the present peasant workers are still temporary ones, who are employed when production demand is great and are sent back to the countryside when the production declines.

III

We have given a detailed account of peasant workers and their present state, but how do we evaluate them?

First, we must examine the effect of peasant workers on the town's construction. A county town encounters a lot of problems in its development. Apart from the shortage mentioned previously, there are also financial problems and problems of taking over farmland for use. The proper employment of some peasant workers will help solve these problems. Let's look at a survey of 1,050 peasant workers of Zhenze: 599 of them are commuters — living in the countryside and working in town. They account for 57 per cent of the total. The rest either have their homes in town while still maintaining personal domiciles in the countryside (called "semi-resident households"), or else live in the dormitories of their enterprises and go home to the countryside during holidays. That means, over half of the peasant workers do not need to establish living quarters in town, and considerable savings can be made in building housing for the rest. This much reduces the expenses and land required in town construction and therefore speeds up its pace.

Secondly, we must look into the effect which peasant workers have on the countryside. To study this effect, we need to take a close look at the townships which these peasant workers come from, and also at their residential places. (See Table V.)

The distances between the peasant workers' home in the countryside and their working places are manifested in Table VI. (These statistics are based on a group of 427 people.)

The Tables V and VI indicate that Zhenze Town's peasant workers come from the nearby rural areas, and that most of them come from the areas nearest to Zhenze Township. The township has a total of 18,791 labourers, with 807 of them employed in town, or 4.3 per cent of the township's total labour force. Let's say, a peasant worker's average annual income (wage plus bonus) is 500 yuan, then every year they bring back 400,000 yuan to the countryside. These two figures clearly illustrate the role which peasant workers play in absorbing the surplus rural labour force, increasing peasant income and accumulating funds for rural construction.

In most cases, the surplus rural labour force is seasonal, but peasant workers are not subject to seasons. They work not far from home and over half of them commute every day, so they can help with heavy work at home, and, during the busy season in farming they can take part in agricultural production in their spare time. From the investigation in Waiyi Brigade, Zhenze Township, which is 4 km. from town, we know that during the busy season, the peasant workers employed in town can devote two and a half hours to farm work in addition to

Table **V**

COMPOSITION OF ORIGINAL LOCALITIES OF ZHENZE'S PEASANT WORKERS

Source	Number of people	Distance (km.)	As % of the total
In and near town	1,024		77.2
Town's vegetable grow-ing brigades	90	in town	
Zhenze Township	807	near town	
Badu Township	127	near town	
Within 12 kilometres (including in and near-town)	1,305		97
Qingyun Township	65	6.5	
Tongluo Township	23	8.5	
Miaogang Township	111	9	
Nanma Township	19	9.5	
Meiyan Township	26	11	
Qidu Township	10	12	
Taoyuan Township	7	12	
Other townships in the county	20		
Other counties	19		
Unknown	7		

Note: Tongluo and Nanma townships are located near county towns. Because there are flourishing market town in the townships, the number of peasant workers who leave them to work in county towns is comparatively small. The number of peasant workers from Miaogang Township far surpasses that from other townships the same distance away because it has a contract with the town.

working eight hours in the enterprises, a total of ten and a half hours a day, which is the usual practice in our rural areas. During the busiest farming season peasant workers work even longer. We personally witnessed some of them carrying a load of grain to a feed-processing mill on their way to work in the

Table VI

A SAMPLE SURVEY OF PEASANT WORKERS' COMMUTING DISTANCES TO WORK

Distance (km.)	Number of people	Distance (km.)	Number of people
0.5	158	3.5	14
1	44	4	5
1.5	88	4.5	3
2	28	5	9
2.5	22	5.5	—
3	45	6	11

morning and bringing the ground feed back home when they got off duty in the evening. During the busiest season, they go to work in the morning after an hour's toil in the fields, and after work they often directly head for the fields on their bikes. They join their family members in the farm work and then go home together with them for supper.

This is good both for agricultural and sideline production and strengthens family solidarity. Dong Qinhua, a girl in Wai-yi Brigade, was adopted by her uncle to look after him. She works in a commune-run factory near town. If she worked in a place too far away to commute from every day, her uncle would be left unattended, thus posing a social problem.

According to the commune's stipulations, peasant workers are not assigned "responsibility land" but rather "land for growing their own rations". The peasant workers living in town leave their land to their relatives or other agriculturally-engaged households after consulting with them, and work out an agreement as to how the grain ration is to be provided for. This contributes to the relative concentration of separated farmland. Peasant workers, bringing back from town skills, knowledge and information almost every day, have been exerting a far-reaching influence on the rural areas by raising them from their present state of technological and cultural backwardness.

Thirdly, let's examine, in the context of China's macro-economic performance, the significance of peasant workers, their form of work as well as their way of life, to China's construction. In the course of "the four modernizations" county towns and small cities of various kinds are bound to develop significantly. An unavoidable problem arising from this development is the subjection of city development to restrictions imposed by the level of grain production. We should by no means wait till we have sufficient grain before we start building up towns. On the contrary, we should make great efforts to build the small towns and take advantage of their position as links between the city and the countryside, intensifying the tie between the two areas, improving services before and after agricultural production, raising the level of socialization of agricultural production, thus speeding up the development of agriculture, including grain production. In this process, in view of the fact that our present macro-economic situation does not permit a big increase in town residents who consume marketable grain, it is feasible to employ labourers in county towns and rural towns who grow their own grain. Later, when grain becomes abundant and other economic conditions permit, we can, at any time, convert the non-agricultural labourers who grow their own grain into those who consume marketable grain, to meet the needs of production and social development. By so doing, we can keep the initiative in our own hands.

Fourthly, peasant workers merits our study both in their form of work and way of life. In building socialism that has Chinese characteristics, our socialist system ensures that our peasants will never repeat the experience of those farmers who during the early stage of capitalism flooded into the cities after going bankrupt. Rather, our peasants will switch gradually from being integrated with state-owned agricultural means of production (mainly land) to being integrated with the state-owned industrial means of production. This "gradual shift" is a process by which the peasants are transformed into workers, which is shown in the work and life of peasant workers.

The city-countryside relationship in our country is approaching a state of integration, not of opposition. The merger of the two, as Engels pointed out, should be our goal. The starting point for this process of merger can be the towns and small cities, as they are nearest to the countryside. The fact that peasant workers are engaged mainly in industry while still living in the countryside and not totally separated from agriculture, is good for these industrial workers' physical and mental health. At the same time, it causes the countryside to be influenced by cities and also speeds up the tempo of urban construction. This might very well be a form of socialist labour which conforms with the actual situation of our country. Even after the limitations on grain production mentioned earlier are done away with, the maintenance of the peasant workers' form of work and way of life will be beneficial to the establishment of a new type of city-countryside relationship in our country.

September 1983

THE RISING OF RURAL INDUSTRY AND PROSPERITY OF TOWNS

— A Survey of the Town of Tangqiao in Shazhou County

Huang Bingfu, Xu Weirong and Wu Daqian

Since the Third Plenary Session of the Eleventh Central Committee of the Chinese Communist Party held in December 1978, the town of Tangqiao in the Tangqiao Township of Shazhou County has prospered quickly along with the growth of rural industry. This ancient town, which has experienced ups and downs in the past, is now playing an increasingly important role in China's modernization programme and helping change the face of the whole township.

I. The Historical Development of Tangqiao Shows That the Scale and Speed of the Construction of Towns Are Determined by That of the Growth of the Social Forces of Production

According to the *Annals of Tangqiao*, the town came into being during the latter Yuan Dynasty (1271-1368). Located between grain and cotton producing areas and easily accessible by water and land, the town was frequented by nearby grain and cotton growers who, by using their hands, shoulder poles or boats, carried their farm and sideline produce there for exchange. The place thus became a rural market town. During the last years of the Qing Dynasty (1644-1911), the town, well-known for its fine-quality handwoven cloth, was "crowded by merchants, and became prominent due to its large daily volume of business transaction", thus developing into a trading centre for the nearby rural areas. At that time, the residents of the town numbered 500-600. Later, the town experienced numerous vicissitudes. In the early post-1949 period, the town had more than 100 shops of various kinds, with more than 1,000 residents. After the founding of the People's Republic, Tangqiao thrived once again. However, the town's economic growth and construction work later slowed down due to the disruption caused by erroneous "Left" ideology and of other mistakes in our work. Especially during the period when undue emphasis was put on growing grain, a large number of the town's residents were sent to settle down in the countryside and the existing shops also closed during the busy seasons in farming so as to concentrate labour on farming. As a result, the economy of the town dwindled.

Beginning in the mid-1970s, the rise of rural industries run by the people's commune and production brigades brought vitality back to the town. Since the Third Plenary Session of the Party's Eleventh Central Committee, the Party's various rural economic policies have been implemented in Tangqiao and its rural industries have grown rapidly, resulting in great change in the town.

Tangqiao is now composed of two streets, an old one in the south and a new one in the north, reflecting the town's past and present respectively and showing that its construction has entered a new period of development.

The old street in the south, 600 metres long from east to west and less than two metres wide, is lined with clusters of low-roofed dwelling houses. Before the creation of the new street, the old street was crowded with tea-houses, restaurants, groceries, stores and workshops dealing with metals, bamboo and wooden articles, sauce and pickles. A 100-metre-long section in the middle of the street bears the vestiges of the "Great

Leap Forward": many old buildings were dismantled and street was widened for the purpose of reshaping the town. But, because of its weak material foundation, few new buildings were added and the housing shortage was aggravated. In a word, Tangqiao, like many other rural towns in China, looked old and shabby at that time. Nevertheless, considerable progress had been made since 1949: Roads and bridges had been repaired, garbage dealt with properly and epidemic diseases controlled. There has also been development in the town's handicraft and processing industries, including iron and other metals, wood, bamboo, grain, cotton, edible oil and wine; and in commerce, in the form of establishing supply and marketing cooperative. Accordingly, communications, transportation, and cultural, educational and public health undertakings have grown gradually. In the period before Third Plenary Session of the Party's Eleventh Central Committee of 1978, the Tangqiao People's Commune had a single-product agricultural economy, and in the economy of the town of Tangqiao, the political, economic and cultural centre of the whole commune, commerce, service trades and a small number of handicraft industries still occupied the dominant position. Restrained by its underdeveloped economy, the town could only carry out some repairs and minor construction projects.

The new 1,300-metre-long street in the north, which was constructed after the Third Plenary Session of the Party's Eleventh Central Committee, presents a sharp contrast with the old one. Its eastern section is an industrial area composed of commune- or brigade-run enterprises, including a factory producing computer chips, a bakelite electrical equipment plant and a plastics factory; its western section contains a grain supply centre and a cement factory; and its central section is a busy shopping centre with an asphalt road, 12 metres in width and 400 metres in length. The street is lined with Chinese parasol trees and row upon row of newly-built two-to-four-storeyed buildings. They include government offices, sales departments of industrial corporations, a department store, grocery stores, hotels, a cultural centre, a bookstore, a hospital and a post and telecommunications office. Obviously, the street has become the political, economic and cultural centre of the whole township. With the creation of this new street, the floor space of the town's buildings has expanded from an original 30,000 square metres to 130,000 square metres, and the size of the town has also increased by 400 per cent.

It is the growth of rural industries that has brought vitality to the town of Tangqiao.

Apart from the money spent in building workshops in the commune- or brigade-run factories, direct investment in the town's construction during the past four to five years totalled more than 1.6 million yuan, and has been used for such projects as creating the new street, digging a river, building 17 bridges, running the cultural centre, supporting school and hospital construction, and adding sanitary facilities and other public utilities. This sum was derived entirely from the after-tax profits of rural industrial enterprises. In addition, the cement factory (with an annual output of 15,000 tons), the lime factory (with an annual output of 18,000 tons) and the brick and tile factory (with an annual output of 30 million pieces) have provided principal building materials for the construction of the town. Obviously, it would have been impossible for Tangqiao to carry out the above-mentioned construction projects if it had relied solely on accumulation from agriculture without the material foundation provided by rural industries.

The historical changes which have taken place in Tangqiao show that the growth of towns and small cities are based on the development of social productive forces. In the 30 years between 1949 and 1978, Tangqiao's agricultural, sideline production and industrial output value totalled only 150 million yuan. However, in the short space of the five years between 1979 and 1983, the figure rose to more than 320 million yuan. This indicates that carrying out large-scale town construction has only been possible in the period after the Third Plenary Session, not before.

II. Rural Industries Are Bringing About Profound Changes in Tangqiao's Characteristics, Function, Population Composition, Residents' Living Standards and Way of Life

The most outstanding characteristic of Tangqiao's prosperity is that the growth of its rural industries has promoted construction in the town, while the relatively rapid and sound development of the Tangqiao Township's rural industries is the result of its special conditions.

Just like many river and lake regions south of the Changjiang River, the township has a big population and scanty land. Still worse, the total combined area of its water surface is quite small. It has an average of only 0.053 hectare cultivated land per capita and 0.033 hectare of water surface, thus resulting in a surplus of labour in the rural areas. In this township, which was once well-known in the province and the country for its high yield of wheat, annual per capita income averaged only about 100 yuan before 1978. Although the township has a small variety of natural agricultural resources, it has a lot of favourable conditions for expanding its rural industries. Close to main lines of communication and near a ferry stop along the Changjiang River, Tangqiao is easily accessible by land and water. Its population contains a large number of dexterous artisans and maintains close links with nearby big and medium-sized cities including Shanghai, Suzhou, Wuxi and Changzhou. Therefore, after the town's inhabitants came to better understand its advantages and characteristics and decided upon direction of its development, they established commune- and brigade-run industries in response to the requirement of the times. The Tangqiao Township's rural industries first emerged in the mid-1970s, in the form of one or two multi-purpose factories which relied mainly on manual operations. However, since 1978 its industries have rapidly expanded, now comprising 96 factories, of which 24 are run by the commune and 72 are brigade-operated. With light textile industries comprising the majority, they include building materials, electronics, machinery and chemical factories. In 1983, the township's industrial output value reached more than 92 million yuan representing 90 per cent of its combined agricultural, sideline production and industrial output value. Its industries netted a profit of more than 9.6 million yuan and delivered more than 6.7 million yuan to the state in taxes, accounting for about 90 per cent of the whole township's tax deliveries.

The rise of rural industry has resulted in the most profound changes of the town of Tangqiao. Apart from the construction of its newly built street, houses, factories, stores, cultural establishments and public utilities, other more extensive and profound changes have also taken place.

First, the town's economic pattern has changed from one centred on commerce, service trade and handicraft industry to one centred on industry in which industry and commerce have both prospered. Tangqiao has also changed from a rural type town to one of industrial type. Formerly, Tangqiao was a rural town which had evolved along with the growth of agricultural production and rural handicraft industry, and with the increased exchanges of farm and sideline produce and the growth of commercial activities. During the long course of development, the town confined itself in commerce, service trade and handicraft industry. The town's annual commercial turnover of several million yuan was the main expression of its economic activity and its economic exchange with the rural areas.

Since the establishment of rural industry in the town, it has become a relatively strong economic entity within the space of several years. Today, apart from a dozen brigade-run factories, 21 of the 24 commune-run factories have been built in the town. In the past, peasants went to the town mainly to sell their farm and sideline produce and to buy the means of production and daily necessities or for recreation and entertainment. Now, most of the people who go to the town are workers in the commune- or brigade-run factories. As a result, great changes have also taken place in the customers and services of many of the town's departments, including banking, supply and marketing, commercial, post and telecommunications, transport, financial and taxation departments, which have all played a role in promoting the growth of rural industry. There, the former tranquility and monotony which typifying a rural town have been superseded by the scenes of vitality and activity which characterize a newly emerging industrial town.

Second, Tangqiao has broken through the restrictions imposed by its original administrative set-up and economic division, and expanded the scope and contents of its activities, as well as its function and role in the interflow between the town and rural areas. In the past, Tangqiao, like many other rural towns, played the role of a "link" between urban and rural areas by exchanging, through its own channel, urban industrial products for rural farm and sideline produce, including grain, cotton, oils and pigs. Therefore, it had connections with only a few nearby cities, the nearest being Changshu, and Shanghai the farthest, with Suzhou and Wuxi in-between. But today the situation has changed. Goods shipped from cities to the town include not only industrial products but also a larger quantity of raw materials and fuel needed by rural industries. On the other hand, goods shipped from the town to the cities comprise not only farm and sideline products but also a large quantity of industrial products, mainly textile and light industrial products.

To meet their developmental needs, the commune- or brigade-run enterprises have to establish links with more cities by breaking through the bonds of their original administrative and economic divisions. Today, they have set up sales departments in such big and medium-sized cities as Daqing, Tangshan and Urumqi.

The Xidan Department Store in Beijing has also set up a special counter commissioned to sell their products. The bakelite electrical equipment plant alone has established regular business links with 36 second-grade wholesale stations and more than 40 lamp shops and factories throughout the country. Because of their reasonable prices and good quality its products have gained popularity among the consumers. On the basis of contracts with the town, Shanghai sells 300,000 pieces of knit goods, 100,000 door locks and other industrial products on its behalf annually. Here, we can see that great changes have taken place in the scope of city-country links and in the contents of their commodity exchanges.

The second change is of more far-reaching significance. With the rise and expansion of rural industries, interflows between cities and countryside have progressed from the exchange of manufactured products to further include scientific and technological links, with cities providing modern science and technollogy for rural areas. Of the Tangqiao Township's 24 commune-run factories, 11 have established various kinds of links of technical co-operation with universities, colleges, scientific research institutes and large factories and mines in big and medium-sized cities. The town's computer chip factory, for example, has invited as its technical advisors 18 professors, associate professors, research fellows and engineers from 14 organizations, including Qinghua University, the East China Teachers University, Nanjing University, a research institute under the Science and Technology Commission for National Defence, and the institutes of computers, mathematics, electrical engineering and physics under the Chinese Academy of Sciences. These advisors, mostly of whom are computer specialists, provide guidance in the fields of technology, business, information and other areas, and have trained a group of local experts through the means of factory-organized training courses. This spreading of technology to the rural areas has yielded good results. The semi-conductor memory designed and manufactured by the factory itself has passed inspection and been praised by the Information Group of the China Computer Society. While visiting the factory, we saw students from the Changzhou Radio School doing their practice work there. We were told that several vocational schools had sent students to this factory for training and practice work.

The chemical fibre textile mill has taken the same road. Its management invited 48 retired cadres, technicians and skilled workers from the Wuxi No. 2 State-Run Cotton Mill to serve there for two years to pass on their knowledge and help train workers. Later, the textile mill invited specialists and professors from universities and colleges in Shanghai and Wuxi to give lectures at the workers' spare-time school in the mill. All these measures have achieved quick results. Now, the mill's chemical fibre products have reached the same level as similar Suzhou products, and its pure polyvinyl alcohol fibre yarn has been included in the state production plan.

From Tangqiao's practice of establishing technical co-operation between urban and rural areas, with rural industries taking the lead, we can see that technical exchange between the cities and countryside has very bright prospects. In such co-operation and exchange, the big and medium-sized cities should use their scientific and technological advantages to help provide the tens of millions of rural towns with modern industry, transport, commerce, service trade, education, science, culture and public health facilities. Only in this way can the towns throughout the country become bases for transforming the vast rural areas.

The third change is that Tangqiao has absorbed a sizable amount of surplus labour from the local rural areas, thus accelerating the historical course of the transformation of the agricultural population into an industrial population. In this way the town has absorbed the flow of workers which would otherwise have gone to big and medium-sized cities. In the early post-1949 days, Tangqiao had a population of 1,000. Later, the population grew yearly, reaching its peak in the late 1950s, when it numbered 2,400. Then, subsequently it decreased year after year until the early 1970s, when it began to rise again, reaching the level of the early post-1949 period. This peculiar curve in population change resulted from the slow growth or gradual shrinking of the commodity economy of towns and small cities during this period. Over the course of many years, educated urban young people were sent to either settle down in countryside or else work in other localities. Most of those remaining in towns were old workers from the commercial and service trade departments and some family dependents. This decrease in quantity and quality of population had a negative effect on the economy of towns, making it shrink even further.

The rise of rural industries has fundamentally changed this

situation. Today, the workers in Tangqiao's rural enterprises total 8,700, accounting for 60 per cent of the township's total labour force. Of the workers, 4,400 have jobs in the commune- or brigade-run factories in the town. Their homes are in the rural areas but they work in the town. This is in essence a transformation from agriculture in narrow sense to agriculture in broad sense, from an agricultural population to a non-agricultural population, and from a rural population to an urban population. The course of the transformation of the towns is also a process by which they have been increasingly flourishing. It should also be mentioned that while absorbing a large amount of surplus rural labour, the rural industries have also absorbed many educated urban young people and residents. At present, 420 of its residents, or one-fourth of Tangqiao's population, have worked in commune-run factories in the town. This has prevented outflow of population from towns, thus reducing the pressure of population growth on county seats and towns directly under county administration.

Today, China has an imbalanced distribution of population. On the one hand, population of big and medium-sized cities is growing continuously and the size of the labour force in the rural areas is becoming excessive; on the other hand, the population of the rural towns has increased slowly for a long time. How can we change this situation? How can we make living arrangements for the additional 200 million people by which the population of China is expected to increase by the end of this century? We are faced with a pressing task — to effect a rational flow of population.

In the past, we resorted to administrative measures to make rural labour force stay in the countryside and have some urban residents settle down in rural areas. Practice shows that this method cannot solve the problem. On the contrary, it has only increased the imbalance of population distribution. The example of Tangqiao has taught us that a positive method of effecting rational and balanced population flow is to develop the economy of towns and small cities, absorb surplus rural labour locally, and make the residents of towns remain there. At the same time, it is necessary to encourage big and medium-sized cities to run branch factories, shops and schools in towns and small cities, so as to attract and transfer part of the population of big and medium-sized cities to towns.

The fourth change is that the rise of rural industries and the increasing prosperity of the economy of towns have brought great changes to people's living standards and habits of life. Tangqiao is no longer a township with high agricultural output but low per capita income. In 1983, per capita income distributed by the collectives averaged 344 yuan. This figure was more than four times that of 1973 and represents an increase of 150 per cent over that of 1978. Income derived from household sidelines has also doubled, and is still increasing. Peasants can now earn a considerable income by doing some piecework assigned by rural enterprises. The annual income from sewing nylon shirts alone came to more than 1.4 million yuan, an average of 60 yuan per person. Since the piece rate wage system and the floating wage system were implemented, each worker in the rural enterprises has earned an average annual income of more than 700 yuan, a sum almost equal to the annual income of a worker of an enterprise in a medium-sized city. With the increasing economic prosperity of towns, more than 130 self-employed households have arisen in the township, the monthly income of each household reaching 100 to 200 yuan. In recent years, most of the local peasants have moved into new dwellings, more than 600 households now living in new buildings of two or more storeys. People's demand for manufactured goods of daily use has also gradually changed, with the demand for high-grade articles increasing.

Now, every family has one or more electric fans and there is one television set for every 10 households. Garments made of handwoven chequered cloth have been superseded by thin, light dresses made of chemical fibre fabrics. Many women in rural areas have become unwilling to spend time making shoes, now preferring to buy cloth shoes, plastic sandals and various kinds of leather shoes. The people's demands for a richer cultural life have also increased. Their interest in films shown in the open air by mobile projection teams has greatly diminished, while the town's 1,000-seat theatre and two story-listening halls always play to full houses, except during the busy seasons in farming. In the cultural station, hundreds of people can be seen reading books every day, while others take part in sports and other recreation activities. This is all evidence that the gap is narrowing between the living standards of the peasants in the Tangqiao Township and that of the residents in big and medium-sized cities.

In a word, the growth of rural industry has helped the town of Tangqiao to create a new situation in its socialist construction. It is now undergoing a process of shifting from quantitative change to qualitative change. From the case of Tangqiao, we can see that the distinctions between town and country are being reduced remarkably by the transformation of rural-type towns into ones of industrial type, a transformation resulting from the growth of their commodity economy. As the big agricultural population is gradually transformed into a non-agricultural population the distinction between industry and agriculture is being reduced. The introduction of the advanced science and technology of the big and medium-sized cities to the countryside, and the training of local technicians by well-educated experts and specialists has opened a new way to gradually reducing the distinction between mental and physical labour. We think that therein lies the strategic significance of the directives given by central authorities on energetically developing towns and small cities.

III. Some Problems in the Process of Development of Tangqiao

Today, Tangqiao is advancing on the road of modernization, but it has also encountered some problems which need study and solution. We believe that these problems are by no means unique to Tangqiao, but that other towns and small cities of the same type will probably encounter or have encountered them as well.

(1) The question concerning agricultural growth. The expansion of rural industry has provided a great deal of funds, materials and technical equipment for agriculture, increased peasants' income by a big margin, and contributed a lot to the all-round construction and public welfare undertakings of the rural areas. Rural industrial expansion and agricultural growth are complementary. Under the present circumstances in which the price of grain deviates from its value, rural areas near Suzhou have subsidized agriculture with industry, thus promoting steady agricultural growth. But, it is also possible for us to go to the other side and affect agricultural production if we fail to use the economic lever of the profits of rural enterprises properly in carrying out infrastructural adjustment of the collective economy, and to deal appropriately with the differences between the income of people engaged in agriculture, sideline production and industry, differences resulting from the price scissors between industrial and agricultural products.

The Tangqiao Township has paid attention to this problem. Formerly, a considerable number of peasants were reluctant to engage in agriculture. Of the township's 6,400 peasant households, 2,000 wanted to contract for less land or even give up agriculture, and only 77 hoped to contract for more land. Most of those who gave up agriculture wanted to find jobs in factories. Since some peasants lost their enthusiasm for agriculture, the local tradition of intensive and meticulous farming passed into oblivion. In view of this situation, the township authorities took measures this year to increase the extent to which "industry subsidizes agriculture". As a result, each commune member engaged in farming now receives 180 yuan derived from rural industrial profits as against 140 yuan last year (1982), thus further reducing the differences between the income of those engaging in farming and those working in industry. In essence, this is an effort of the rural industries to share the state's burden of subsidizing grain prices, when the state lacks macroscopic adjustment measures. This is correct and necessary, and is also of significance to the construction of towns. Just as the single-crop agricultural economy does not bring prosperity to the towns, they will also not prosper if the development of rural industry fails to promote agricultural growth. All areas with relatively developed rural industries will probably encounter this problem, and they adopt appropriate measures to solve it.

(2) The question concerning non-staple food supply. With its increasing affluence and the rapid growth of its population, the demand for non-staple food in Tangqiao has more than trebled. The supply of various kinds of vegetables has especially fallen far short of demand. At present, most of the fish and fresh vegetables on the rural fairs are sold at very high prices, because they are shipped in from such relatively distant cities as Changshu, Suzhou and Shanghai, instead of from local areas. The market price survey we made in August 1983 showed that the prices of young soya beans, wild rice stems, bean curd, egg-plants, towel gourds, young green vegetables, and string beans were more than 20 per cent higher as compared with those in nearby big and medium-sized cities. Aquatic products, including fish and shrimps, were very rare and sold at prohibitive prices. The root cause of the problem is that the town lacks a vegetable production base which can keep up with its increasingly rapid growth. The 24 big canteens in the town also lack steady supply of vegetables. It seems that these two problems, namely, towns depending on big and medium-sized cities in vegetable supply and the living expenses of the residents in the former being higher than that in the latter, must be solved. Otherwise, towns will lose their appeal, and their residence will tend to move out. Moreover, residents in big and medium-sized cities will balk at moving into towns and the population transfer will not be realized as we wish.

In order to solve this problem, Tangqiao has begun to establish a rather stable vegetable production base. It has made arrangements with each vegetable grower, and major consumers in the town have direct contacts with households specializing in vegetable production and have signed contracts with them. Just as industry was earlier made to subsidize grain production, measures of "making industry subsidize vegetable production by using profits from rural industry" have also been adopted, thus increasing the income of vegetable growers and rousing their enthusiasm. In addition, under the slogan of "turning the factories into orchards, flower gardens and vegetable gardens", some factories in the town have made use of their odd pieces of land to grow vegetables and plant trees, thereby solving their problem of vegetable supply through self-reliance. This is a good solution, but, unfortunately, only seven factories in the town have the conditions to do this, the others having little or no spare land.

(3) The question of economizing on land. Saving every inch of land is China's basic national policy. It is all the more essential to do so in the rural areas south of the Changjiang River where "land is more precious than gold". However, the development of rural industry and the construction of towns will inevitably use more land. Since 1978, the construction of new factories, roads and rivers in the Tangqiao Township has occupied 30 hectares of land, or about 2 per cent of the township's total cultivated land. Of these 30 hectares, 16.7 were used in expanding the town. Although the heyday of occupying cultivated land has passed, this problem still must be taken seriously. During the course of its development and construction, Tangqiao, like many other towns, has encountered the problem of lacking the financial resources to dismantle its old dwelling houses and replace them with new ones. Therefore, the town has adopted the method of building a new street while retaining the old one, thus occupying some additional land. The township Party committee has drawn up an overall plan for town construction according to which it is preparing to renovate the old street. Under this plan, bungalows will be replaced in stages and in groups by multi-storeyed buildings. The land thus saved will be used for other construction, under the condition that the residents' housing conditions are improving gradually.

(4) The problem concerning leadership of the management of towns. The work of leadership at township level has always focused on rural areas, and this practice should continue in the future. But for a newly emerging industrial town like Tang-

qiao, improving its leadership has become a very pressing task. Today, one-third of the total population and two-thirds of the Communist Party branches of the township are concentrated in the town of Tangqiao. Country fair trade has thrived along with the town's economic growth. According to a survey made between 3:00 a.m. and 7:00 a.m. on August 13, 1983, people entering the town numbered 8,243, 1,051 of them on bicycle. At the farm produce fair along a 200-metre-long street lined with 503 stalls, the volume of transaction within the four hours amounted to more than 14,000 yuan. Under such circumstances, the tasks of improving ideological and political work, economic management, social order and market control have become more arduous. Who will take charge of this work and how to carry it out? These are also important questions, demanding prompt solution. At discussions we organized, leading officials of the Tangqiao Township expressed a consensus of opinion that the former administration exercised solely by the powerless neighbourhood committee was in no way suitable to the town's present scope. They maintained that a general town Party branch or a town administration committee should be established as early as possible and that men of action and vision should be chosen to take the charge of it and invested with power. Under the direct leadership of the Party committee and government, those who are in charge of the town should do their utmost to develop the town's material and spiritual civilization, co-ordinate the work of the town's various departments, and ensure its sound development and continued prosperity.

September 17, 1983

ECONOMIC CONNECTIONS
BETWEEN A SMALL TOWN AND
ITS NEARBY CITIES

— A Case Study on Songling

Xu Dawei, Meng Chen and Zou Nonglian

A number of small towns are invariably found around a large or medium-sized city. How to make use of this favourable condition to speed up the small towns' economic growth is a question worthy of study. We have made a survey of the town of Songling to this end.

Located in the northeast of Wujiang County, the town of Songling is 16 kilometres from Suzhou to the north, 60 kilometres from Jiaxing to the south, 100 kilometres from Shanghai to the east, and 85 kilometres from Wuxi to the northwest. Because of its location, the town has had close ties with Suzhou over the ages. According to historical records, as early as 238-251 a fort was built on the present-day site of Songling to defend Suzhou, the then capital of the Kingdom of Wu. By 909, it had been made the seat of government of Wujiang County under Suzhou Prefecture. After the completion of the Grand Canal linking Beijing in the north to Hangzhou in the south, Songling gradually became a sort of satellite "tourist spot" of Suzhou and was much frequented by men of letters. Before the founding of new China in 1949, Songling's connections with Suzhou were mainly political, military and cultural in nature, and economic ties between them were virtually non-existent.

Today, as the seat of government of Wujiang County, Songling is not only the political and cultural centre of the county, but also the headquarters for directing countywide economic construction. Since the 1970s when factories were first sei up there, and in the course of its subsequent economic growth, the town has established and strengthened its economic links with neaiby cities, and with Suzhou in particular. This article will focus on this type of economic link and, at the same time, touch on ties in the fields of science, culture and education.

I. The Establishment of Economic Connections — a Historical Necessity

In retrospect, it is clear that the town's economic connections with Suzhou have grown out of its industrial development, and the increase in the number of the town's factories was directly related to its strengthening its economic links with the city. This trend can be seen in the table below:

Table I

ECONOMIC CONNECTIONS OF SONGLING'S FACTORIES
WITH SUZHOU AND OTHER CITIES

	1969	1974	1980	1982
Total number of factories	8	23	34	43
Number of city-linked factories	3	11	23	32
Number of factories linked up with Suzhou	2	10	22	31

The table shows that before 1969 the town's industrial base was very weak with only eight workshop-like factories which existed mainly to serve the needs of the local population, engaging in such tasks as making simple farm tools and wooden and bamboo articles, grain processing and printing. Only a few of them had any links with cities. Local industry began to gather speed after 1970, and its growth further accelerated after 1978. By 1982, the number of Songling's factories had risen to 43.

In addition to its original industries, the town now had its own machinery, chemical, textile, building, electronics, garment and shoe-making factories, and a number of other light industries. Most of the raw materials needed by these newly established factories came from other counties and provinces, and most of their products were sold out of the town. During this period, a growing number of these factories established ties with nearby cities. By 1982, 32 factories had linked up with cities, of which 31 forged ties with Suzhou. This shows that Songling's economic connections with nearby cities grew in direct proportion to the increase of the number of the town's factories.

These kinds of economic connections are both an outcome of the socialization of production and an essential condition for Songling's industrial growth. The phenomenon of the interdependence of economic connections and industrial growth has its own social origin.

It may be of interest to recount the process of how these factories were set up in the town. During the "cultural revolution", many factories in large and medium-sized cities stopped production or closed down, and large numbers of cadres and middle school graduates were sent down to the countryside. This gave the town a chance to expand its industry rapidly by using the raw materials, energy (mainly electric power) and markets relinquished by city factories, and the technical knowhow of those who were sent down to the town. However, because of their weak industrial foundation, most of the town's factories were of low quality. In 1978, fixed assets were estimated at 1,344 yuan per capita for the town's industrial population, its factories' equipment was out-of-date, and the technical and managerial competence of their workers and cadres was relatively low. These favourable conditions for Songling's industrial growth were eliminated after the "cultural revolution" ended in 1976, as production in city factories returned to normal. The town's industry thereupon entered a period of repeated trials, which were especially acute when there were energy shortages. In order to survive and expand, the town's factories found that the only way out was to establish ties with city factories and to seek help from them.

Another real challenge was employment. Almost all factories in Songling were established for the purpose of creating more job opportunities. Although Songling's 43 factories have taken on 6,270 workers in recent years, the town still has 204 jobless people. Not far from the town is a township called Hubin with a labour force of 24,000. The head of this township said that grain production and a diversified economy could not absorb so much manpower, and consequently he had a surplus labour force of 4,000 on his hands. In 1982, more than 2,000 peasants had to leave this township to do odd jobs. Thus, as the seat of the county government, absorbing large amounts of surplus labour from neighbouring rural areas has also become one of Songling's major tasks.

The strengthening of economic links between the town and its nearby cities not only caters to the needs of the town but also is essential to the cities. City factories are now facing problems such as scarcity of land and lack of space for work-shops, shortage of labour and the urgent necessity of upgrading their equipment. Under these circumstances, it is hard if not impossible for them to expand production. Take the Suzhou Synthetic Fibre Textile Factory. With a history of 87 years, this big factory has sufficient funds and a sizable contingent of qualified technicians, its fixed assets totalling 27.04 million yuan and its staff and workers numbering 7,132. About 70 per cent of its products are sold on the international market. In order to better suit the needs of the overseas market, the factory planned to renew the equipment of two of its workshops, but not having sufficient land and buildings, it had to suspend pro-duction for at least two years to carry out the plan. Take the Suzhou Electric Fan Factory as another example. The "Great Wall" brand fans produced by this factory sell well on the home market, but its output falls short of the market demand because the factory is short-handed and under-equipped. Factories in small towns, however, have some favourable conditions which those in the big cities lack. If city factories establish ties with factories in small towns, they can easily overcome their difficulties and each side can make better use of its respective strong points.

Economic links between cities and towns are based precisely on the objective needs of the two sides. With regard to the town of Songling, it has benefited exceptionally from forming economic connections with Suzhou.

Located just 16 km. away from Suzhou, Songling is easily accessible both by a highway and the Grand Canal which connects Beijing and Hangzhou. There is a bus service with 140 buses running daily between the town and the city, and a ferry service whose passenger ships make 14 trips per day. In 1982, passengers carried by highway transport totalled 740,000, and by waterway, 84,000. The town's location and convenient transportation conditions facilitate business trips and information transmission, while also lowering energy consumption and raising work efficiency.

Over the years, there has been a close connection between the populations of Songling and Suzhou. In the early 1950s, more than 100 households moved from the town to the city. Statistics made at the end of 1983 show that 228 people from 194 households lived in Songling but commuted to work in Suzhou. On the other hand, 101 people who lived in Suzhou worked in Songling, of these 78 in factories, 5 in commercial departments, and 18 in schools. During the ten years' domestic turmoil of the "cultural revolution", nearly 200 cadres and middle school graduates were sent down to the Hubin Township in the suburbs of Songling. Most of them have now returned to Suzhou, but have maintained close links with the township in one way or another. Furthermore, many people in Songling have relatives and friends in Suzhou. Such close links between people are a very important medium in forming economic ties between a town and a city.

In sum, it is only natural that the town of Songling has established close economic ties with Suzhou in the course of its development, because there are social needs and favourable conditions for establishing them.

II. Forms and Benefits of Economic Links

Roughly speaking, the establishment of economic links between Songling and Suzhou has gone through three stages:

The first stage took place before 1979. At this stage, it was
through the medium of Suzhou's commercial system that most
factories in Songling sold part of their products, purchased part
of their raw materials or established connections with factories
in Suzhou or other cities. For example, eight factories in Songling, including the Bakelite and Electrical Equipment Factory,
the Chemical Plant, the Garment Factory, the Silk Factory and
the Painted Can Making Factory, formed ties with related factories in Suzhou during this period through the city's Metals,
Chemicals, Transport and Electrical Appliances Corporations.
Some factories, like the Chemical Plant, turned out products
needed by the corporation based on the information it provided.
The rise of this practice owed much to Suzhou's commercial
system, and particularly to its quick access to market information. Songling thus benefited from its favourable location.

The second stage took place beween 1979 and March 1983.
With the implementation of the policy of invigorating the domestic economy, more channels for production, circulation and
information have been created between cities, towns and townships, and a large number of factories have begun to shift from
the mere production of goods and enter the field of combining
operations and management. During this period, not only did
more factories in Songling establish ties with those in Suzhou, but they further formed links with these factories directly,
rather than going through the city's commercial system. For
example, the Hubin Sofa Factory, the Silk Factory, the Garment
Factory, the Printing House and the Wire Rod Plant, which
were set up during this period, formed direct ties with Suzhou's
No. 3 and No. 8 Plastic Factories and Electric Fan Factory respectively, with the help of the cadres and middle school
graduates who had been sent down to Songling from Suzhou.

The third stage commenced after March 1983. During this
stage, the system of placing counties under the administration

of cities has been put into practice, and the administrative barriers between them have been dismantled. With the support of the Party and government leadership and the relevant departments of the city, the county and the town, the conducting of economic relations between Songling and Suzhou is now carried out by the relevant departments, as compared with before, when these matters were left up to the local people themselves. These ties have changed from being informal to formal, and most interfactory links have gradually stabilized. As a result, six more factories in Songling have formed new economic connections with those in Suzhou, and more advanced economic links have come into being, including the joint operation of Wujiang County's Hongguang Textile Factory, the Suzhou Synthetic Fibre Textile Factory, the Wujiang Chemical Plant and the Suzhou Dyestuff Plant, and a joint venture — the Zhenhua Woollen Mill — run by the state, the province and the county.

From the above-mentioned stages, we can see that although economic ties between Songling and Suzhou are determined mainly by their own needs, they are also affected by the state policies and administrative structure. When the policies and administrative structures were not compatible with economic development, the expansion of such economic ties was restricted. When the reverse is true, expansion is promoted, and new and more advanced ties come into being.

Today, the following five forms of economic connections exist between Songling and Suzhou:

1. Processing customers' semi-finished goods. Some factories in Suzhou have their semi-finished goods processed by factories in Songling, which only charge processing fees. Factories undertaking the task do not need to have a great deal of equipment or circulating funds so long as they have ample manpower. If factories are short of labour, they can assign jobs to households. For instance, part or all of the products of the Embroidery Factory, the Silk Factory, the Garment Factory and the Hubin Electric Meter Factory are turned out in this way.

By processing semi-finished goods, Songling's factories have formed links with city factories, some of which are relatively

stable, others, rather loose. The stability of the links is determined by whether a given factory can fulfil processing tasks
in terms of quality and quantity. Since the institution of the new
system of placing counties under the administration of cities,
factories in Songling have been receiving support from relevant
city departments, thereby improving the quality of their products. As a result, their links with city factories have become
closer and more stable. Some factories, like the Hubin Electric
Meter Factory, are able to process such rather sophisticated
semi-finished products as stators and rotors of electric fans.
However, this is generally a rather simple form of economic co-
operation.

2. Contract for sale of products or co-operation in production and marketing. The relevant departments and factories in
Suzhou provide part of raw materials; and Songling factories
turn out finished products, with Suzhou contracting for the
sale of the bulk or all of the products. For example, the Painted
Can Factory turns out cans, with the Suzhou Paint Factory
supplying part of iron sheets and other raw materials at slightly
lower than market prices. In 1981, the factory produced 190,000
cans, of which 160,000 were purchased by the Suzhou Paint
Factory. The Songling Wooden Article Factory is another example. After the town was placed under the administration of
the city, the Suzhou Furniture Corporation and the Suzhou
Clock Factory supplied some timber to the Songling factory
which turned out furniture and clock cases in accordance with
the two city enterprises' blueprints and technical requirements.
The two enterprises purchased or contracted to sell all of its
products. Today, nearly half of the town's factories operate in
this way. Its seven collectively-owned factories, which are
directly under county administration, have been saved from
bankruptcy as a result of this form of economic link. This form
offers the advantage of safety to the factory, as it merely
undertakes process of production, without having to worry
about obtaining raw materials or marketing its finished products. This is a more advanced form of economic co-operation
than the first one.

3. Technical service. Suzhou factories and relevant departments send people to Songling to help solve knotty technical problems in exchange for service fees. For example, the rice-puffing machines produced by the town's Grain Processing Machinery Factory sold well. But, when the machines were used in the northern part of China, their key elements would change shape. For a long period of time, the factory could not discover the reason for this. Later, it asked help from technicians of Suzhou Scientific and Technical Service Centre. The technicians found that the deformation of machine parts resulted mainly from their being unsuitable for use in the northern climate. Necessary measures were adopted and the problem was solved. One more example: The quality of the graphite washers manufactured by a Songling factory was unstable. The city's Scientific and Technical Service Centre dispatched four engineers to help the factory solve its technical problems, and as a result, the quality of this product stabilized. Although technical assistance is a supplementary form of links which came into being after factories had basically solved the problems of production, marketing and supply of raw materials, it is nevertheless still vital to successful production. Since quality is the life of products, products will find no market and production will be pointless if quality is not ensured. In order to ensure quality, the town's factories must receive technical assistance from big and medium-sized cities.

4. Serving as intermediate experimental bases of scientific research institutes. The Suzhou Chemical Industry Research Institute came up with a new product, sensitive nylon, but could not find a suitable factory in Suzhou to carry out intermediate experiments and small batch production. The Hubin Chemical Plant in Songling was considered an ideal factory for such a task, and so the institute and the plant established co-operation in scientific research and production. In distributing the income which was earned from the manufacture of the products the plant took the bulk and the institute the rest. This is a form of economic co-operation which is both stable and has great future prospects.

5. All-round co-operation. This is a kind of economic co-operation established on the principle of mutual benefit and carried out by meeting each other's needs and making use of each other's advantages so as to seek common progress. This kind of co-operation takes two forms: (1) Co-operation in production, supply and marketing. An example of this is the joint operations now conducted by the Wujiang Hongguang Textile Factory and the Suzhou Synthetic Fibre Textile Factory. The former uses part of its workshops and equipment to turn out the low- and middle-grade products of the latter, thus enabling the latter to concentrate on high-grade, precision and advanced products. In return, the latter helps the former raise economic results in technology, operation and management, as well as increase the variety and improve the quality of its products. The latter also helps the former to sell products through its marketing channels. (2) Specialized co-operation. The relationship between the Wujiang Chemical Plant and the Suzhou Dyestuff Plant is an example of this. They originally turned out products of the same kind, but used different trade marks and competed on the market. Since their raw materials were supplied according to the state plan, the Ministry of Chemical Industry and the Jiangsu provincial bureau in charge of the matter had the two factories enter into an arrangement of specialized co-operation in management, in accordance with China's current policy of readjustment. As a result, the two factories now manufacture and sell same kinds of products with same quality standard and the same trade mark. These two forms of co-operation represent an even higher level in terms of scope and thoroughness.

The following Table II lists the five forms of co-operation and the number of factories which are linked to counterparts in Suzhou by each of these forms respectively.

As a matter of fact, some factories engage in two or three different forms of co-operation with the city simultaneously. This is because different forms of co-operation evolved along with the different stages of the development of economic ties. While retaining original forms of co-operation, some factories

Table II

DIFFERENT KINDS OF CO-OPERATION BETWEEN SONGLING'S FACTORIES AND THOSE IN SUZHOU

Form of co-operation	Number of factories
Processing customers' semi-finished goods	6
Contract for sale of products or co-operation in production and marketing	14
Technical service	7
Serving as intermediate experimental bases for scientific research institutes	2
All-round co-operation	2

have gone on to establish new forms of ties with the city's other factories. There are also cases in which different workshops within a single factory have different forms of ties with various factories in the city. It is also because, in the course of forming economic links, factories in both the town and the city have come to see the great importance of technology in aiding the interests of both sides. As a result, big factories have tried their best to help small factories technologically, and the small ones have striven earnestly to learn from the big ones. Incomplete statistics show that during the period between 1980 and 1983, Suzhou dispatched 465 technicians to Songling to help the town factories solve their technical and managerial problems, and that Songling sent 1,550 workers to Suzhou factories for study and training. With the increase in technical competence and the growth of technical co-operation, economic links have become more stable and their forms have evolved.

The choice of forms of co-operation cannot be made haphazardly, but is rather restricted by a number of factors, including geographical location, relations between people, trade, products, funds, the needs of the city's factories, and the production capacity of the town's factories. Of these factors, the latter is the most important.

Following is a table showing average per capita fixed assets of factories which are engaged in different forms of economic co-operation with the city.

Table III

AVERAGE PER CAPITA FIXED ASSETS OF VARIOUS
SUZHOU FACTORIES

Form of links	Average per capita fixed assets (yuan)
Processing customers' semi-finished goods	898
Contract for sale of products or co-operation in production and marketing	3,342
Technical service	4,751
Serving as intermediate experimental bases for scientific research institutes	1,546
All-round co-operation	3,501

In the above-mentioned statistics, we have eliminated the overlapping caused by factories engaged in several forms of co-operation. The table shows the average per capita fixed assets of factories engaged in the first form of co-operation amount to only 898 yuan. This indicates that these factories are short of equipment and incapable of producing finished products from raw materials. Hence, they can only co-operate with another factory by relying on the manual dexterity of their workers to process its semi-finished products. The table also shows that the average per capita fixed assets of factories in the second, third and fifth categories are more than three times that of factories in the first category. Although the figure for factories in the fourth category is much lower, it is still nearly double that of the first category. Marx summed up this situation succinctly: "These social relations into which the producers enter with one another, the conditions under which they exchange their activities and participate in the whole act of production, will naturally vary according to the character of the means of production."* Social relations among people often play a great role in promoting the establishment of economic connections between Songling and Suzhou. Superficially, contingency seems to play role in forming the ties, but, in fact, the choice of forms which such ties take is governed by inevitability because the nature of economic co-operation is independent of people's subjective desire, and is determined mainly by the factories' production capacities. For instance, the Hubin Plastics Factory and the Shanghai Plastic Products Factory once co-operated in production and marketing, and the Hubin factory sent workers to Shanghai to receive training. Later, it was found that Shanghai factory's equipment was so advanced and technical requirements were so high that workers from the town could hardly master the technology within a short period of time, and that even if they did master it, it still could not be applied in their factory because of its lack of compatible equipment. Afterwards, the Hubin factory contacted Suzhou's No. 8 Plastics Factory. There was no big difference between the equipment of the two factories, and after receiving training the workers from the town could master its use and apply it to their own factory. Thus, the two factories formed close ties, with the Hubin factory processing the Suzhou factory's semi-finished products.

Although all-round co-operation has many advantages, it is not suitable for all factories. On the other hand, even a poorly-equipped factory can also achieve fairly good economic results, so long as it proceeds from its reality and engages in co-operative projects compatible with its production capacity. For example, although the Embroidery Factory, the Silk Factory and the Shoe-making Factory have simple and relatively backward equipment, the economic links of processing semi-finished products have brought women workers' dexterity into full play. In 1982, the six factories engaged in such co-operation produced

* Karl Marx, "Wage Labour and Capital," *Karl Marx and Frederick Engels Collected Works*, Progress Publishers, Moscow, 1977, Vol. 9, p. 211.

543 yuan of output value and 23 yuan of profit for every one hundred yuan of fixed assets they possessed. An outstanding example is the Shoe-making Factory, which netted a profit of 300,000 yuan in the year. Naturally, as a factory expands its size and improves its technical set-up, it will seek more advanced forms of economic co-operation. Take the Hongguang Textile Factory for instance. In 1975, the factory, with 420,800 yuan of fixed assets, co-operated with factories in Suzhou and Shanghai in processing, production and marketing. By 1982, the factory increased its fixed assets to 2,408,800 yuan, nearly six times that in 1975, and began to discuss all-round co-operation with the Suzhou Synthetic Fibre Textile Factory. This shows that there are bright prospects for Songling's factories in choosing and deciding on suitable forms of economic co-operation with larger factories so as to promote their own growth.

Various kinds of economic links between Songling and Suzhou have promoted the expansion of the town's industry and brought about significant economic results. In the 1950s and 1960s, Songling's industry grew very slowly. By 1970, its industrial output value had reached only 6,438,100 yuan and its profits merely 301,500 yuan. In this period, only two factories had ties with Suzhou. However, the town's industry achieved very rapid growth during the 13 years between 1970 and 1982, with output value increasing seven times, rising from 6,438,100 yuan to 45,222,000 yuan; and profits increasing nearly 11 times, rising from 301,500 yuan to 3,274,500 yuan. This period also saw a boom of economic co-operation with Suzhou, with 31 factories establishing ties with the city by 1982. This indicates that rapid development of economic links with Suzhou was the result of big industrial growth in Songling.

By analysing the development of some typical factories in a more detailed way, we can clearly see the role such links played.

Roughly speaking, Songling's factories can be divided into three groups:

1. Factories which were set up rather early, but have not made much progress because they have not established economic links with cities. The Songling Wooden Articles Factory, the oldest factory in the town, is a case in point. It started as an individually-owned handicraft workshop in the early years after the People's Republic was founded in 1949, and then operated as a wooden articles co-operative before it became a factory. Since it confines its business activities to the town and surrounding county, its production has shown little progress in the past 30 years. By 1982, its output value reached only 244,000 yuan, with profits of less than 10,000 yuan.

2. Factories which were set up early, developed slowly, and even encountered financial difficulty, but whose situation has taken a turn for the better and developed rapidly since establishing links with Suzhou. During the initial 12 years after it was set up in 1958, the Wujiang Petroleum Machinery Fittings Factory had a very small annual output value, never topping 230,000 yuan. In 1970, with the help of Suzhou Metals, Chemicals, Transport and Electrical Appliance Corporation, the factory adjusted its production by turning out box spanners instead of axle sleeves. In 1972, with the help of the No. 526 Factory in Suzhou, it also contacted units directly under the Ministry of Petroleum Industry and contracted to produce petroleum machinery fittings, thus ensuring its source of raw materials and market. As a result, the factory increased its output value from 230,000 yuan to 4,436,000 yuan in the eight years from 1970 to 1978. After the implementation of the policy of placing counties under city administration in 1983, the factory began receiving even more production orders.

3. Factories which established ties with big or medium-sized cities almost as soon as they came into being and which have made steady progress as a result, some of them developing very rapidly. Take the Hubin Sofa Factory for example. Established in 1980, it immediately entered into a co-operative arrangement with a copper factory in Shanghai to process its semi-finished products, and its output value came to 170,000 yuan in the same year. In 1981, it began producing sofas by co-operat-

ing with Suzhou's No. 3 and No. 8 Plastics Factories through the co-ordination of the city's Plastics Corporation. Its output value reached 330,000 yuan in 1981 and 760,000 yuan in 1982, and the profits it realized during these two years were 45,000 yuan and 53,000 yuan respectively. The Hubin Universal Joints Factory is yet another example. In 1974, it began to produce universal joints for motor vehicles, its raw materials coming from the Motor Vehicle Fittings Corporation and the Yuejin Factory in Suzhou. By 1979, its output value came to 830,000 yuan, and profits 250,000 yuan. After 1980, the factory's annual output value and profits went down because of the decrease of market demands for its products as a result of a price adjustment and petroleum shortage. In 1982, it had a deficit of 30,000 yuan. In 1983, the Yuejin Factory dispatched 15 engineers to the town's factory to help design new products and carry out technical transformation and training. As a result, the variety of universal joints produced by the factory rose from one to ten, and it netted a profit of 60,000 yuan in the same year. Its profits are expected to exceed 200,000 yuan in 1984.

What is noteworthy is that different forms of economic co-operation have brought about different economic results: the more advanced and comprehensive the co-operation, the better the economic results. Take the Hongguang Textile Factory for example. It originally co-operated with factories in Suzhou and Shanghai in production and marketing. On May 1, 1983, it entered an all-round co-operation agreement with the Suzhou Synthetic Fibre Textile Factory. Five months later, its output value reached 14,740,000 yuan, or a 41.3 per cent increase over the corresponding 1982 period. The profits earned for every 100 metres of fabric it manufactured rose to 4.79 yuan, as compared with 4.48 yuan before it entered the agreement, an increase of 6.92 per cent. The daily output value of each loom rose from 96.64 yuan to 176.96 yuan, an 83.11 per cent rise. Thus, all-round co-operation has brought about marked results. The facts show that Songling's establishment of various kinds of economic links with Suzhou has a bright future.

III. Scientific, Educational and Cultural Links
Which Serve Economic Construction

The upsurge of economic construction is invariably accompanied by an upsurge in cultural undertakings. Before 1970, although Songling had educational and cultural connections with Suzhou, few of them served economic construction. After 1970, with the strengthening of economic ties between the town and the city, their scientific, educational and cultural links began to grow rapidly. Today, all kinds of vocational schools in Songling have close links with Suzhou in one way or another, while the Public Health School and the Art School in the town are directly run by the city. The 12 associations which comprise the Songling Society for Research on Small Town Construction established in 1982, included the Associations of Enterprise Management, Science and Technology, and Adult Education, and Physical Culture and Sports Associations, Scientific and Technological Consultation Service Centre, Training Centre for Enterprises, Gardens and Parks Management Department as well as Suzhou University and the Suzhou Silk Engineering College. These types of scientific, educational and cultural links have become a motive force of Songling's economic growth and an important guarantee for promoting economic ties between the town and the city.

The restoration and expansion of the Songling Workers' Spare-Time School is a case in point.

In the second half of 1978, the Songling Workers' Spare-Time School was restored due largely to the fact that the town's industrial growth and increased economic links with Suzhou called for higher levels of technical competence on the part of its workers. While partly relying on short-term training courses run by Suzhou's factories, the town has also endeavoured to expand its spare-time education facilities.

One of the major features of the school is to improve teaching quality and train qualified personnel through firmly relying on Suzhou's technical and intellectual forces. Since its restoration, the school has always received the city's support in the three following aspects:

(1)   Dispatching teachers. The school invited 36 teachers, including three associate professors and 14 lecturers, from Suzhou University, Suzhou Silk Engineering College, and the city's Workers' University, Teachers' Advanced Study College and Electronics Research Institute. Teaching a total of 20 subjects at the town's school, these teachers stay there for periods varying from half a year to three years, most of them staying for one year. Hence, the school's teaching quality is ensured.

(2)   Providing laboratories. Experiments are essential to training students' practical ability. Students of the Songling Workers' Spare-Time School performed simple experiments at the town's middle school and factories, and more complicated ones at Suzhou's No. 15 Middle School, Silk Engineering College and Teachers' Advanced Study College and Suzhou University. During the summer vacation in 1981, 22 students attending the school's engineering telecourse went to Suzhou University (then called the Jiangsu Teachers College) and stayed in the laboratory building of the Physics Department for seven days. Under the guidance of that university's teachers, the students did 10 different electronic, atomic and optical experiments. Each student in the first class of the engineering course performed an average of 65 experiments within a period of three and a half years, exceeding the number stipulated by Jiangsu Provincial Television University. The spare-time school thus raised its teaching quality, and, as a result, students' average marks ranked first in the county during the last term, as compared with ranking last during the first term.

(3)   Guided graduation projects. Graduation projects are a key link in training students' ability to solve practical problems. In 1983, all graduation projects undertaken by the students attending the school's engineering telecourse were based on production problems existing in the town's factories. In order to ensure the success of the projects the school's teachers were aided by three associated professors, three lecturers and three engineers from Suzhou University and other units in guiding

the projects and presiding over their graduation oral examinations. With the support of the teachers from Suzhou, the students did a good job in their graduation projects, and seven of the projects were directly applied to production. For instance, the high-pressure dyeing machine designed and manufactured in the electrical equipment factory has benefited the factory a lot, and was commended by several departments in Jiangsu Province.

With full support of Suzhou's relevant departments, the town's spare-time school has started to offer specialities to meet a wider range of social needs, a departure from its beginning, when it only offered courses which catered to the pressing needs of production.

The evolution of the spare-time school can be divided into the following stages.

(1) Offering literacy classes. There were two classes. One was for workers studying primary school subjects, and the other, junior middle school subjects.

(2) Offering special engineering courses. At first, the school trained technicians by offering some courses at special or technical secondary school level, which covered electrical engineering, machinery, electronics, industrial accounting, commercial accounting, economic statistics and enterprise management. These courses were both badly needed and directly applicable in production. Later, the school concentrated on training technical personnel for scientific research by offering telecourses in engineering, its students being selected from among technicians or secondary school graduates who had failed to pass university or college entrance exams.

(3) Offering some special secondary school courses which cover a wider range of subjects, including calligraphy, fine arts, photography, childcare, cooking, garment making, literary and artistic creation, and music and dance. This broad variety of courses suits people of different inclinations while also serving production, both directly and indirectly. For instance, the calligraphy, fine arts and photography courses are applicable to factories' advertising; the childcare, cooking and garment mak-

ing courses are indispensable to daily life; while those in literary and artistic creation and music and dance help enrich the cultural life of the factory workers.

(4)   Offering special classes to meet a wide range of social needs. These classes include news reporting, rudiments of writing, Japanese language, English language, Esperanto, and tele-courses in the liberal arts. Although these courses do not serve production directly, they benefit the students a lot. Since most of the students return to their factories after graduation, they can use their knowledge to enrich factories' social activities or engage in further study for their factories' sake.

Today, the school has attracted a large number of the town's young workers. Some students are taking several courses simultaneously, others take one class at a time. Towards the end of 1983, the school expanded its programme, offering 38 classes as against two when it was restored in 1978. To date, it has enrolled a total of 9,477 students, and graduated 5,589. About 88 per cent of the town's young workers under 35 have received training there.

The school has played a remarkable role in aiding production. Most of the graduates from the school's college telecourses and special secondary courses have become key technicians in their factories, and 76 have joined various groups for tackling key technical problems. Since 1981, these graduates have completed 123 technically innovative projects, of which nine have brought their respective factories 2.4 million yuan in profit. One graduate has succeeded in developing an A.C. contactor for the Electrical Equipment Factory, which can be used in examining the quality of complete sets of electrical equipment cabinets. In two years, this new device has saved the factory 80,000 yuan, about one-third of its annual circulation fund. Another student has helped the Wujiang Switchgear Plant tackle a key technical problem related to a contactor pressure testing instrument for stepping switches on load voltage regulators — the plant's main product. Well received at a product assessment meeting held in Suzhou, the testing instrument was considered as good as a similar instrument imported from Japan.

From the example of the workers' spare-time school, one can see to what extent these scientific, educational and cultural links have promoted Songling's economic growth and helped strengthen economic ties between Songling and Suzhou.

December 1983

RESEARCH OF THE DISTRIBUTION OF THE VILLAGES AND TOWNS OF GAOCHUN COUNTY

Jin Qiming, Shen Guoming, Dong Xin and Lu Yuqi

Villages and towns are the places where people engage in production and commerce, and where they live, dwell and rest. Within the limits of a given region, villages and towns jointly constitute an organic whole. The overwhelming majority of villages and towns in China existed in a state of economic self-sufficiency or semi-self-sufficiency for a long period in history, which made them ill-adapted to present needs of developing rural commodity production and agricultural modernization. Along with the economic development in rural areas and increase of peasants' income, the people's demand for the development of villages and towns has increased. For this reason, establishing a system of rational distribution of villages and towns of various grades and types in accordance with different characteristics of various regions, is thus a very pressing task. By using the distribution of Gaochun County's villages and towns as examples, we try to make some initial approaches on the above-mentioned problems.

I. Analysis of the Present Conditions of the Villages and Towns

Gaochun County is situated along the southwest border of Jiangsu Province with an area of 763 sq. km. It is under the jurisdiction of the city of Nanjing and is bounded by counties

of Lishui and Liyang, as well as the counties Langxi, Xuan-
cheng, Dangtu of Anhui Province. Currently there are 1,006
natural villages and towns throughout the county, with a total
population of 391,600, and an average of 389 persons in every
village or town. However, the difference between individual
places remains quite large. A big town can contain several
thousand inhabitants, while a small one only a few hundreds.
There is an even greater disparity between villages in this regard. There are small villages with only a single household and
large ones with seven or eight thousand inhabitants. As for
the number of villages and towns in each township, some have
more than ten while some have over one hundred, a tenfold
difference. With respect to regional distribution of villages and
towns, there exists very notable difference between the diked
region in the western plains and the hilly land region in the east
of the county. The villages and towns in these two areas differ
greatly in population size, distribution density and in the relative proportion occupied by large, medium-sized and small villages respectively.

DIKED REGION TYPE In regions of this type, inhabited
areas are broad and scattered, laid out in belts, and have many
big or fairly big villages. Most villages and towns of this kind
are located alongside the dikes and ridges of the low-lying areas,
scattered but connected. The land in this region is low-lying
and so floods occur frequently. During the time when the forces
of production were still undeveloped, people lacked the ability to transform nature, and so they were compelled to draw
close to dikes and ridges located on the higher ground and live
in concentrated communities so as to pool their efforts to strug-
gle against floods. As a result, the interior of the diked regions
were left uninhabited. The combined influence of various
factors which condition the formation of inhabited areas have
given rise to the large size of the villages and towns of this
region. The whole region has 259,519 inhabitants, concentrated
in 493 natural villages and towns, with an average of 526 persons in each village or town, one-third larger than the county
average. Eighty per cent of the county's fairly large villages of

over 500 residents are distributed in this region, and villages
with over 1,000 people account for as much as 86 per cent of
the county's total of this group, whereas this region accounts
for only 28 per cent of the small villages with less than 100 inhabitants in the county. The county has quite a few considerably large villages and towns. For example, Xuecheng, where
the local government of Xuecheng Township is located, has
7,176 inhabitants, amounting to 25 per cent of the total population of the township. Neighbouring Changle Village is even
larger, with 8,597 residents, accounting for nearly one-third of
the total population in the whole township. There are five villages and towns with populations of over 1,000, accounting for
36 per cent of its total number of villages and towns, while the
total population of the five villages and towns make up more
than 85 per cent of the population of the whole township. For
villages and towns, when they are large in scales, the smaller
their density and the sparser their distribution. The densities
of the distribution of villages and towns in all the townships
in the diked region are generally less than 1.6 villages or towns
per square kilometre, Xuecheng Township being the lowest,
with only 0.4.

Establishing villages and towns on dikes and ridges in low-
lying areas has numerous advantages. On the one hand, it permits people to make full use of sloping fields, inferior lands,
and scattered plots of inutilized lands, without taking over
high-yielding fields. On the other hand, as the rural areas become economically prosperous and their external relations develop steadily, building villages on dikes and ridges is advantageous to communications and transportation as well as to carrying out commercial activities. In the meantime, the concentration of population on dikes and ridges in low-lying areas is also
advantageous to setting up various kinds of service facilities to
meet the material and cultural needs of the broad masses of the
people. This distribution also makes it able to prevent damages caused by the catastrophic floods which occur almost once
every century, and also conforms to the habits and customs
which the people have formed over a long period of time.

However, over-concentration of the population also affects production to a certain extent, one problem being that long distance between cultivated lands and villages increases the radius of cultivation and thus causes inconvenience.

HILLY LAND TYPE In regions of this type, inhabited areas assume the form of small and dense groups, and many are small and medium-sized villages.

Regions of this type account for 40 per cent of the land area of the whole county, forming a sharp contrast with the diked region. Natural villages and small towns mostly take the shape of blocks in their plans and are spread all over the region. There are 483 natural villages and small towns throughout the whole region, about the same number as that of the diked region, yet they contain a total of only 112,422 residents, an average of only 233 persons for each village or small town, less than half that of the diked region. As for density of villages and small towns, each township has an average of 1.6 villages and small towns per sq. km. Dingbu Township has the highest density, with 2.9 villages and towns per sq. km., almost twice the average density of the whole county. In this township there is an average of only 169 persons for each village or small town. There are as many as 51 small villages with less than 200 inhabitants, accounting for 70 per cent of the county's total of villages and small towns of this group, and making up 96 per cent of the total if those villages and hamlets of the 200-500 group are further included. This form of scattered distribution of villages and towns is closely related to the area's geography. Topographical conditions characterized by undulation and unevenness not only makes communications inconvenient but also brings about the scattering of the farmlands. Under the conditions in which the level of productive forces is not high and people are still reliant on nature, they have no alternative but to establish their residential areas near their farmlands. In the meantime, the low density of population in this region has resulted in a larger area of cultivated land per person and smaller residential quarters.

Scattered distribution of residential quarters is quite favourable to agricultural production. For instance, the small radius of farming is convenient for management and administration. Particularly under present conditions in which a lot of the processes of agricultural production are still mainly done manually, this kind of distribution may save time in going to and from farmlands, and therefore is advantageous to intensive farming. However, this sort of distribution is not only unfavourable to the peasants buying their means of livelihood without going afar, but is also unfavourable to their improving their level of scientific and cultural knowledge. Furthermore, it is impossible to set up various kinds of welfare facilities in small-scale villages and hamlets. Meanwhile this pattern of distribution occupies too much land, and is not appropriate under the present conditions, in which cultivated fields have kept decreasing. From the point of view of long-range development, scattered villages and small towns are also disadvantageous for carrying out farmland capital constructions and agricultural mechanization.

Villages and towns are two different types of rural residential areas. Towns are characterized by having fairly large populations, being rather big in scale, and being not only bases of relatively centralized industrial and sideline production, but also being collection and distribution centres as well. Accordingly, the vitality of a town is directly determined by the scope of the services. Studying the scope of services in towns provides an important basis for dividing them into grades.

There are currently 19 towns in Gaochun County, all of which, with the exception of the county seat Chunxi Town, do not have the organizational system of towns, but are merely the natural towns which are the seats of township governments.

However with regard to the economic activities of these towns, some are confined within the townships themselves, some extend to several other townships and some reach as far as other counties and provinces. There are numerous factors conditioning the scope of the economic activities of towns. First of all, they are determined by the given town's geographical location. Big towns are usually well-situated in places which are convenient for transportation and where there are fairly big markets which can draw peasants from a large area all around to carry out the exchange and trade of goods and commodities. Take Chunxi Town as example. Situated in the centre of diked region in the west, it is the seat of the people's government of Gaochun County and its scope of attraction extends across provincial boundaries, reaching an area within the boundaries of Anhui Province of nine townships with a population of 150,000. Secondly, their distance from county seats is also an important factor. For its two townships of Yongning and Dingbu, which are located along the eastern border of the county, there is a highway connection but the transportation cost of materials is high due to their long distance from the county seat. And this plus the fact that they are near Liyang County has subjected them entirely to the commercial influence of Liyang. Furthermore, the bigger a town is, the more complete will be its various service facilities, the larger will be its essential facilities, such as shops, and the wider will be the variety of commodities they have on sale.

Table I

THE VARIETY OF COMMODITIES AVAILABLE AT DIFFERENT TOWNS
(April 10, 1983)

	Daily consumer goods		Durable goods	
	Cigarettes	Toilet soap	Wrist watch	Clock
Chunxi Town (county seat)	24	14	27	19
Qiqiao (regional centre)	18	14	4	7
Cangxi (seat of township government)	20	6	—	14
Hongqi (administrative village)	7	3	—	—

From the above table one can see that in the big towns commodities supplied by shops are numerous in variety giving people a big room for choice. At the same time, large towns where trade is flourishing offer a good market for commodities, and so peasants would rather travel a long distance to these places to choose goods and take their farm and subsidiary products there to sell for better prices. It is precisely for this reason that the residents of Tanggou Town and several other towns in Anhui Province, neighbouring Xuecheng Town, would rather travel an extra 2.5 kilometres to Xuecheng for fairs rather than go to Tanggou Town which is smaller in size than Xuecheng. Besides this there are certain influential historical factors which should not be ignored. Take Dongba Town as an example, its scope of services covers most of Langxi County in Anhui Province. This is partially a consequence of the large size of Dongba, but it is also inseparable from the historical customs and practices of the area.

There are also regional differences in the distribution density of the towns. The whole county has 19 towns of which 12 are distributed in the diked region of the western plains, whereas there are only 7 towns in the hilly region in the east, which is more or less comparable in size to the western diked region. The existence of such regional differences is the result of a combination of factors, including the topographical conditions of these two regions, the distribution and size of their residential areas, the developmental level of their productive forces and their communication and transportation conditions.

II. System of Grades of Villages and Towns

Villages and towns are an organic whole. Every town functions as a centre for its surrounding villages. However, all the towns differ in their functions as centres. Towns are different from villages, which take agriculture, forestry, animal husbandry or aquatic production as their primary production activities. Although towns still retain certain elements of these primary activities, as for example, when part of their inhabitants engage in agriculture or divide their time between agriculture and industry, nevertheless their economic functions in industry, commerce, communications and transportation, along with their cultural and administrative functions, are already quite conspicuous, forming sharp contrast with villages and hamlets. The higher the grade of towns is, the bigger role as centres will be, the wider their scope of service will be and the more the service items it will include.

We can divide all the towns of Caochun County into four grades based on their total industrial output values, commercial turnover, volume of business in catering trade, their population scales, and sales volume of three kinds of durable goods (sewing machines, wrist watches and clocks) as well as that of three kinds of consumer goods (cotton clothes, cigarettes and wines).

Chunxi is the only grade I town. The four grade II towns include Yaxi, Qiqiao, Dongba, and Gucheng; the seven grade III towns include Cangxi, Xuecheng, Zhuanqiang, Hancun, Zhengjuesi, Gulong and Dingbu; and the seven grade IV towns include Hecheng, Caotang, Xiaba, Qingshan, Gangkou, Shishu and Gubai.

Chunxi Town, the only grade I town in the whole county, is the county's political, economic and cultural centre. Chunxi Town has a definite place in local history. In the fourth year of the reign of Hong Zhi in Ming Dynasty (1491), at the time when Gaochun County was formed by detaching seven townships and towns from Lishui County, Chunxi Town was made the county seat. By the eve of the founding of the People's Republic Chunxi already had a population of over 2,000 inhabitants. After 1949, the people's government of the county re-established its seat here again, its contacts with the county's other villages and small towns were strengthened, and priority was given to developing its various public service facilities. Chunxi Town has highways linking it with all the other towns of the county, and also has good water transport services. Situated close to Gucheng Lake, it can maintain economic contact with places within and outside the county through the

Guanxi and Xuhe rivers. These favourable conditions of communications and transportation have played an important role in speeding up Chunxi's economic development, and strengthening its role as the county centre.

The four grade II towns of Gaochun County are distributed in the central and eastern parts of the county, there are none in the diked region in the western part of the county. This situation is mainly due to existence of Chunxi Town, the county's largest centre in the west, which exerts an influence over the whole western region of the county, making it impossible for a grade II town to come into existence. The four grade II towns in the eastern area, Dongba, Qiqiao, Yaxi and Gucheng all have ready access to both water and land transportation. In addition, the eastern region is a bit far away from Chunxi Town and so they are not influenced by it as much as those in the western diked region. On top of this, each town has its own strong points, which is what made it possible for four such regional grade II centres to have arisen. With the exception of Gucheng, the three other towns all have a very large scope of service.

There are seven grade III and grade IV towns respectively, distributed throughout the county. They function as sub-centres to the grade I and II towns. The spheres of attraction of these towns are all quite small, generally limited only to the townships they are located. However, they differ greatly for their sizes, appearances, and number of shops.

A town is the centre of economic activity within a region. Towns of various grades provide services to the units and inhabitants within the respective area of their influence. From Tables II and III one can see the function of service trade in different towns as well as sizes of service area they represent.

The comparison between the service scope and grade of each of the towns shows that the service scope of Gaochun County's towns basically tallies with their grades. High grade towns have a large scope of service, while low grade towns have a correspondingly small scope of service.

Table II

1982 SALES VOLUME OF SERVICE TRADE IN DIFFERENT GRADE TOWNS IN GAOCHUN COUNTY

(Unit: yuan)

	Hotel	Photo-graphy	Hair-cutting and hair-dressing	Public bath-house
Grade I town: Chunxi	139,461	6,821	28,869	16,527
Grade II town: Dongba	4,749	1,096	2,608	5,394
Grade III town: Cangxi	1,275	0	993	4,202
Grade IV town: Hecheng	325	0	802	805

Table III

AVERAGE SERVICE AREA AND RADIUS IN DIFFERENT GARDE TOWNS

	Average service area of all service trades (km^2)	Service radius (km)
Grade I town: Chunxi	540.4	13.5
Grade II town: Dongba	68.5	4.8
Grade III town: Cangxi	36.9	3.3
Grade IV town: Hecheng	11.4	1.9

Differentiating the grades of villages and hamlets is quite complicated. Taking into consideration such various factors as their population, administrative status, commercial service, we determine that 21 out of the 943 villages in the whole county are grade I villages, 256 are grade II and 666 are grade III.

As a matter of fact, grade I village actually has an embryonic form of small town.. In sum, villages can be roughly divided into the following types:

1.   Those with fairly good original foundations.   Peiqiao, Miaogang, Changle, Nantang are the kind of villages which used to be flourishing towns before 1949.   It is only because they did not later become the commune seats that they have declined into rural places, which, nevertheless, still have some service facilities.   Peiqiao, for example, still retains a section of small street, and has more than 20 persons who are engaged full-time in various kinds of commercial activities.   There are co-operative stores (cigarettes and wine shops, department stores and hardware stores, one of each), five bean-curd stands, two snack bars, two barber shops and also tea-houses, flour and oil-extracting mills.   They are service centres for several administrative villages.

2.   Large villages with favourable conditions for setting up some service facilities.   Zhaoqianwei in Xuecheng Township is an example of such a village.   With more than 5,000 inhabitants, it is the centre of five administrative villages and has a relatively large comprehensive stores.

3.   Among the villages which are far from towns.   Various service facilities have been set up in those which are well situated and are considerably large in scale, in order to make things more convenient for the people.   Jingtang of Qiqiao Township, Shangyi and Xishe in Yongning Township are examples of villages of this type.

4.   Central villages formed through the large investments made as a result of competition between the different administrative units.   Take Zhuanqiang Township's Shuibiqiao for instance.   In order to compete against bustling Shuiyang Town in neighbouring Anhui Province, it set up a supply and marketing station to draw the local people to buy goods and sell their farm products.   Yet another example, Beigengchen Village in the northern part of this township, separated from Shishu Township by only a river, has become a grade I village in the process of competing with the latter.

5.   Villages which are the bases of commune-run industry. Villages such as Sunjia in Xuecheng Township and Xiaqiao in Cangxi Township have become commune-run industrial zones

thanks to their close proximity to county seat and their plentiful electric supply and good transport services.   The former boasts a brickyard, iron forging and casting mill and pharmaceutical factory; the latter has such industrial enterprises as a plastics factory, chemical fibre mill, ramie processing factory, prefabricated housing components plant and so on. In order to meet the needs of the workers in those factories, some service facilities have been correspondingly set up for the two villages.

6.   Villages whose existence is connected with historical custom.   Take Yangjiawan Village in Cangxi Township for example. It is close to Anhui and there is a check gate in its vicinity through which many people pass.   As a result of this, it has become customary for peasants to set up their sales stands and stalls here, transforming the place into a small market with shops, public bathrooms and other facilities, and making it a centre for the nearby villages and hamlets.

7.   Villages which were established as the result of the transfer of the seat of an administrative organ.   Xidoumen is an example of such a village, having been established right after the offices of Danhu Commune moved to its present location in 1978.

As for the numerous grade II villages, all of them are the seats of the managing bodies of the administrative villages, and are generally provided with the public facilities needed by the residents in their daily lives, including primary schools, cultural stations, clinics and purchasing and marketing agencies. However, due to a number of reasons, some administrative villages still do not have any purchasing and marketing agencies. Firstly, some have no need to set up such agencies since they are located near market towns or grade I villages. The administrative villages of Dongba, Liuxia and Dongfeng near Dongba Town are cases in point.   Secondly, there are villages which lack the economic strength to establish such facilities.   For instance, the fact that two-thirds of the administrative villages in Gubai Township still do not have any purchasing and marketing agencies is, to certain extent, the result of their low level of economic development.

Grade III villages, which are even more numerous, are the most essential residential areas in countryside where productive activities of farm and household sideline production are carried out, and at present most of them still lack basic service facilities.

Above we have presented an analysis of the system of villages and towns of Gaochun County. Although we have adopted various sorts of indexes in dividing them into grades, yet the focus of our attention has been on the role played by the commercial and service trades in the residential areas, so we have only made reference to the population figures, industrial output value, administrative positions of the places, and not made them the basis of our investigation. It is actually very difficult to create a sharply dividing line between villages and towns. A lot of grade I villages play the role of complementing towns and some are gradually becoming fairs. Those grade II villages which have small purchasing and marketing agencies are also significant in supplying peasants with daily necessities. Therefore, one can coherently divide the whole county's villages and towns into seven grades on the basis of the amount of their commerce and service trade. The higher the grade is, the smaller the number of such villages will be.

In this system of grading villages and towns, not every higher grade residential area is surrounded by lower grade residential areas. This is because each region is a mosaic-like system which is formed by villages and towns of different grades which connect, influence and interact with each other. The low-grade commodities found in the purchasing and marketing agencies and supply-and-marketing co-operatives of grade I villages or grade IV towns can also be found in the grade II villages and grade I towns; whereas grade I villages and grade III and IV towns are not supplied with, or are not completely supplied with, either the medium- and high-grade commodities found in the grade II towns, including such commodities as radio sets, sewing machines, wrist watches and bicycles; or the high-grade goods like recorders, TV sets, washing machines supplied to the grade I towns. Therefore people living in the vicinity of grade I towns are able to purchase the entire range of low-, medium- and high-grade goods, and consequently their surrounding areas do not have the conditions necessary for the development of grade II towns. As for areas a bit farther away, the only possibility is to set up some purchasing and marketing agencies selling daily necessities such as salt, soy sauce, matches and stamps. The chart below shows the pattern of distribution of villages and towns:

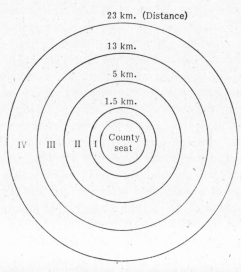

I. Suburbs where there are only grade III villages or grade II villages, but which have no commercial facilities.

II. Areas which contain grade I and grade II villages which have purchasing and marketing agencies but have no towns.

III. Areas which contain grade III and IV towns as well as grade I, II and III villages.

IV. Beyond a range of 13 kilometres of a city, there appear grade II towns and villages below that grade.

In the areas surrounding grade II towns there also appear a similar pattern of distribution of towns and villages, but on a smaller scale. These different patterns link and overlap with each other. This kind of pattern provides us a basis for rationally arranging the system of distribution of villages and towns.

III. Rational Distribution of Villages and Towns

Although tremendous progress has been made in the construction of villages and towns in Gaochun County since the founding of the People's Republic there are still quite a few remaining problems. The main problem is that the county lacks an overall plan, and therefore lacks planning in the choice of location for towns at various levels and in determining the appropriate sizes and rational distributions of villages and hamlets. In the construction of towns, only the initial construction of the seats of all the township governments has been carried out. In fact, some of the seats of township governments should be expanded into grade I towns, some are only appropriate for being built into small towns with a relatively small scope of services, and some are not suitable for being built into towns at all. There are still other townships which are large in area but whose government seats are located at outlying places, making it necessary to establish two towns within them.

1. There should be a grade I town in the east part of the county. As Gaochun County is long from east to west and narrow from north to south, and its only grade I town (Chunxi Town) is situated in an outlying area in the west, its location is obviously inconvenient for most places in the east. Therefore it is necessary to establish a grade I collection and distribution centre in the east. This centre should be established in the town of Dongba. Firstly, being located at the centre of the east part of the county and traversed by the Xuhe River and a highway linking it with Chunxi, Lishui County and Anhui's Langxi County, this town is well situated with regard to both

water and land transportation. Secondly, the town's presently existing foundation is quite good, as it already has factories, banks, post offices, supply and marketing co-operatives, restaurants, hotels, public bathrooms, cinemas, theatres and other enterprises and institutions, constituting a fairly complete set of economic, cultural, and living service facilities. The streets of the town have been paved with cement and street lamps have been installed. Thirdly, Dongba has a long history and was formerly the most flourishing town in Gaochun County, having had more than 100 rice stores, and served as the collection and distribution centre of agricultural and subsidiary products for the surrounding regions in the period before 1949.

2. In order to suit the needs of rural economic development, of raising people's living standards in countryside and of reducing the burden of Chunxi Town, a sub-centre should also be established in the western area of the county. All the existing grade II towns are centred in the east of the county. In the future the towns of Zhuanqiang, Hancun and Zhengjuesi should all be expanded into grade II centres. Giving a brief rundown on these towns will make the reason for this clear:

Zhuanqiang is located in the centre of the southwestern part of the county, far away from Chunxi Town but near Shuiyang Town in Anhui Province. It has a good existing foundation, there are many villages and hamlets in its vicinity, and the living standard of peasants in the surrounding diked region is generally fairly high. The diked region is crisscrossed by streams and brooks which offer much convenience to water transportation.

Zhengjuesi is situated along the bank of Shuiyang River, on the western border of the county, the meeting place of two provinces and three counties. Its geographical position is rather favourable to its development. In the days to come, planning and construction should be stepped up and work should be done in its widening streets, expanding the sizes of its shops, and increasing their variety of commodities. Furthermore, there is also need to add photo studios and other service facilities and to increase the scope of its present services so as to catch up with and even surpass the town of Yanchi in Anhui Province.

Hancun is linked by a highway to Chunxi, from which it is separated by a distance of 13 kilometres, making it inconvenient for peasants to carry on commerce there. Besides, Hancun is close to Tuanjiewei, an area of land which was reclaimed in 1969, where there is quite big potentiality for development and a grade II town with a fairly wide range of services is needed.

3. In order to make things more convenient for the people, it is necessary to add some grade II centres in the eastern part of the county. When Dongba becomes a grade I centre, the scope of its services will be expanded to cover the entire area of the eastern part of the county. However this will cause waste if the service radius is made too big. For this reason sub-centres are urgently needed to co-ordinate with the grade I centre. The original grade II towns of Yaxi, Qiqiao and Gucheng should continue to play the role of regional centre for the areas in which they are respectively located. These three towns have good bases and fairly complete service facilities, but they need to be further developed to meet the ever-growing needs of the people in their material and cultural life. Shuangpaishi, located one kilometre north of Qiqiao at the intersection of three main highways, can be developed with a stress on making use of its favourable transport conditions. With regard to Yaxi at the eastern border, despite its remote location far away from Chunxi, it is not only traversed by Shuanlang Highway but also connects with Liyang County via the Yaxi River, providing it with fairly favourable conditions for development. Nevertheless, at present, Yaxi's streets should be re-paved and its service facilities should be improved by erecting a multi-storeyed service building and a post office, and by perfecting the town waterworks. Gucheng has quite favourable conditions for development due to its location at

a strategic point along the waterway between Gaochun and Dongba, making it accessible by both water and land traffic. In addition to this, the county-run cement plant, ceramic plant, building materials factory, coal mine and other industrial enterprises situated in its vicinity also enhance its development potential. In future Dingbu Town may be developed into grade II centre. With its river boundary, Dingbu belongs to both Jiangsu and Anhui provinces, and is also the point where the Xuhe River and Shuanglang Highway intersect, giving it an important geographical position. As it develops, it may extend its service coverage to some places in Anhui Province.

4. The number of the existing towns is on the small side. In the future, grade I towns should be increased to an appropriate extent. At present there are 19 towns in the whole county, averaging only one for every 53 villages and hamlets, a relatively small number. Later small towns should be further developed for the following reasons:

(1) It will be beneficial to production and make things more convenient for the people, enabling peasants to use less time and travel shorter distance to purchase the means of production and daily necessities which they require.

(2) The surplus rural labour force may be used to increase the size of towns, and at the same time also help support the nearby rural areas. Therefore some big grade I villages, which already have numerous existing installations and are appropriately located and accessible to transportation, may be developed into towns. For instance, Shangyi Village of Yongning Township, Jingtang Village of Qiqiao Township, Shucun of Qingshan, Shengqian of Gucheng, Yangjiawan of Cangxi, Xiaohua of Danhu as well as the Tuanjiewei Farm and Fujiatan Tree Farm are all examples of this type.

5. Qingshan Town should be abolished and reduced to a grade I village. Qingshan Town is only two kilometres from Dongba and established in 1962 when the northern border area of the Dongba Commune was set aside to form the Qingshan Commune. Although now the political, economic and

cultural centre of Qingshan Township, its residents have always maintained the habit of going to the markets in Dongba. Up to now, more than a dozen public service facilities, such as supply and marketing co-operatives and so on, have been set up in this town, but they have not been able to play their proper roles. Therefore, Qingshan Town should be abolished and reduced to a grade I village. The major development projects planned for Qingshan Township may be transferred to Shucun to its north.

In sum, we can conclude that a more ideal arrangement of the gradation of the towns in Gaochun County would be as follows:

Grade I: Chunxi Town and Dongba Town;

Grade II: Yaxi, Qiqiao, Gucheng, Dingbu, Zhuanqiang, Hancun and Zhengjuesi;

Grade III: Cangxi, Xuecheng, Gulong, Caotang, Xiaba, Gubai, Hecheng, Shishu and Gangkou; and

Grade IV: Shangyicun, Jingtang, Shucun, Shengqian, Yangjiawan, Xiaohua, Tuanjiewei Farm and Fujiatan Tree Farm. (See the diagram on p. 267.)

6. The number of grade I villages and their service facilities should be further increased, enabling them gradually to be built into small town centres of fair size and service capacity. There are currently only 21 grade I villages in the whole county, accounting for only 2.2 per cent of the total number of the villages. In order to make it facilitate production and daily life, there is an urgent need to increase the number of grade I villages. In the future, the objects for development into grade I villages should be: (1) well-situated grade II villages; (2) grade II villages with rather complete existing service facilities; (3) villages of larger sizes; (4) villages with highly-developed economies. The existing grade I villages generally already contain comprehensive shops, bean-curd mills, barber shops, medical care stations, cultural stations, primary schools and other service facilities. In the future, along with the development of production, facilities for country fair trade should be set up; and in order to meet the needs of the people

DIAGRAM OF RATIONAL SELLING OF GOODS BY TOWNS OF DIFFERENT GRADES OF GAOCHUN COUNTY

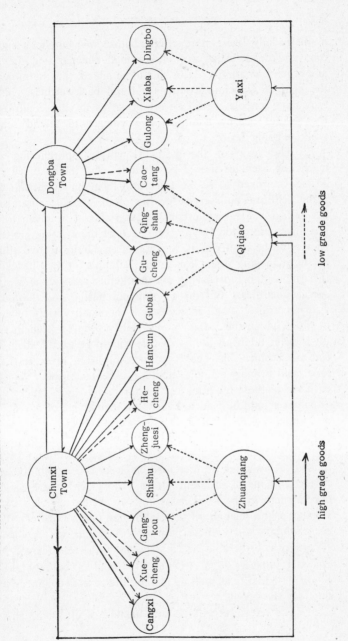

in their daily lives, more public bathrooms, butcher's shops, food and drink shops as well as small cinemas and theatres and other recreational places should be added. Furthermore, in the light of Gaochun County's cultural backwardness, junior secondary schools should be set up so as to enable pupils in the several nearby administrative villages to attend school without going far.

7. The scale of the grade II villages' purchasing and marketing agencies should be expanded and their service conditions improved so as the transform them into political, economic, cultural and service centres of their whole administrative villages. Meanwhile consideration should be given to expanding some grade II villages. Each of the existing grade II villages in the county is the location of an administrative village or the managing organ for several administrative villages, so they all contain purchasing and marketing agencies and other service facilities. But the existing purchasing and marketing agencies are too small in scale, and the small variety of commodities which they offer cannot satisfy people's need in raising their standard of living, so they should be expanded in the future. Besides this, health stations, libraries, processing factories and primary schools should also be established. At present most of these facilities are already in existence. Henceforth attention should be paid to expanding their scope of operations and improving their service. However, even at present, some administrative villages still do not have any purchasing and marketing agencies and other basic service facilities. In the future, they should be increased in accordance with the specific conditions of different places. Along with the economic development in the rural areas and rise in the people's living standards, the set pattern of establishing one service centre in each administrative village may be broken and some grade III villages of considerable size may gradually be transformed into grade II villages, so as to reach the goal of both obtaining economic benefits as well as making life as convenient as possible for the people.

8. The reform of villages and hamlets of all grades should

take place mainly at their original locations, while making appropriate adjustments with regard to their dispersion or concentration. Most of the existing villages and hamlets throughout the county spontaneously arose and developed on the basis of small-scale peasant economy. Despite these villages' relatively poor present conditions, which are insufficient to meet the needs of their development, nevertheless, from the point of view of saving funds, using less cultivated land, reducing hindrances to production during construction period, it is still necessary to utilize their existing installations and facilities and adopt ways of reforming them at their present locations. However, the county's villages presently exist in sharply different states of distributions, scattering at the east while highly concentrated in the west. The villages' distributional arrangements have, to varying degrees, influenced the production and life in them. In the diked western region most villages are concentrated on the dikes and ridges of the low-lying lands, with few being distributed in the inner diked areas as these places are too far from farmland and therefore inconvenient for production and management. In the hilly eastern region by contrast, the villages are scattered in distribution and occupy a lot of lands, making it inconvenient to set up a network of various kinds of welfare facilities, and also hindering farmland capital construction and the realization of agricultural mechanization. At present, the newly reclaimed areas such as Tuanjiewei, Yongshengwei, Xihutan and so on in the western part of the county still remain vacant and uninhabited, so arranging for the appropriate distribution of villages is still both necessary and possible. Because the big villages are inhabited by many people living in compact communities, their houses tend to be crowded together and have poor lighting and ventilation. This leaves little space for activities and tends to make the roads in villages narrow and winding. In order to have a comfortable environment to live in which is also in convenient proximity to farmland, people must move and settle down in the newly reclaimed region. Besides, there is a scarcity of land for building new housing since the land on the dikes and ridges is limited, thus increasing the possibility of moving people to newly reclaimed region to set up new villages of around 100 households. However, at present, there are some problems which must be overcome with regard to establishing new communities in areas in the newly reclaimed region, such as their long distances from service centres, inconvenience to transportation, relatively lack of security in the event of catastrophic floods, as well as the people's own reluctance to break-up their present long-standing living arrangements.

Appropriate arrangements should be made to gather together in groups those natural villages now scattered in the eastern part of the county. Some grade II or sizable grade III villages which are well situated and convenient to transportation could be made to serve as nucleuses for these new groupings, small villages of 100 or 200 residents located in their vicinity being amalgamated with them to form medium-sized villages of 500 residents. However, in the hilly region of the east, cultivated fields are scattered, and the amount of land area per capita is rather large, so it is unadvisable to establish large villages of several thousand inhabitants such as those in the diked region of the western part of the county.

May 1983

GIVE FULL PLAY TO THE ROLE OF SMALL TOWNS

— An Investigation of Yiling Town in Jiangdu County

Wu Rong, Wu Defu, Qian Guogeng

The thousands of small towns situated between the urban cities and rural villages serve as an important link between them. The construction of small towns in a vigorous and planned way has an important bearing on the country's modernization programme, and particularly on the acceleration of its agricultural modernization and gradually narrowing the gap between town and country, between industry and agriculture. However, in the past, we paid little attention to the conditions in small towns. For the purpose of finding out about the developmental trends of small towns with comparatively well-developed commodity production, and examining thoroughly how to give further play to the role of small towns, we have recently conducted a investigation at Yiling Town in Jiangdu County, Jiangsu Province.

I. The Rise and Decline of Yiling Town

Yiling Town is located along the central section of Yang-Tai Highway (the highway links Yangzhou with Taizhou in Jiangsu Province). With more than 30 million yuan in annual industrial output value it compares favourably with some developed towns in southern Jiangsu, ranking first among the small rural

towns in northern part of the province.   In 1982, its annual
turnover from the retail sale of social commodities exceeded 20
million yuan, greatly surpassing the level of most towns of its
size.   Its annual revenue topped four million yuan, outstrip-
ping even the level of certain counties.   Some of its products
are popular throughout the province.   For instance, its production of royal jelly ranked second in the province, and some
of its other products such as cast iron, nodular cast iron, MS80
softener and 566 resin are well known both inside and outside
the province.   The whole town has become the economic and
cultural centre of the rural area within a radius of 50 square
kilometres.

The town of Yiling has a long history, and references to it
can be found in *The History of Prefectures and Kingdoms in
the Later Han Dynasty*.   During the Tang and Song dynasties,
Yiling had evolved into a populous commercial port with quite
a few warehouses, academies of classical learning and temples
and monasteries.   It used to be a good place with prosperous
economy and flourishing culture.

During the years of Japanese occupation, the town suffered
severe damages and its economy withered up.   Most of its shops
were shut down and went out of business, its economic and
cultural life not recovering until quite a long time after the
victory of the War of Resistance Against Japan in 1945.

After the founding of the People's Republic, Yiling was revived and regained its former prosperity.   At that time there
were 40 shops trading in manufactured goods for daily use,
including groceries, refreshments shops, department stores,
hardware stores; 91 households dealing in purchasing, processing and selling farm and sideline products such as grain and
fish firms, oil mills, meat stalls and so on; 53 establishments
engaging in service trades, including restaurants, barber shops,
public baths, hotels and other catering services; 37 households
engaging in service trades, such as dyehouses, cobblers' shops,
repair shops and so forth.   It then had 221 shops in all.   In
addition, there were 80 odd households engaged in peddling.
This dense network of trading establishments drew the peas-

ants living in a radius of about 80 square kilometres to its country fairs. In the town, people were bustling about, coming and going from morning till night. Nevertheless, the whole town did not have a single industrial enterprise, but remained a centre of commercial consumption.

In the 1950s the establishment of the state monopoly for the purchase and marketing of grain and the socialist transformation of capitalist industry and commerce helped stabilize market prices and establish China's socialist planned economy. Nevertheless, it objectively affected the development of the commodity economy in Yiling. Twenty-nine grain trading companies, the biggest commercial firms in the town, were closed down; catering and service trades which served the purpose of exchanging grain between the peasants in the surrounding villages were also closed down one after another. In particular, the "Left" ideological trend in economic construction became increasingly pronounced, resulting in the commercial enterprises being artificially merged and the system of single-channelled state monopoly was adopted in commodity circulation. Thus the enterprises lacked the pressure of competition, management lost its elasticity and the town's whole economy became vigourless.

This situation did not end until 1978 after the Third Plenary Session of the Party's Eleventh Central Committee which was a great turning point for both the economic development of the country as a whole and for the economic and cultural development of Yiling Town in particular.

Industry and construction took the lead in invigorating the town's economy, which has been developing rapidly by an annual average increase of 23 per cent. The total industrial output value of Yiling shot up to 31.59 million yuan in 1982, accounting for 62 per cent of township's economy, thus changing the unitary rural economic structure and taking the place of commerce as the backbone of the town's economy. The opening of the country fair trade has brought vitality and prosperity of the town's economy. On an average day, the fair is attended by 300 small tradespeople, pedlars and persons selling farm and sideline produce, and is visited by 4,000 shoppers. The volume of business of the country fair trade has been increasing year by year, amounting to 1.44 million yuan in 1982, or doubled the figure of 1978.

Progress in culture, education and public health has kept abreast of the development of the economic construction. The town has taken a lead in the whole county in its drive for cultural and ideological civilization, in organizing spare-time performing entertainment for the peasants, as well as in its family planning, patriotic health campaign and pre-school education work and so on. As social order is good and people's standards of social conduct has attained a high level, people live and work in peace and contentment. Yiling is now in the initial stages of being converted into a rising rural market town with flourishing economy and culture.

II. An Economic and Cultural Centre

With the rapid growth in its economy, Yiling has been playing a decisive role in stimulating economic and cultural development in its surrounding rural areas, as is borne out by the following:

1. Yiling has tapped new sources of employment for urban labour, so that people in general have now got steady incomes and public order has been strengthened. During the ten or twenty years prior to the end of the "cultural revolution" marked by the smashing of Gang of Four in 1976, there had been quite a number of residents without fixed occupations. Having no fixed income, these people were never free from worry, and as a result, they often quarrelled among themselves and created disturbances. Along with the development of the market town's economy, the residents have gone to work in factories and shops. Thus not a single idler or unemployed person can be found in the town now. The town has an average per capita monthly income of 29 yuan, reaching the level of average medium and small cities, eight yuan lower than that of Chang-

zhou, which has a high level for our country. However, the real benefits which they derive are equal to 37 yuan per capita monthly income of Changzhou residents, as the cost of living in this town is low. The living standards of the townspeople have kept rising; men and women, old and young, dress neatly and their housing conditions have been much improved. They have raised demands that their cultural life be further enriched.

The town comprises 1,000 households, of which 270 have TV sets, accounting for 23 per cent of the total. In 1982, there was an annual average of 40 film showings per person, greatly exceeding the provincial average of 27. The improvement of people's life has promoted unity among the townships in the neighbourhood, causing a reduction in the incidence of crime and civil disputes.

2. Yiling has recruited surplus labour force from the countryside, which has given rise to a new generation of peasants engaged in industry or trade who have left the land but not their hometowns. The township of Yiling has a total of 33,000 people engaged in agriculture, and 28,000 *mu* of cultivated land with only about 0.8 *mu* of land per capita. There are 15,000 full and part-time workers, of which 40 per cent (or 6,000) are surplus to agricultural production. At present, the industry, commerce and building industries run by township and the town employ 4,371 workers and tradesmen, accounting for 29 per cent of the township's labour force, 73 per cent of its surplus labour.

It has been proven that the development of town-run industry and commerce is well-sorted to our country, with its conditions of a large population and a limited amount of farmland. We should strengthen the construction of small cities and towns, continuously strive to expand town-run industry and commerce, and draw to them a large number of rural surplus labourers. This is an inevitable trend in our rural economic development and in the formation of a new urban-rural pattern.

3. Yiling has provided a large amount of funds, materials and technical equipment for rural construction, thus stimulat-

ing the continuous growth of agricultural production. Under the circumstances in which prices deviate from values and the impossibility of the price scissors between agricultural and industrial products being narrowed within a short period of time, the only way out for agriculture is to practise local self-compensation.

An important approach to developing town-run industry and commerce is to distribute a portion of its profits to assist agriculture, and in particular to support production by practising "using industry to supplement agriculture". In the six years since 1976, the town's industry and commerce had provided 550,000 yuan for the support to agriculture, proportionally, 4.9 times the size our national investment in agriculture during the corresponding period. Compared with 1976, the agricultural output value of the town in 1982 amounted to 3.69 million yuan, representing an increase of 46 per cent, and an annual increase rate of 6.5 per cent.

4. The town has raised the level of the peasants' distribution thereby arousing the more enthusiasm for labour among those who are engaged in farming. The village is a place with a dense population and a limited amount of land, and agriculture here was formerly focused on grain production. In recent years, in order to encourage grain growing, the country has already raised the purchase price of grain, but because of the big gap between the income derived from growing grain and that gained from diversified undertakings, the peasants regarded grain growing as carrying out a commitment and making a contribution. Even in 1982, when an exceptional bumper harvest was gathered, the annual per capita income of the town from the grain production alone was only about 60 yuan. By means of wage income and "using industry to supplement agriculture", the gross income of the town's rural population from industry, commerce and sideline production amounted to more than 4 million yuan, representing an average annual per capita income of about 120 yuan, or more than double the figure from farming. When the income from family sideline occupations and other sources was added, the per capita in-

come approached 300 yuan. The increase of income has stimulated the peasants' enthusiasm for agricultural production and helped to further consolidate the foundation for agricultural production.

5. The town has changed the economic structure in the countryside, and created the conditions for narrowing the gaps between town and country and between industry and agriculture. The emergence of the town-run industry has smashed the bonds of agriculture in a narrow sense and the unitary economy. It has helped to integrate the occupations of planting and breeding with the industry of processing farm and sideline products, to carry out the diverse economic undertakings of agriculture, industry and commerce, and to gradually change the usual practice whereby all farm products, and especially the cash crops used as raw materials, were transported to the cities for processing and then sent back to the countryside for sale. The Yiling Royal Jelly Factory united with both the town's own rural bee-breeding households as well as with those in its neighbouring townships in processing royal jelly on the spot, carrying out a joint operation involving agriculture, industry and commerce. By doing so, the expenses of transporting raw materials and products between town and country were saved, and economic benefits raised. This method of operating has a broad future for development. We can clearly see from the upsurge in Yiling's industry and commerce that in carrying out overall development of farming, forestry, animal husbandry, sideline occupation and fishery, and the diverse economic undertakings of agriculture, industry, commerce, transport and building, the countryside is bound to rely on small towns. The rural area of our country is handicapped by a large population and limited farmland, so the commodity rate of most farm and sideline products cannot possibly be as high as that of some other countries. We do not have the conditions to permit each agricultural production management unit to run the diverse economic undertakings of farming, industry and commerce on its own. They can only march towards the depth of produc-

tion by association in which small towns may play the link role.

As agriculture develops from self- or semi-self-contained economy into commodity production on a larger scale, the conditions for transforming the small towns into processing bases for diversified farm and sideline products become much riper. This creates favourable conditions for future elimination of the gaps between town and country and between industry and agriculture.

6. It has widely opened up the market for industrial and agricultural products, invigorated business and promoted the development of production.

Small towns serve as a bridge for the exchange of goods and a hub of circulation for the interflow of materials between town and country. Through the small towns large amounts of urban industrial products are supplied to the vast countryside in a steady stream, while the rural grain, cotton, edible oil, pigs and other sideline products are transported to the cities for sale.

To ensure the free flow of industrial products for sale, it is vital to improve rural townships' commercial enterprises. Yiling, through restructuring its commercial system, has created several diverse co-existing economic sectors and unclogged numerous channels of circulation. All these economic sectors and channels, each trying to outdo others, competing with one another, making up each other's deficiencies and developing in harmony, have brought vitality to the market. In 1982, the following things were sold through these different channels: 3,000 bicycles, 39 TV sets, 1,293 wrist watches, 258 sewing machines, 791 radio sets and cassette recorders and 66,800 metres of chemical fabrics; compared with 1981, this represents increases 200 per cent, 34 per cent, 190 per cent, 65 per cent, 50 per cent, and 12 per cent respectively. The gross volume of retail sales rose by 48.5 per cent, as against 1981. These figures are a clear illustration of the broad market for consumer goods which exists in the rural areas. Provided that the reform of the circulation system is carried out in earnest, the overstocking of consumer goods will be eased and still greater development will be achieved in industrial production.

7. The town has enriched the cultural life in the countryside and become an activity centre for local scientific, educational, cultural and health undertakings.

Yiling has the following cultural, educational, medical institutions and establishments for popularizing science:

Cultural centres, public reading rooms, Xinhua bookstores, broadcasting stations, movie theatres, children's centres, key primary school, comprehensive school, supplementary classes for common knowledge, spare-time mechanic schools, town hospital, key district hospital, pharmacies of both Western and Chinese traditional medicine, instruction centre for agricultural scientific technology, information office for industrial scientific technology, exhibits to disseminate scientific knowledge and scientific research workshops. These institutions have not only become the centres of scientific, educational and cultural in the town, but have also become demonstration sites for the dissemination of spiritual civilization throughout the countryside as a whole. Regardless of the nature of the propaganda or cultural activity, it is first initiated in the town proper, and then extended from there to the surrounding villages. The method of "using rural towns to carry along the rural areas" has been adopted in promoting such activities as pre-school education, and to propagate "the five stresses and the four points of beauty and three loves", family planning and patriotic health campaigns. When these activities which are conducive to the welfare of society as a whole become widespread throughout the countryside, a new generation of peasants nurtured on socialist spiritual civilization will come into being.

III. Enlightenment Which We Have Gained and Problems Remaining to Be Solved

Small towns serve as the economic and cultural centres for the countryside. Speeding up the construction of small towns is the key to transforming the face of the countryside, realizing the four modernizations, and gradually narrowing the gap between town and country. Strengthening the research on small towns, summing up their historical experiences, and exploring their law of the development, are among the important tasks of social science and particularly sociology. As a result of our investigation of Yiling, we have come to the following realizations concerning the development of small towns:

1. Small towns have taken shape step by step in given economic districts in the wake of the development of the forces of production, and in particular progress in the division of labour and the exchange of commodity production. They have their own laws of formation and appropriate patterns of density.

Before "the three transformations" (the socialist transformations of handicrafts, capitalist industry and commerce, and agriculture), Yiling prospered by making good use of the favourable geographical location along the banks of the Grand Canal and beside the highway linking Yangzhou and Taizhou and also situated in a location most favourable for exchanging the rice from "the southwest, with its inexhaustible produce" and the cereals from "the northwest, with its limitless harvest". Yiling solicited both travelling traders from faraway and peasants living in its immediate vicinity to come and do business. As a result, the town has been transformed into a centre of consumption activity of the small commodity economy.

Since the Third Plenary Session of the Party's Eleventh Central Committee, Yiling has taken on a new look. A lot of town-run industries have sprung up; the interflow of commodities has been improved; economic activity both in the town and its surrounding villages have become more and more vigorous; and commodity production on a larger scale is emerging. Now Yiling has become a rising town combining consumption with production and all-round operation of agriculture, industry and commerce. Yiling's development showed clearly that the formation and advances of small towns are decided by the level of the growth of the productive forces.

In southern Jiangsu there is a town every 35.9 square kilometres, while in northern Jiangsu there is a town every 69.8 square kilometres. This distribution is surely not the product of accident, but was absolutely decided by the level of the economic development.

In the old days, the commodity rate was considerably high in the south of the province, therefore commodity collecting and distributing centres were needed for comparatively small areas. In contrast, in northern Jiangsu, a backward place which was not fully economically self-sufficient, the commodity rate was so low that the commodity collecting and distributing centre could not come into being within a small area.

At present, in the Xu(zhou)-Huai(yin) area of northern Jiangsu the commodity rate for the farm and sideline products is constantly growing and the original small towns which had difficulty undertaking the purchase of the farm and sideline produce and providing for the peasants' life, are gradually being replaced by the former larger townships, now reduced in size, and newly formed small towns.

Of course, there had been cases of artificially establishing administrative centres, which were later made to serve as economic centres. Nevertheless, the establishment of such centres must be based on scientific calculation and forestall sudden economic changes. For example, during the 1960s, Ganxia Township in Wuxi County moved its government from Chenshi, which was fairly large but located in a remote area, to its present location, which is well-situated and has good transport facilities. As a result of vigorous expansion of commune- and brigade-run industries in the 1970s, it has grown rapidly from a town of about 400 people into a town of more than 4,000 people, with prosperous industry and commerce and developed science and culture. However, it is rather difficult to build up small towns within a short period if, for the sake of convenience in the administrative management, one arranges the administrative divisions as he pleases and sets up a new township with its government situated in a place which offers few attractions to the peasants living in the surrounding areas because it lacks the necessary economic and cultural conditions.

The township government seat near Yiling has already been in existence for over twenty years, but due to certain historical reasons and other objective factors, its economy has been progressing slowly. It still looks like a rural village which has failed to play a role as an economic and cultural centre. Therefore, a new administrative centre and a new town must be established in conformity with the level of local productive forces and based on scientific calculation. It is necessary to weigh the pros and cons of the location as well. On no account must one be blind, rash and subjective in making such decisions.

2. The development of the small towns' economies must be in line with local conditions, be based upon the countryside and aid the harmonious development of the economy of both the small rural towns and the countryside.

The essential part of Yiling's economy is its town-run industry. Its rapid development was brought about by carrying out the principle of suiting measures to local conditions, having one's feet firmly planted in rural areas and serving agriculture.

Yiling Royal Jelly Factory was established in 1970. At that time, there were around 20 bee-breeding households and more than 300 apiaries. The factory sent people to learn techniques in the city of Wuxi and began trial production of royal jelly products. The source of materials, marketability of the products and guaranteed quality helped the jelly factory grow more and more vigorous. The factory has now adopted a modern production assembly line. There has been a big increase in production, and the output value of the factory had jumped from 950,000 yuan in 1978 to 9.06 million yuan in 1982. With an output of 1,400 tons of cast iron of a quality matching advanced standards, the Yiling Foundry leapt to the fourth place among the iron and steel mills in the province, putting it just behind the three major plants in Nanjing, Wuxi and Suzhou.

The development of the small towns' industries has given an impetus to the development of rural brigade-run enterprises. They have adopted the method of "dispersing components and spare parts, transferring manufacture of initial products to a lower level", thereby linking the commune- and brigade-run enterprises closely together. The Yiling Foundry distributed the screws and casings of the buckle products to be manufactured in the factories run by Guoyun Brigade. The royal jelly factory, using the method of "the big assisting the small", transferred the manufacture of the ampacity flasks, large and small packing boxes and small aluminium cases and other by-products to 25 enterprises run by brigades like Yunhe. The annual output value of these factories which revolve round the royal jelly factory had shot up to 1.10 million yuan.

In addition, a large amount of funds accumulated by the brigades from the profits of commune-run industries on the basis of taking 10 per cent of the total wages of the workers and staff engaged in industrial production, had been spent on modernizing agriculture, thereby mobilizing the enthusiasm of the agricultural labour forces, enhancing the ability to resist natural calamities and further consolidating the agricultural foundation. Since 1978, Yiling's grain output has kept rising with each passing year, its average annual per capita grain ration increasing from 230 kg. to more than 250 kg. At the same time, production of rapeseed rose from 117,000 kg. to 297,250 kg. As a result of having solved the problem of adequate grain production, the rural labourers engaged in town-run industry and commerce have been able to keep their minds more on their work and exert all their strength in production. The stability of agriculture has in turn helped to accelerate the development of town's economy, thereby creating a positive cycle.

Practice has proved that the principle of "suiting measures to local conditions, and planting one's feet firmly in the countryside" is vital to the joint prosperity of small rural towns and villages. Nevertheless, in the process of developing their economy, some small towns in a certain districts of northern Jiangsu blindly applied the experience of southern Jiangsu to running small rural towns' enterprises. They devoted themselves single-mindedly to the engineering and electronics industries, neglecting to adopt measures suitable to the local conditions. These districts did not make efforts to develop their farm and sideline product processing industries and mining and handicrafts enterprises in the light of their own concrete conditions and advantages. Consequently, capital funds and labour forces were consumed without obtaining the due economic results. Rather than aiding the rural economy, this resulted in the indiscriminate equalization and transfer of funds, labour force and arable land in the countryside. As a result, the enthusiasm of peasants was dampened and the development of agriculture was affected. This is a lesson which deserves to be borne firmly in mind.

3. The major key to invigorating the small rural towns' economy is to unclog the commercial channels and adopting a circulation system which permits the co-existence of various sectors and the free flow of numerous channels.

Emphasizing production over circulation has become a custom through long practice. Under the present circumstances of the increasing growth in the scale of commodity production, if the commercial circulation system is not improved, even greater losses will surely occur, it will be difficult to continue production. Yiling has made a correct appraisal of the situation and spent over half a year resolutely reforming its commercial system, which has produced obvious results. What was originally difficult to buy is now obtainable, what was difficult to sell before is now salable. Both production units and peasants are satisfied and the residents of towns feel content. Furthermore, tax revenues paid to the national government have increased.

In order to invigorate the economy, one must transform the existing commodity circulation system, with its few economic sectors and unified state purchase and marketing of goods, into one with diverse channels which gives more decision-making power to enterprises. That is to say, one must establish an open, multi-channel circulation system with a dense network of circulation points, in accordance with the principle of making the guidance of state planning primary. Now in the town of Yiling, commerce takes such varied forms as state-operated enterprises, supply and marketing co-operatives, co-operative enterprises, town-run enterprises, and businesses run by educated youth or individuals. The number of networks has more than doubled, as compared with previous years. With the increase in channels and networks, competition is increasing, thus external pressure is brought to bear on management, and vigour within the enterprises is unleashed.

Now every shop is trying to raise the quality of its service, and to do more business by every means, thus gradually ensuring the free flow of commodities. People say, "In the past, the single channel was just like a drainage ditch in the wheat fields. If one foot of it was clogged, it would be useless no matter how long it was. All of us were worried to death, but couldn't do anything about it. Now all the channels are flowing smoothly, so that we select our purchases from different shops, and get better bargains."

At the beginning of the reform, some people were afraid that with the increased number of channels no one would have enough business to do. But practice has shown that these people underestimated the purchasing power of the countryside and the initiative of the enterprises' staff members. The volume of business of the seven or eight channels in the town of Yiling has increased greatly in the past few consecutive years, with the average annual rate of increase ranging from 10 per cent to more than 30 per cent. With the passage of time, the benefits of the restructuring of the town's commercial system become more and more obvious. Yet some people still failed to understand the reform. They frowned upon the fact that peasants were being allowed to engage in commerce. The pretext for their opposition is that they thought the division of agriculture and commerce represented social progress, and peasants engaging in commerce a kind of retrogression.

As a matter of fact, the above two-thirds of Yiling's commerce involves supplying materials and products needed by its town-run industries, constituting an important component diverse rural economic undertakings jointly run by the agricultural, industrial and commercial sectors. In order to thoroughly change the rural economic structure, the peasants must stride boldly to enter the field of circulation. To a certain extent, the purchasing, transportation and sales undertakings jointly run by the agricultural, industrial and commercial sectors have unblocked the clogged circulation channels and done away with excessive links between state-operated commerce and supply and marketing organizations, thereby reducing the expenditures and increasing the income of the peasants.

The other one-third of Yiling's commerce mentioned above has also, to a certain extent, done away with centralized management in supply and marketing, which is not harmful but beneficial. The reason why the peasant-run commerce continues to thrive and develop is that it is accommodated to the market and suits the needs of the masses.

Everything that keeps pace with the market and suits the people's needs is a great productive force.

4. It is imperative to pay attention to the corresponding development of cultural and scientific undertakings in establishing small rural towns of this new type.

While stressing the development of economic construction Yiling has also made great efforts to establish cultural and educational undertakings. Much attention is now being paid to the appraisal of cultural proficiency in selecting cadres, promoting staff members and recruiting new workers. Studying science has become the order of the day. In 1982, the local Xinhua bookstores sold 5,400 scientific and technological books and 2,900 copies of scientific newspapers and periodicals were distributed to subscribers through the local post office; increasing 5.5 times and four times respectively over the sales and distribution figures of 1978.

In order to meet the needs of the masses in studying science and technology, the town set up 24 training classes for agriculture, sideline production, industry and commerce; held about 30 lectures on science and 15 supplementary classes in basic education; and selected 30 people to be trained in Nanjing and Yangzhou. Some of the town residents were even sent to universities to audit classes. They have also organized varied and colourful cultural and sports activities by making good use of their recreational facilities, so as to help the local people enrich their mental world and live by high moral standards.

This set of cultural and educational activities has improved spare-time cultural life, added vitality to rural towns and villages, and stimulated the growth of labour productivity.

Yet even at present, there are still quite a few rural towns which only stress improving material civilization to the neglect of spiritual civilization. Their cultural and educational undertakings do not meet the requirements of the broad masses. Certain towns have no bookstores, reading-rooms, theatres or places for holding cultural activities. The task of universalizing scientific education and technical training has not been carried out and little attention has been paid to primary and secondary school education.

In these places, the widespread illiteracy, lack of education in sciences, dull cultural life, and unhealthy atmosphere characterized by frequent quarrels and disturbances have hampered the expansion of production.

5. It is necessary to solve the problems connected with planning and the system of organization in developing rural economic and cultural centres.

1) Problems in planning.

Yiling is confronted with the problem, like most small rural towns, of developing blindly and in an unplanned way. Every unit went its own way in building houses, trying to make use of every bit of available space, and the resultant disorder in the distribution of housing seriously decreased the amount of cultivatable land.

Compared with the initial post-1949 period, the amount of floor space within the whole town has tripled. One of the main causes of the above-mentioned situation is the fact that the town has too many leaders to formulate a unified plan.

The town of Yiling has the following administrative units, institutions and enterprises: a district affairs office, town government, primary and secondary schools, post office, tax bureau, bank, town clinic, hospital, state-operated factories, county- and town-run factories, supply and marketing co-operatives, state-run shops and a grain administration office. These units are prone to attend merely to their own development to the neglect of unified planning; their concern frequently extends no farther than the facilities within their own office buildings, while neglecting the necessary additional installations outside their building. Therefore, in building small towns, a programme which simultaneously takes into account both the immediate effects and the long-term impact of the planned changes is advantageous to production, and makes daily life more convenient. This programme has the effect of law once it is ratified by the people's government at a higher level. In order to put an end to the indiscriminate occupying of cultivated land, the procedures for examination and approval must be further restricted and the requisition charges for taking land must be raised.

For the sake of doing a good job in the building of towns, full-time committee members in charge of such work should be provided to towns which are relatively large in scope (peopled 4,000 or above), so as to help make a unified plan and carry out unified management.

2) Problems concerning the system of organization.

There are altogether 1,897 small cities and towns in Jiangsu Province, of which only 132 have their own organizational systems, and the rest are seats for the township governments.

Some towns with nearly 10,000 people are still under the leadership of townships, so they have no rights of self-determination of their own. Yiling, which originally had a population of over 7,000 residents, was also under the jurisdiction of the township government. Under such a system, it is **very** difficult for small towns to fully play the role of rural cultural and economic centres.

In carrying out the structural reform of separating out government administration from commune management, Xinfeng Commune in Dafeng County held that the early reforms in which towns had been incorporated into counties, becoming county-run towns and thereby separating off from villages, did not meet the requirements for the harmonious development of both the urban and rural economies. If towns remain under the leadership of townships, their rights of self-determination will not be respected; the requirement of giving priority to the work in the cities and towns will not be met and they will not be able to play their full roles.

The Xinfeng Commune having learned from the experience of placing counties under the administration of municipalities established Xinfeng Town, and with approval of the provincial people's government implemented the new system of placing villages under town administration there on a trial basis. This had the effect of establishing closer economic, cultural and scientific ties between the town and township, so that they formed a unified entity. With the approval of the provincial government, the township of Yiling annulled its township system and established the town of Yiling under the new system of towns exercising administration over villages, enabling it to give full play to its role as an economic and cultural centre, and prompting its neighbouring villages to develop even faster.

THE FORMATION AND DEVELOPMENT OF THE SILK TOWN SHENGZE

Ju Futian and Wu Dasheng

The silk town Shengze has developed from a former collection and distribution centre for farm and handicraft products into a small industrial town.   Located in the southern tip of Wujiang County, Jiangsu Province, it borders on Wangjiangjing Town of Jiaxing County, Zhejiang Province.   It is 48 kilometres from Suzhou in the north, 118 kilometres from Hangzhou in the south and 68 kilometres from Huzhou in the southwest. During the Ming and Qing dynasties, Shengze enjoyed equal fame with Suzhou, Hangzhou and Huzhou, which were known collectively as the "four silk centres" of China.   Shengze has now become a base of silk industry and one of the main areas producing pure silk for export.

Shengze was originally named "Qingcaotan", meaning "green grassland".   During the period of the Three Kingdoms (A.D. 220-280), this place was used by General Sima Shengbin of the Kingdom of Wu as the site of his military camp.   Hence it was called "Shengzhai", meaning "camp of Sima Shengbin". As it is surrounded by lakes, it was renamed Shengze or Shenghu (*ze* and *hu* both mean lake) in Southern Song Dynasty (1127-1279).   In 1647, Emperor Shun Zhi of the Qing Dynasty ordered the establishment of Shengze Town, but it was not until 1740 when the county seat was moved to Shengze that the town was formally founded.   With the development of its silk industry, Shengze gradually expanded.   Since Shengze first became a market place during the reign of Emperor Jia Jing (1522-65) of the Ming Dynasty up until the present, more than 560 years have elapsed, during which time it has witnessed its mode of production evolve from cottage handicraft to workshop handicraft, and its economic system change from capitalism to socialism.

I. The Formation and Development of an Entrepot of Rural Handicraft Products

1. The rise of Shengze's cottage handicraft.

According to the *Annals of Wujiang County*, silk production in Shengze started in the reign of Emperor Xi Xuan (1425-34) of the Ming Dynasty. At first, being unfamiliar with the technique of silk weaving, the local people had to get some workers from Suzhou to do the job. The people in Shengze learned from the skilled weavers of Suzhou and gradually mastered the craft. By the time of the reigns of Emperors Cheng Hua and Hong Zhi (1465-1505) of the Ming Dynasty, some people in Shengze had become quite proficient in doing this work. With the popularization of silk weaving skills, the people in Shengze and Huangxi became largely engaged in silk making. As a result, it developed from a sideline occupation into being the main occupation of the peasants, and consequently there arose a number of households, which, while still doing some farm work, took silk weaving as their regular occupation. During the period between 1522-65 (in the reign of Emperor Jia Jing), about 100 households gave up field work to devote themselves entirely to silk production. This separation of handicraft production from agricultural work indicated that silk making in Shengze had attained the status of a commercial trade. The development of silk production on the basis of cottage handicraft industry brought about a gradual transition from natural agro-economy to commercial economy in both Shengze and the surrounding villages, while also quickening the process of their population's shift from engaging in agricultural to non-agricultural pursuits.

2. The emergence of workshop handicraft production.

During the reign of Emperors Long Qing and Wan Li (1567-1619) of the Ming Dynasty, silk production increasingly expanded in the villages surrounding Shengze, and the number of households specialized in commercial production of silk also grew. "The quantity of silk production and the price of silk greatly affected the income of silk weavers" (from *Annals of Wujiang County*, Vol. 38, published in the reign of Emperor Qian Long of the Qing Dynasty). This statement indicates that silk weavers had come to rely on the commodity economy. With the expansion of the commodity economy, "the rich employed workers to weave while the poor did the job by themselves", and the polarization between the rich and the poor became more and more acute. By the latter Ming Dynasty, several thousand workers were employed as weavers in the Shengze area. The emergence of "employed weavers" indicated that some rich silk handicraftsmen had become owners of handicraft workshops. In his novel *Stories to Enlighten Men* Feng Menglong, a writer of the Ming Dynasty, gives an account of how a weaver named Shi Fu in Shengze became rich, which is quite meaningful. He describes how formerly Shi Fu had only one handloom on which he and his wife worked. But due to his expert weaving skills, the silk he made was of exceptional quality and fetched high prices from the silk traders. Within a few years of time, Shi Fu became quite well-off, setting up three or four looms in his home. Before long, his profits from silk making increased several times over, and he planned to buy some more looms. It so happened that his neighbour was manufacturing silk at a loss and could not go on with it. So Shi Fu bought his neighbour's two rooms and turned them into workshops. The novel recounts: "Within ten years, by dint of his unremitting efforts, the total value of his property increased to several thousand taels of gold. He then purchased another big house in the immediate vicinity, bought 30-odd looms and hired some workers, thereby establishing a thriving business" (from *Stories to Enlighten Men*, Vol. 18, by Feng Menglong). This description on how Shi Fu built up his family fortune epitomizes the development of silk trade from cottage handicraft to workshop handicraft in the Shengze area. Judging from the level of development of the handicraft industry and commodity economy of that time, it was quite possible for this kind of workshop handicraft to emerge in Shengze. But due to the fact that it was more profitable to engage in silk trade than in silk production, there were only few rich families who went in for production. As a result, the workshops in Shengze did not gain superiority in silk production till the end of the Qing Dynasty, while its cottage silk industry flourished all along.

3. The formation of an entrepot of rural handicraft products.

It was probably in the reign of Emperor Jia Jing that Shengze became a market town. "At the beginning of the Ming Dynasty, Shengze was just a village with 50-60 households. In the reign of Emperor Jia Jing, the number of households doubled. The local people began engaging in silk weaving as their regular profession and Shengze became known as a town." (From the *Annals of Shenghu*, Vol. 18, published in the reign of Emperor Tong Zhi (1862-75).) Later, along with the development of silk production and trade, the population in Shengze also increased. According to the *Annals of Wujiang County*, in the reign of Emperor Kang Xi (1662-1722), the total number of households in Shengze surpassed 10,000. Most of these new inhabitants were migrants from Shaoxing, Zhejiang Province and they were mainly engaged in the scouring, dyeing and finishing work required in silk production. One of the silk producing areas in Zhejiang Province, Shaoxing's silk printing and dyeing techniques were quite advanced at the time. Due to the various skills introduced by the people from Shaoxing, the technology of silk production in Shengze became more sophisticated and comprehensive. As a result, the silk fabrics produced in Shengze became more and more refined and therefore increasingly competitive on the domestic and world markets. "Different varieties of exquisitely woven silks and satins were made in Shengze — printed and plain, long and short, heavy and light." (From the *Annals of Shenghu*, Vol. 1.) Many

traders came to Shengze and vied with each other in buying the
numerous varieties of marvellously patterned silk products. The
expansion of its markets spurred the further development of
silk production in Shengze and the surrounding areas, and,
under such circumstances, Shengze naturally became a silk collection and distribution centre.   The flourishing of silk production and trade in Shengze was vividly described by a local
poet Zhou Can in his poem:*

> On border of two kingdoms** of the ancient day,
> Great expanses of mulberries lay.
> Though a little place out of the way,
> Into the world its silk made its way.
> Merchants flock there from afar,
> Many leaving rich and gay.
> Dusk and morning come and go;
> At the looms the weavers stay.

By the end of the Ming and the beginning of the Qing Dynasties along with further development of silk production and
trade, silk firms and shops sprang up in the town.   At that
time, out of the 16 streets in Shengze, four and a half were
occupied by these firms and shops.   According to the statistics
made at the end of the Qing Dynasty and the beginning of the
Republic of China, there were about 50 raw silk firms and
70-80 silk fabric shops and firms in Shengze, conducting transactions in a fairly big scale.   The boom in the silk trade promoted the development of the silk weaving machinery industry.
In the reign of Emperor Qian Long (1736-95) of the Qing
Dynasty, there were already households specially engaged in
making looms and spare parts of weaving machines, such as
shuttles, reeds and pirns.   Peopled by numerous artisans and
technicians variously skilled at weaving, dyeing, polishing and
weaving machine making, Shengze Town thus became a collection and distribution centre for handicraft silk products.

---

* Annals of Shenghu, Vol. 1.
** The kingdoms of Wu and Yue of the Warring States (475-221
B.C.).

4. Features of a collection and distribution centre for rural handicraft products.

The reason why Shengze was referred to as a centre for the collection and distribution of silk products was that the town did not have a concentration of silk handicraft workshops and cottage handicraft households. As mentioned above, in the reign of Emperor Kang Xi, Shengze had already developed into a big town with 10,000 households. However, of these, only 300 families were engaged in silk weaving and dyeing, whereas in the areas within a radius of 25 *li* (unit of Chinese measurement, 1 *li* is 0.5 kilometre) surrounding Shengze, there were more than 6,000 silk weaving households. The silk produced in Shengze accounted for less than 5 per cent of that produced in the immediate surrounding rural areas, so the silks purchased by merchants there originated mostly in the countryside. However, most of the trades that served silk production such as processing, marketing, machine repair and transportation were concentrated in Shengze. Besides this, Shengze was also a port town. Every day, between 400 and 500 boats from rural areas would moor here and take away raw silk and silk fabrics. Firms and shops that dealt in raw silk and silk fabrics in Shengze served not only as links between other towns and the surrounding countryside, but also as bridges between Shengze and the weaving households in other towns.

Due to the short supply of raw silk in the countryside surrounding Shengze, the weavers had to rely on Jiaxing and Huzhou for their supply. The silk firms' primary business consisted of buying raw silk from Jiaxing and Huzhou and then sending it to the rural weavers in Shengze. The silk shops conducted transactions directly through the permanent buying and selling stations in Shengze, while the silk firms purchased silk fabrics from the silk shops and then sent them to other towns. At that time, one could find branches of Shengze silk firms in many important trading centres throughout China. The silk shops purchased the fabrics from the "silk agents" rather than buying them directly from the weavers themselves. These agents were the product of the highly developed silk trade, and played the exploitative role of middlemen between silk producers and silk shops. They received a service commission when they sold the silks produced by the weavers to silk shops. At the beginning, these silk agents went from house to house to collect the silks and then sold them to silk shops. Later, with the expansion of silk production and trade volume, the silk agents no longer went to the villages to collect silks. Instead, they had the silks sent to them by ferryboat and then sold them to silk shops. Likewise, the weavers entrusted the owners of the ferryboats to buy for them the raw silk they needed from the silk firms. The owner of a ferryboat served concurrently, in modern terms, as both a village's "section chief in charge of supply and marketing" and "section chief in charge of transportation". In the course of silk trade, the silk agents to a certain extent also played the role of regulating silk production. The production of silk at that time was completely governed by the market. Scattered in various towns and villages the weaving households had no access to any market information and they carried on their production blindly to a large extent. As a result, the specific varieties of silk most needed by the firms were often not available. Being familiar with the demand of the market, each of the silk agents would provide loans to some weaving households and ask them to produce silks according to given designs and specifications within a fixed period of time. After purchasing the silks, the agents would grade them and sell them to different silk shops, thereby serving as a medium linking the forces of production to the market.

To sum up, the main function of Shengze served as a centre for the collection and distribution of handicraft products can be outlined as follows: rendering both pre- and post-production services to the silk handicraft workers in the rural areas and manipulating silk production through the regulation by the market, thus serving as a bridge between production and marketing. The pre- and post-production services were, of course, geared to the aim of making profits for the commercial entrepreneurs. But objectively speaking, they linked up production and marketing, kept the commodity flow between them smooth and unimpeded and stimulated the development of the silk handicraft industry in Shengze.

5. Reasons for continuous growth of silk handicraft in Shengze.

Silk production and trade constituted the material basis for the formation and development of Shengze. The reasons for this prolonged flourish in Shengze, which is only one of the many small towns scattered all over the Lake Taihu area, are as follows:

(1) Bordering on Jiangsu and Zhejiang provinces, Shengze is within a close distance from Suzhou, Hangzhou, Shaoxing, Huzhou and Jiaxing. The techniques of silk weaving and dyeing developed in these cities had a great influence over the development of silk production in Shengze. As is mentioned above, the people in Shengze learned the technique of weaving from craftsmen of Suzhou, while the craft of scouring, dyeing and finishing was brought to the town by migrants from Shaoxing.

(2) Enjoying a warm and humid climate and high-quality fresh water, the Lake Taihu area is suitable for the cultivation of mulberry trees and the rearing of silkworms. Adjacent to silk producing towns like Zhenze, Nanxun, Shuanglin, and Puyuan of Jiangsu and Zhejiang provinces, Shengze could always get adequate supplies of raw silk.

(3) As most of the land in the rural areas around Shengze was owned by the landlords, the peasants there had to work as tenant farmers and could hardly make a living due to their cruel exploitation. However, if a peasant wove a bolt of silk, he could earn a profit equivalent to 25 kilogrammes of rice. As a result, the peasants preferred silk weaving to farming. Those who could not afford to buy looms found employment in the town doing weaving work for others. Hence there was adequate manpower in the town to develop the silk handicraft industry.

(4) By the beginning of the Qing Dynasty, the silk handicraft in Shengze had already basically become specialized. The

different procedures of silk making such as winding, drawing, picking up, beaming, wefting, weaving, bleaching, dyeing and finishing were already being shared out among the different households on the basis of the division of labour. At the same time, there were also households specializing in the repair and construction of weaving machines. This specialization in the town's silk handicraft was conducive to passing on technical know-how and raising production efficiency.

(5) The waterways which criss-cross Shengze have made it convenient for merchants from other areas to come here for silk business. As the town's commerce flourished, its silk market expanded and its silk production grew. Like twin brothers, the silk industry and commerce enhanced each other, sharing the same ups and downs.

(6) The silk production in Shengze expanded gradually from the countryside to include the cities. In history, the feudal bureaucrats' control over silk production in the rural area surrounding Shengze was rather loose, and its silk production was never under the yoke of the guild system, as it was in Suzhou. All these were advantageous to the development of the silk handicraft in Shengze.

In short, the expansion of silk trade in Shengze was attributable to various factors such as its favourable climate, rich natural resources and the industriousness of its peasants.

II. From Rural Handicraft Centre to Industrial Town

1. The birth of the silk industry.

Shortly after World War I, the capitalist world tided over the economic crisis of 1920-21 and its economy entered a new phase of development after emerging from a period of recovery. With the increased demand for silk on both domestic and world markets, the silk products turned out in Shengze could not meet the need. Under the influence of some silk factories in Shanghai and Suzhou which had expanded their production by introducing electric looms, a few entrepreneurs engaged in the silk business in Shengze also set up silk factories furnished with power looms. In 1929, the Meilichou Factory (meaning "Beautiful Silk Factory") succeeded in the experiment of starting two iron-and-wood looms using electricity generated by diesel engines, which created a stir by increasing output. In 1930, using electricity supplied to Shengze by the Suzhou Electric Light Factory, Wang Mingquan, a silk entrepreneur, opened four silk factories in Shengze with a total of 146 electric looms. Then, Lang Meichun followed suit by replacing the handlooms in his silk factory with electric-powered looms. Soon afterwards, several Shanghai silk factories moved their operations to Shengze. The bosses of these silk factories were merchants who had formerly been involved in the silk trade and had shifted to the silk industry after accumulating some capital. This course of development can be regarded as typical of China's national capitalists at the time. They generally first started some small silk factories in Shanghai and, after accumulating enough funds, they moved these factories back to Shengze. The reasons for this are first, that the town's silk industry already had a sound technical foundation; second, its labour costs were low; third, it was easier to procure labourers here; and fourth, Shengze was close to raw silk producing areas. By 1936, the total number of electric looms in the town's different factories had increased to 1,360, and the number of workers to 908. The introduction of power looms in the silk factories prompted some of the handicraft households in Shengze to also install electric looms. However, due to the limited supply of electricity, (two hours a day), the majority still preferred the traditional wooden handlooms.

The introduction of electric looms and concomitant increase in productivity brought about a transformation of the relations of production, which could be termed an "industrial revolution" in Shengze's silk production. First of all, there was a change in the town's class structure, namely, the first generation of industrial silk workers and national capitalists came into being. Second, the transition from cottage handicraft to capitalist industry was completed. Previously limited in scale, the town's silk cottage handicraft enterprises did not have modern work-shops or fixed workers. Most of their employees were part-time weavers, some engaging in trade by day and doing weav-ing work at night. The handlooms were simple, crude and inefficient. When these were replaced by electric looms, both production and variety were increased, quality improved and the products sold better.

2. The decline of Shengze's silk industry during the War of Resistance Against Japan (1937-45).

After "September 18th Incident" of 1931,* Japanese rayon was dumped onto China's market at low price, and the sale of Shengze's pure silk products began to suffer as a consequence. In order to maintain production and find market, the town's silk factories began using rayon as the main material for making coarse textiles. In 1937, the Japanese launched a full-scale invasion of China. After occupying Jiangsu and Zhejiang prov-inces, they set up the Huazhong Raw Silk Company, which exercised control over China's entire silk industry. As a result, the good quality raw silk produced in Jiangsu and Zhejiang provinces was all shipped to Japan and large numbers of mul-berry trees in these two provinces were felled. This eventually led to an abnormal phenomenon in Shengze market: the price of indigenous raw silk became even higher than that of silk fabrics. At the same time, the Japanese dismantled some silk workshops in Shengze and took away the motors. Besides this, they also damaged the road linking Suzhou and Jiaxing, blockaded a canal in southern Jiangsu leading to the town and cut off the silk trade between Shengze and other towns and cities. Consequently, the silk factories in Shengze were forced to close down, with only a few silk handicraft households re-maining in operation by using a small amount of indigenous raw silk.

Devastated by the Japanese, the silk industry in Shengze suf-fered badly. After the victory in the War of Resistance Against

------

* The incident of the Japanese seizure of Shenyang which was the first step in their invasion of entire China.

Japan in 1945, some former silk factories were transformed into cotton mills. In 1947, the silk factories in Shengze mainly produced cotton textiles. From 1947-49, the silk production and market in Shengze were under the control of the bureaucratic capitalists, driving many small weaving households into bankruptcy. By the eve of the founding of the People's Republic in 1949, all the silk factories in Shengze had been turned into cotton mills and its silk production had virtually stopped.

3.   The recovery and expansion of silk production in Shengze after 1949.

After 1949, silk production in Shengze resumed as if spring had come to a withered tree. During the initial period after 1949, Shengze Town had a total of 126 factories, workshops and handicraft households, with 450 electric looms and 840 silk and cotton textile workers. Under the leadership of the people's government, and with the aid of loans provided by the People's Bank and orders for processing placed by the state-run cotton and silk companies, silk production in Shengze quickly recovered. Between 1949 and 1956, silk and cotton production had been further developed. In 1956, shortly before the realization of joint state and private ownership of the enterprises, Shengze had 68 silk and cotton mills, 74 individual handicraft households and 1,641 textile workers.

After the completion of the transformation of private enterprises in 1956, the silk and cotton mills as well as households with electric looms were merged to form six textile mills. In the year 1956-57, the state invested a total of 1,319,690 yuan in updating their equipment and modernizing their workshops, resulting in a fairly big rise in production. In 1957, Shengze's total output value for textile industry reached 7.88 million yuan, an increase of over 12 times as compared with the early post-1949 period.

In order to meet the need of the gradually restoring silk production in 1957, the state reorganized the town's six cotton mills into three silk factories. Another silk factory was formed in 1958 by merging some of the individual weaving households which were using wooden looms. From 1957-69, these factories mainly produced rayon products and blend fabrics with rayon as the main material. It was not until 1970 that some of the pure silk fabrics were again produced. After 1975, the quantity of pure silk fabrics produced registered a gradual rise. At the same time, weaving equipment was updated or transformed, with old looms replaced by the new iron-and-wood looms equipped with automatic shuttle-changing devices.

The main reason for the slow development of silk production in Shengze between 1957 and 1975 was its outdated equipment and the lack of the ability to produce fine silk fabrics for export. Besides, the domestic market was quite limited as the purchasing power of the people had been rising very slowly. As a result, the development of silk trade in Shengze was restricted by its own productive capacity and the limited demands of the market.

4. The boom in Shengze's silk industry since 1978.

After the Third Plenary Session of the Party's Eleventh Central Committee held at the end of 1978, the policy of readjusting the national economy was implemented throughout the country. Since then the silk industry in Shengze has been reoriented to mainly produce pure silk for export. To this end, great efforts have been made to transform and renovate existing equipment and modernize such various production processes as designing, sampling, printing, dyeing and finishing. In the past four years, old-fashioned iron-and-wood looms have all been replaced by automatic looms, and more than 900 sets of key equipment for winding, drawing, twisting-in, warping, drying and dyeing have been made with imported steel. To meet the need of the world market for wide-width and figured silk fabrics, looms making narrow-width and plain fabrics have been replaced by those making wide-width and figured fabrics, made by the mills' own technical personnel. The number of wide-width and figured silk looms accounts for 50 per cent and 37 per cent of the total number of weaving machines respectively. The goal of having looms making fabrics of different width has been basically realized. In order to keep the temperature and moisture of the workshops constant so as to ensure the quality of pure silk fabrics, 101,880 square metres of workshops have been completely or partly rebuilt and installed with air conditioners and humidifiers. In the meantime, a silk research institute, a design centre and a silk sample factory have been set up. Increasing attention has been paid to intellectual development and technical training, emphasis being laid not only on the training of technical personnel for scientific research, designing and sampling, but also on the work of producing new varieties and patterns. As a result, a comprehensive silk industry has come into being in Shengze that embraces weaving, dyeing and the making of weaving machinery and equipment. Furthermore, a specialized production line for making pure silk fabrics for export has been set up, ensuring the swift expansion of production of silk fabrics, and especially pure silk fabrics. In 1982, the total output value for Shengze's silk industry reached 222.9 million yuan (not including that of the township- and commune-run silk factories), which was twice as much as in 1978. In 1982, 39.31 million metres of silk fabrics were produced, double the production of 1978, with the amount of silk fabrics and pure silk crepe for export increasing by one and five times respectively. As the quality of the town's silk products has improved, certified products now account for 97.47 per cent of the total. In the 1982 National Appraisal of Silk Products Competition, Shengze's Nos. 01, 02 and 07 bleached double crepe and the dyed double crepe won first place awards.

5. Favourable conditions for the development of Shengze's silk industry.

Shengze owes the rapid expansion of its silk industry since 1978 to the wise policies adopted by the Third Plenary Session of the Eleventh Party Central Committee and the increasing demand of silk on the world market. In addition to this, it has also benefited from the following favourable conditions.

(1) Help from big cities. The silk factories in Shengze benefit from their proximity to large cities like Suzhou, Shanghai and Hangzhou by often sending personnel to these places

to study production techniques and learn from their experiences in updating equipment and enterprise management.   Shengze's factories also turn to these large factories for help in solving difficult problems which crop up in their production and work. For example, with the help of Shanghai No. 1 Silk Machinery Plant, the Huasheng Looms Factory in Shengze succeeded in producing a type of loom which has now become the main item of weaving equipment in all the silk factories in the town. Another example is the Wujiang Printing and Dyeing Factory which introduced the method of cation dyeing but was unable to maintain colourfastness.   The factory sent people to Shanghai No. 1 Silk and Satin Printing and Dyeing Factory to study their technique of cation denaturation and succeeded in improving colourfastness.   One last example is the Xinhua Silk Factory of Shengze, which raised the quality of its pure silk fabrics by learning from Hangzhou's Fuhua Silk Factory the technique of finalizing the design of raw material.

(2) A solid foundation in traditional silk weaving and exquisite workmanship. Having developed as a result of the town's long tradition handicraft silk production, Shengze's silk industry has a good technical foundation. Most of the families in town have silk weavers among their members. Many families have been in the trade for generation and are well known for their silk weaving skills.   We conducted a survey by taking a random sampling of the occupations of the members of 283 households out of a total of 8,490 residing in 16 streets in Shengze.   The result shows that 268 families (94.7 per cent) have people working in silk industry, among which 83 families (31 per cent) are entirely engaged in it. Out of the 268 families, 101 families (37.69 per cent) have worked in the industry for one generation, 152 families (56.71 per cent) for two generations and 15 families (5.6 per cent) for three generations. Many weavers come from well-known silk making families, having acquired the traditional weaving skills from their parents in their youth. Familiar with all the processes of silk weaving, they continue to perfect their skills and excel at both plain silk and brocade weaving. The tradi-

tional silk weaving technique which Shengze has evolved over the course of the past 500 years has been handed down from generation to generation and has become the town's common heritage. As Prof. Fei Hsiao Tung has pointed out, Shengze's traditional silk weaving technique "has even insinuated itself into the people's genes and has become part of their biological foundation". The majority of the 1,000-odd young women workers who entered the town's silk factories in the last two years are from traditional silk making families. On the average, they mastered the technique and started to work independently within three months, which is estimated to be four or five times faster than people from ordinary backgrounds.

(3) Good co-operation from departments of industry and foreign trade. Foreign trade departments have provided Shengze's silk factories with both funds and material for the replacement of old equipment so that their productive capacity can meet the needs of the international market, thereby providing a material base for the development of Shengze's silk industry. Shengze's Department of Silk Industry has also done its utmost to meet the demands of foreign trade by ensuring the fulfilment of silk production quotas according to the stipulated time, quality and quantity. As a result, when there was a slump in the demand for silk on the world market in 1982, Shengze's silk sales abroad increased by 20 per cent as compared with 1981.

6. The position and role of the silk industry in Shengze.

First of all, Shengze is one of the bases of the silk industry in Jiangsu Province and also one of China's major pure silk producing areas. Shengze has 16.7 per cent of the silk weaving looms and 15.5 per cent of the silk workers in the whole of Jiangsu. In 1982, the value of the town's silk output, excluding that of township- and town-run factories, amounted to 16 per cent of the total silk output value of the province and 32.2 per cent of that of the city of Suzhou (including that of Wujiang and Wuxian counties which are under the jurisdiction of Suzhou Municipality). In 1982, Shengze's export of silk fabrics accounted for 46.8 per cent of the total of the province, that of pure silk one quarter of the whole country, and that of crepe silk more than one-third of the nation's total. Its pure silk was sold to 52 countries and regions. In 1982, Shengze's foreign exchange earnings from the export of silk accounted for 34.3 per cent of the total of Suzhou Municipality.

Secondly, Shengze is the centre of the silk industry in Wujiang County. Apart from the silk factories in Shengze, Wujiang County has 223 others, of which 33 are run by the township and 190 by production brigades. Scattered in various towns and townships of the county, these small factories have a total of 4,500 looms. In 1982 they produced 30 million metres of silk fabrics, of which 35 per cent was pure silk. These factories were all set up after 1975 with the help of the five county-run factories in Shengze. These five factories were respectively responsible for aiding them with obtaining equipment, machine installation, product design, technical personnel training and marketing. To help these township- and town-run factories solve technical problems, a technical service team comprising one experienced technician from each of the five factories was set up and has been making the rounds among these factories for three successive years giving technical guidance. As a silk design centre, the Shengze Silk Sample Factory specializes in creating new and marketable designs for the local factories.

Thirdly, by turning in a large amount of profit and taxes to the state, Shengze's silk industry has augmented state revenue. In the four years between 1979 to 1982, Shengze's five county-run silk factories and one printing and dyeing factory handed in 58.4 million yuan as profit and taxes, the equivalent of 1 8 times the total state investments and bank loans they obtained during the same period. In 1982 alone, they turned in 15.53 million yuan, which accounted for 19.1 per cent of the total profit and taxes paid by the silk industry of Suzhou Municipality in the same year.

Lastly, the development of the silk industry in Shengze has provided employment for job-awaiting youths in the town and the surplus labourers in the countryside. From 1978 to

1982, twelve of the county-run silk factories in Shengze recruited more than 3,200 job-awaiting youths as workers and another 1,709 surplus rural labourers as temporary workers, thus contributing to the improvement of social security and the raising of people's living standards.

7. The formation of a small industrial town based on silk industry.

Shengze's industry has a history of more than 50 years, commencing in 1929 when the first electric motor was installed in one of the town's factories. After 1949, it has undergone several expansions. Most notably, the rapid development which took place after 1978 greatly changed the nature and function of Shengze, transforming it into a small town with a respectable sized industry. Here are some of the salient facts concerning this development.

(1) The output value of industry, mainly the silk industry, accounts for a large proportion of the whole town's gross output value.

In 1982, the gross output value of the town's agriculture and industry was 279,280,500 yuan, of which the output value of industry amounted to 279,061,500 yuan, or 99.92 per cent of the total, while that of agriculture came to 219,000 yuan, or 0.08 per cent of the total. The average per capita (permanent registered residents) industrial output value of the town reached 10,659 yuan, nearly equalling that of the two urban cities of Changzhou and Nantong. In 1982, the value of the town's silk output (including that of the town- and county-run silk industries) was 252 million yuan, accounting for 90.3 per cent of its total industrial output value.

(2) Most of the factories in Shengze are county-run, and the majority of these are silk factories.

Out of the 33 factories in the town in 1982, 20 were run by the county (seven state-owned and 13 collectively-owned), ten by the town and three by the neighbourhoods. If classified by trade, there were 17 silk factories, among which 12 were run by the county and five by the town (including the one by the town's Labour Service Company).

(3) The majority of the work force of the town is comprised of industrial workers and most of the industrial workers are employed in silk industry.

In 1982, there were 15,432 industrial workers (including temporary workers employed according to plan) in the town, accounting for 86.2 per cent of the town's total work force of 17,906. Silk workers numbered 12,602 (including temporary workers), or 81.7 per cent of the total number of industrial workers.

In 1982, there were 11,312 industrial workers who were registered residents of the town, accounting for 81.96 per cent of the total number of employees (13,802 persons) in the town. The silk industry alone had a working staff of 10,893, comprising 96.3 per cent of the total number of industrial workers in the town.

(4) Over the past three decades and more, great changes have taken place in the town's employment structure. Of the town's total work force, people employed in commerce have dropped from 62.4 per cent in 1949 to 11.3 per cent in 1982, whereas those employed in industry have risen from 29.4. per cent in 1949 to 81.6 per cent in 1982.

(5) So far as the composition of the population is concerned, there is a certain proportion of non-registered residents, of whom the majority are peasant-workers. See the table on the next page for the figures concerning their numbers.

Of the town's population (permanent residents) in 1982, 89 per cent were registered residents and 21 per cent non-registered, among whom 45 per cent were its 3,094 peasant-workers. If we add the 1,050 land-workers (peasants who are permanently employed as irregular workers by factories which requisitioned their farmland), the number of peasant-workers totalled 4,144, which was 12.5 per cent of the town's permanent residents, 23.1 per cent of its work force and 30 per cent of the workers and staff who are registered residents (13,802 persons). The emergence of large numbers of peasant-workers are indications of the fast development of Shengze's industry, the manpower shortage among its registered residents

RESIDENTS COMPOSITION OF SHENGZE

Item	1949	1978	1982	1982 increase over 1949 (%)	1982 increase over 1978 (%)
Registered residents	24,632	21,510	26,179	6.3	21.7
Including agricultural people		1,123	1,123		
Non-registered residents		3,878	6,954		79.3
Including peasant-workers		780	3,094		296.7
Total number of residents in the town	24,632	25,388	33,133	34.5	30.5

as well as the shift of the population from agricultural to non-agricultural occupations.

(6) The population density within Shengze proper is high.

The town proper covers an area of 2.58 square kilometres, with a density of 12,842 persons per square kilometre (counting only the permanent residents). The built-up area of the town is 1.75 square kilometres, of which one-third is used for industry.

(7) A good foundation has been laid in Shengze's town construction.

As a result of the more than thirty years of effort since 1949, a good foundation has been laid in Shengze's town construction. The total floor space of its residential houses amounts to 226,076 square metres, averaging 6.3 square metres per person. The town's water processing plant supplies 5,000 tons of water daily to 70 per cent of its residents. Besides this, the town's 16 factory-owned deep wells produce another 16,000 tons of water daily to meet the needs of the industry and part of its residents. There is a sub-station which ensures the supply of electricity for both industrial and residential use. Automation in telephone exchange in the town proper has been realized. The town has a long distance bus station and two wharves. Its buses and steam boats can reach cities like Shanghai, Suzhou, Jiaxing and Hangzhou. The town also has a cinema, a story-telling house, a cultural station, a TV relay station and a broad-casting station. It has also five primary schools and two middle schools.

III. The Two Problems Shengze Must Solve in the Course of Its Further Development

The density of Shengze's factories and population indicates that the town's development has reached its saturation point. In what way should such a small industrial town develop in the future and what are the problems to be solved?

1.   In the production of silk, extension should give way to intension, to intensive processing. Shengze should develop in the following direction.

Firstly, to expand its silk printing and dyeing industry. At present, fine plain silk constitutes the bulk of pure silk fabrics it sells abroad. In 1982 for example, it accounted for 93 per cent of the pure silk exported. Therefore, more funds should be invested in silk printing and dyeing so that modern equipment can be imported, the technical level of printing raised and production of printed silk for export increased. At the same time, there must be improvement in the work of design-ing a wider variety of more stylish articles so that the town's products will compete better on the market.

Secondly, to develop various kinds of other pure silk products for export, such as garments, shoes and caps, quilt covers, pillow cases and arts and crafts works. This will not only greatly increase the output value of silk fabrics but also improve the quality of the products by catching defects in the course of printing, embroidering, tailoring and sewing. What is more, the scope of production will be enlarged and more jobs provided for surplus rural labourers.

Thirdly, to meet the increasing demand on the domestic and world market for jacquard and wide-width silk fabrics, continuous efforts should be made to transform and update the existing looms and install new equipment so as to expand the production of new varieties and styles like jacquard and wide-width silk fabrics.

The following key measures should be taken to guarantee that development will take the above-mentioned direction.

First, concerted effort should be made to train technical personnel. The silk industry is highly technical and artistic. It faces a world market that is highly competitive and therefore silk factories must be staffed by a certain number of technical personnel to improve their competitive ability by constantly improving the variety, the style and the quality of the products. At present, the proportion of engineers and technicians to workers in Shengze's silk industry enterprises (including silk weaving, printing and dyeing, looms and other equipment manufacturing) is only 0.94 per cent, which is lower than that of the big cities like Shanghai (3.5 per cent), Hangzhou (3.6 per cent) and Suzhou (2.2 per cent). Among the 118 engineers and technicians they have at the moment, 95 (80.5 per cent) have been conferred professional titles and 23 (19.5 per cent) have not. As mentioned before, Shengze's silk workers have traditional skills, which are an important factor in securing the position of its silk industry. However, only when such traditional skills are integrated with the advanced technology and equipment of modern industry can they play a bigger role. A number of senior middle school graduates qualified for college enrolment have already been selected by Shengze's silk enterprises and sent to the Suzhou Silk Engineering College to receive training. Though an important aid in alleviating the technical personnel shortage, it is still only one channel, and therefore takes too long to train too few people, rendering it unable to fulfil the town's silk industry's pressing developmental needs. In the future, the training of technical personnel should be done locally. The Wujiang Silk Research Institute located in Shengze should be expanded and strengthened. Silk engineers and technicians from other places should be invited to work or lecture in the institute, which should take the training of technical personnel for various factories as one of its tasks. For this reason, the Wujiang Silk Research Institute, which has already been in existence for three years but not yet officially been approved of by authorities concerned, should try to get the approval from competent departments in the province and the Suzhou Municipality. The silk sample factory should be incorporated into the institute as a laboratory, and serve as a base for training technical personnel and trial producing new products. At the same time, determined efforts should be made to run Shengze's newly established silk professional middle school and speed up preparations for setting up a secondary specialized school for silk workers. There should be no grudging on spending money on personnel training and intellectual investment, as it is an important step in raising the competitiveness of Shengze's silk industry.

Second, solve the problem of labour shortage. The problem Shengze faces at present is not unemployment but rather serious labour shortage. It is estimated that in the ten years to come, the number of women reaching working age will average 167 a year, which will not be enough to fill up the posts left vacant by retirement and natural depletion, to say nothing of the additional female labourers who will be needed to expand production. Silk factories operate on a three-shift system, and the work is not nearly as light as it appears to be. Female job-awaiting youths in other towns and cities are reluctant to leave their homes to become silk workers in Shengze, thus adding to the difficulty in worker recruitment. To make up for this shortage, quite a few young female peasants have been recruited in recent years. However, they often move away, some going back to their home villages after marriage, others becoming so tied down by household chores that they have little time to study technical knowledge and improve their skills. The solution to this problem lies in the adjustment of labour policy (e.g. recruiting permanent peasant-workers) and work time, and the improvement of working conditions as much as possible given the limitations of the actual conditions of Shengze as a small industrial town.

2. In terms of the town's urban construction, the following problems that already seriously hinder production must first of all be solved.

(1) The streets are too narrow and traffic is congested. Most of the streets in the town are about 3.5 metres wide. During rush hours, all of its streets and lanes become jam packed with people. The New South Street and New North Street, the only roads to the Xinmin Silk Factory and Huasheng Loom Factory, are only four metres wide. When a bus passes through, pedestrians have to walk close by the wall, and traffic accidents are common occurrence.

(2) The town's sewers are choked up, causing a lot of difficulties for the residents. Built in the Ming Dynasty, the sewage system of Shengze was damaged and its outlets blocked up in the course of filling up rivers and building roads, factories and houses. When it rains heavily, some places in the town are regularly flooded by water more than 30 centimetres deep. Between June and October 1983, the town was flooded seven times because of sewer blockage, seriously affecting people's life and production.

(3) There is a shortage of housing for the townspeople. Although several big factories have built some housing for their workers which has improved their living conditions, there are still 710 households that lack houses and 230 households that face housing difficulties. Compared with other big towns in Wujiang, Shengze's housing problem is more serious.

(4) Medical and health care facilities are poor. Shengze is a big town with a population of over 30,000, among whom more than 20,000 are workers. The profit it delivers to the state every year amounts to tens of million of yuan. Yet, the town has only one hospital, which is run by Shengze Township and is very small and poorly equipped. Even the big factories do not have clinics. It is difficult for the workers to get medical treatment. Health care for women and children is even more neglected. This problem has been raised at every

session of the town or county people's congress with no result up to now.

(5)   There are too few commercial establishments to meet the needs of the townspeople, especially the factory workers residing in the suburbs. In 1957, the town's 688 commercial establishments were merged into 336, and in the 1960s were further reduced to the present 109, all of which are concentrated on a few streets in the town centre. This is quite inappropriate for Shengze, a town with more than 200 streets and lanes. Furthermore, vegetables and non-staple food are scarce and expensive as some vegetable fields were occupied by factories when they expanded. The town's residents are frequently heard to complain about this.

An architect once compared the economic and social development of a town to the kernel of a walnut, and the infrastructure to the shell. The kernel and shell should grow together. It is bad to have a good shell but a wizened kernel. On the other hand, there are also cases when the kernel grows too plump and splits the shell, which likewise hinders economic and social development. A plump kernel in a small thin shell — that aptly describes the situation in Shengze at present.

The solution to this issue involves tackling a series of problems related to the town's system of leadership, its administrative division and its access to funds for construction.

Being a town under county jurisdiction, Shengze is not entitled to collect revenues for its own use. All profits and taxes from county-run industrial and commercial enterprises must be delivered to the state and the departments concerned in the county. The town's capital construction projects are financed only with the meagre sum of construction funds allocated by the county every year and a small share of the after-tax profit delivered from the town-run enterprises. These two sums of money are not enough to even cover the town's road maintenance expenses. Such being the case, a disproportion between the "shell" and "kernel" of this "walnut" always exists. How should this problem be solved? In view of Shengze's special characteristics, our suggestion is to treat the town as a special region on par with a county in terms of administrative system, so that it will have the power of using the three items of surtax it collects. Besides, permission might be given to such small towns to set aside a certain proportion of the profits earned by their enterprises for urban construction. At the same time, voluntary work can be encouraged and different ways of fund-raising employed to aid such public utility projects as setting up hospitals and repairing sewers.

Second, the contradiction of separate administration of the town and the township must be resolved. Confined in a small area, Shengze has no room for further expansion. The moment one steps out of the town proper, one is in Shengze Township. One solution to the problem is to merge the administration of the town and the township, so as to put the villages under the jurisdiction of the town. Another way is to incorporate a few villages of Shengze Township into the town of Shengze so that, guided by the principle of using land rationally and economically, problems like its shortage of housing and arable land and the narrowness of its streets can be solved by combining the construction of new residential areas with the transformation of old ones.

Third, peasants living nearby should be invited to open shops and engage in commercial enterprises and service trades. Factories should also be encouraged to set up shops nearby the workers' residential areas to serve the workers and staff members. This will help overcome the difficulties encountered by both the state-owned commercial departments and the supply and marketing establishments that intend to expand their commercial networks but are unable to do so because of a shortage of housing and funds.

December 1983

A PRELIMINARY STUDY ON
THE DEVELOPMENT OF TONGLI
— AN ANCIENT CULTURAL TOWN

Zhu Tonghua

I. The Evolution of Tongli and Its Main Features

Tongli Town in Wujiang County, Jiangsu Province, is a typical river and lake region market town south of the Chang-jiang (Yangtze) River. Situated in the northeastern part of Wujiang County, the region has a flat, low-lying topography and belongs to the Lake Taihu plain. The town is surrounded on all sides by four lakes (the Tongli, Jiuli, Yeze and Nanxing), and crisscrossed within by rivers and streams. This is just what the *Tongli Annals* has described as "a market surrounded by ponds" and "a town girdled by various lakes". Though only 6 km. away from Songling, the county seat of Wujiang, and 24 km. from Suzhou, during the ten centuries from the time of its founding in the Song Dynasty up until the end of 1982 it was accessible only by water, not by road.

In the old days of social upheaval when people "went to towns during minor disturbances and to the countryside dur-ing times of major turmoil", Tongli, which enjoyed favourable geographical conditions and was seldom disturbed by wars, became an ideal refuge for the rich to enjoy a tranquil life and for the labouring people to seek a living. The first national census in 1953 shows that there were 506 landlord families out of the total of 2,021 households in the town. This sort of population composition is rare, but by no means accidental.

Tongli has the following features:

1. It is an ancient town with a long history. It was established as a town on its present site in the Song Dynasty. In former days, Tongli was a centre of scholarship and its residents were very active in attending the feudal imperial examinations. From 992 to 1810, it produced one Number One Scholar (title conferred on the one who came in first in the highest imperial examination), 38 successful candidates in the highest imperial examination and 80 successful candidates at the provincial level. The town produced many officials during the Ming and Qing dynasties. Well-known men of letters and scholars like Ni Yunlin[1] and Gu Aying[2] of late Yuan Dynasty, Yao Guangxiao,[3] Dong Qichang[4] and Ji Cheng[5] of the Ming, Shen Deqian[6] and Chen Zufan of the Qing, and Yang Qianli,[7] Liu Yazi,[8] Jin Songcen[9] and Chen Boru[10] of the modern times, either lived or taught in Tongli. Many officials and

---

[1] Ni Yunlin (1301-74) Painter and calligrapher of Yuan Dynasty. Native of Wuxi, born into a rich family. Roved around the area of Lake Taihu and Huanghe River during the years of turmoil at the end of Yuan Dynasty.

[2] Gu Aying Lived during the Yuan Dynasty. Native of Kunshan. Man of letters.

[3] Yao Guangxiao (1335-1418) Native of Changzhou (present Wuxian County). Participated in the compilation of the *Records of Emperor Tai Zu of Song* and the *Yongle Encyclopaedia*.

[4] Dong Qichang (1555-1636) Painter and calligrapher of Ming Dynasty. Native of Huating (present Songjiang County, Shanghai).

[5] Ji Cheng (1582-?) Architect of Ming Dynasty. Native of Tongli, Wujiang County.

[6] Shen Deqian (1673-1769) Poet of Qing Dynasty. Native of Changzhou (present Wuxian County, Jiangsu Province).

[7] Yang Qianli (?-1979) Contemporary poet and calligrapher. Native of Tongli, Wujiang County.

[8] Liu Yazi (1887-1958) Native of Wujiang County. Unswerving patriot, steadfast democrat, great poet of the people and one of the founders of the Revolutionary Committee of the Kuomintang. He organized the Southern Society together with Chen Boru.

[9] Jin Songcen (1874-1947) Native of Tongli, Wujiang County. Joined a patriotic society in Shanghai in 1903. Wrote the first few chapters of the famous novel *Flowers in the Sinful Sea*.

[10] Chen Boru (1874-1933) Contemporary poet. Native of Tongli, Wujiang County, co-founder of the Southern Society Served as director of Jiangsu Provincial Museum after the 1911 Revolution and later as professor at Southeast China University.

scholars when they retired at old age returned to Tongli to build private houses and gardens. At present, one can still see row upon row of big mansions lining the riverside. A survey has shown that houses built during the Ming and Qing dynasties comprise more than one-third of the town's buildings.

Especially worthy of attention is the Tuisi Garden (meaning reflection on retirement) built in 1887 during the latter Qing Dynasty. Constructed by Ren Lansheng, a military officer at the time, he so named the garden to reflect on his faults, as he was removed from his post when its construction was in progress. Occupying an area of over 6,530 square metres, it consists of two parts. The front part is the living area comprises a sedan-chair hall, a tea hall, a main hall and a magnificent building housing the bedrooms. The rear part is a garden built close to water. Professor Chen Congzhou of Tongji University, Shanghai said of the garden to be "unique among landscape gardens south of the Changjiang River, a typical example of a garden built on water". Turned into a factory during the ten years of the "cultural revolution" (1966-76), the garden suffered some damage but has now been restored, thus preserving a master-piece of private gardens.

2. Tongli is also a typical old town in the river and lake region south of the Changjiang. The layout of the town proper is unique. The built-up area consists of about 0.6 square kilometres scattered on seven blocks of land surrounded by embankments and separated by rivers. The rivers run east-west and are spanned by bridges. They form the framework of the town, with everything built along them — the markets, the streets, the houses and the gardens. The rivers, bridges, streets, roads, houses and gardens are woven together so smartly and naturally that they form an organic whole. There are still 20-odd stone arch bridges of different styles constructed in the Song, Yuan, Ming and Qing dynasties. These antique bridges sit on the placid rivers with stone embankments. In front of the white-walled and black-tiled houses which line the riversides are verdant mulberry trees. Here, one can feast one's eyes on those river and lake region scenes typical of the

area south of the Changjiang, characterized by "small bridges, flowing streams and graceful houses".

II. Its Past and Present Functions as a Link Between the Cities and the Countryside

Small towns are the points of junction between the cities and the countryside. As links between the urban and rural areas, they occupy an important position in the urban-rural economic and social structure.

Though an ancient cultural centre, Tongli's evolution and growth was still the result of the development of social productivity, the social division of labour, and commodity exchange.

Historically speaking, the evolution of Tongli's function as a link between urban and rural areas can be divided into three stages.

1. In its early days, Tongli was established as a commercial and consumer town on the basis of its being a collection and distribution centre for agricultural and sideline products.

Tongli commenced its development at a very early date. A neolithic site excavated at Jiuli Village, two km. north of the town, shows that people already lived and worked here as early as 4,000 years ago. During the Tang and Song dynasties, the town was located at the site of present-day Jiuli Lake. When this area later sank and became a lake, the town moved southward to the present site. A paper entitled *Report on the Tongli Neolithic Site in Wujiang County, Jiangsu Province* written by Tongli scholar Wang Jiadong discusses this interesting geohistorical change.

According to the *Tongli Annals*, during the Song Dynasty, the town had "an abundance of produce and was peopled by numerous merchants and dealers as well as persons engaged in various other trades". By the Ming Dynasty, Tongli had already developed into a considerably large town occupying an area of 2.5 sq. km. and containing more than a thousand households, with brisk markets and thriving businesses. It is obvious that by that time, its commercial activities far exceeded exchanges among peasants, rather involving transactions between large numbers of merchants and pedlars who helped to link the urban and rural areas through their exchange of various commodities. The rice produced in Tongli is well-known. Before the founding of the People's Republic in 1949, the economic page of the Shanghai *Daily News* quoted the price of Tongli rice every day. Old people in Tongli recalled that during its heyday the town boasted 72 large and small rice firms. Every year Tongli shipped 20,000 tons of polished rice to Shanghai and kept another 10,000 tons in storage. During harvest time, the more than 100 peasant boats loaded with coarse rice or unhusked rice that came to town would jam the market river.

The abundant farm produce of the extensive rural area surrounding Tongli spurred the development of its commerce, farm produce processing industries and its manufacturing and repair businesses. As a result, Tongli became increasingly prosperous and came to take on the features of a consumer town. Before 1949, there were many tea-houses and restaurants in Tongli. On one 500-metre-long riverside street, there were as many as 14 tea-houses. These tea-houses and restaurants served as resting places for the peasants who came to town as well as gathering places for the townspeople to discuss business and exchange information.

2. Over the years, Tongli's special geographical and historical conditions enabled it to grow into a regional political centre and a cultural town with distinctive features. Quite a few natives of Tongli served as officials in the capital or elsewhere. While serving at these posts, they introduced the traditional culture of their locality to other places, and on retirement, they brought the culture of other provinces back to their native town. Furthermore, when prominent figures came here to serve as officials, or to teach, they also contributed to the interflow of culture. The town's age-old cultural tradition combined with the picturesque scenery of the region stimulated the aesthetic sense of its residents, giving rise to their hobby

of flower cultivation. Furthermore, the labouring people of Tongli turned the whole town into what was virtually a big landscape garden bordering on the water. However, under the feudal system, things created through labour did not belong to the labouring people, but existed only for the enjoyment of the town's exploiting, parasitic class.

3. Tongli's development into a multi-functional town was a big change that took place after liberation in 1949.

In the more than 30 years since liberation, Tongli has experienced many vicissitudes. On the one hand, it has developed from a basically parasitic, consumer town into a multi-functional town with sizable industry in which commerce, the building industry, service trades, transportation, education and health undertakings are all developing comprehensively. On the other hand, in the past years, its traditional culture has withered rather than developed. It was only after 1978 that due attention began to be paid to this problem, and efforts to restore its traditional culture were commenced.

At present, Tongli's industries can be classified into four categories: (1) Farm and sideline produce processing consisting mainly of oil-pressing and rice-milling plants. These plants process the raw grains and oil-seeds purchased by the grain stations. The processing districts include the town and such villages as Tuncun, Jinjiaba, Hubin, Bache and Wanbing. In 1982, a total of 9,130 tons of cereals was processed, with a total output value of 9.98 million yuan, accounting for 36.3 per cent of the town's total industrial output value of 28.72 million yuan. (2) The production of farm machinery and farming materials. The major factories in this category include a farm machinery plant, an electric machinery plant as well as a farm machinery workshop and the brick kiln of the Tongli People's Commune. The total output value of this group amounted to 4.41 million yuan, or 15.3 per cent of the total. (3) The production of spare parts and raw materials for big industries. This category includes factories manufacturing asbestos, transistors, starch, chemicals, silk fabrics and optical instruments. Together, they have an output value of 7.96 mil-

lion yuan, or 27.7 per cent of the total. (4) The production
of industrial products for daily use. The major factories in
this category include a lock factory, a garment factory and a
leather shoe factory. The products of these enterprises are
purchased by the county general merchandise company for sale
in other places. Their output value was 1.38 million yuan,
comprising 4.8 per cent of the total.

Of the above-mentioned four categories, the industrial output value of the first two reached 14.39 million yuan, or 50.1
per cent of the total, while that of the other two was 9.34 million yuan, or 32.5 per cent of the total. This means that Tongli's industry mainly caters to the development of agriculture,
which is good. But on the other hand, it also indicates that
the development of industry in Tongli has been slow and its
strength is still quite limited.

These factories in Tongli have absorbed some rural manpower. At present, there are 1,119 workers employed by
commune-run industries and the construction stations. When
these workers are added to those employed by the county- and
town-run industries, their total amounts to 1,516, or roughly
30 per cent of the surplus manpower in Tongli Township, a
proportion which is not at all high.

So far as commerce and service trades are concerned, under
the influence of the "Left" line of thinking that "the bigger
in scale and more socialist in nature, the better", ever since
1956, the year the socialist transformation was completed, they
have been the victims of excessive and arbitrary amalgamation.
In 1957, there were 109 retail shops and 128 pedlars in the
town. By 1965, there were only 71 retail shops and 47 pedlars
left, a reduction of 35 per cent and 73 per cent respectively.
During the ten years of turmoil (1966-76), private pedlars
were banned all together. The unitary form of commodity
circulation and distribution channels, compounded with the
unhealthy practice of running commerce in a bureaucratic way,
greatly lessened the town's attraction to the peasants. Consequently, the town's commerce and service trades wilted.
The root cause of this, of course, lay in the damage suffered

by the rural commodity economy. The grain output in the surrounding rural areas increased, but the development of the agricultural economy was not diversified, household side-lines were almost prohibited, and rural trade fairs were regarded as "capitalist black markets" and strictly restrained.

Since 1978, various forms of the responsibility system in production have been introduced in the rural areas around Tongli, and they have brought the peasants' initiative into full play and resulted in a rapid development of household sideline production and the diversified economy, as well as spurring the vigorous growth of commune- and brigade-run industries. All this has breathed new life into Tongli's development. In the three years between 1979 and 1981, the turnover of the commercial departments from retail trade rose dramatically from 9,567,000 yuan to 15,348,000 yuan, their profits increasing from 215,000 yuan to 570,000 yuan, or more than 1.5 times. As the political and economic hub of the area, Tongli's function as a link between the cities and the countryside is now being revived and strengthened.

This revival is most obviously reflected in the town's peasant market. In June 1983, we spent three successive mornings inspecting the market in Tongli, a 500-odd metre long street crowded with vendors selling a variety of vegetables, aquatic products, poultry, eggs, bean products, pickles, and fruits, all fresh and reasonable in price. Thanks to the introduction of the responsibility system in commerce, the state-owned and collectively owned shops and stores have improved their service, not only starting business early in the morning but also setting up stalls along this market street. Here, people can choose their breakfast from among the more than 20 kinds of prepared food available. We feel deeply that from the point of view of buying snacks, it is far more economical and convenient to live in a small town than in a large city.

Tongli's role as a link in the fields of education, culture and science is comparatively weak. Lagging behind some recently established towns south of the Changjiang (e.g. some towns and townships in Shazhou County), it no longer lives up to its name as a renowned old cultural centre. The poor road system in the surrounding rural areas is largely to blame for this. The town has only one 800-seat cinema, which is presently under expansion, and a story-telling auditorium with a capacity of 400. In 1982, a total of 413 shows and performances of films, Suzhou ballads, operas and plays were put on for audiences totalling 213,000 persons, among whom 112,000 were peasants. A survey taken of the members of the Tongli People's Commune showed that the peasants go to town to see films and performances an average 4.5 times annually (57 times a year in Shazhou County), or roughly once every three months. The town's cultural station has a space of 60 square metres for recreational activities, but this space has to be partitioned into four cubicles, which serve as a library, a reading-room and a tea-house and a chess room respectively. The monthly fund allocated to the cultural station is a pitiful 18 yuan, which in no way meets the people's needs for cultural life. Managed by the town authorities, this station does not directly involve the peasants in the surrounding villages. The work of popularizing science and technology has not yet been commenced in the town. However, the education of youth in Tongli has a sound basis, the town's middle school having 14 classes with 598 students. As rural students generally attend junior middle school in the vicinity of their townships, the town's junior middle school mainly enrols students from the town itself, with rural students only accounting for 27.6 per cent of the student body. The senior middle school enrols students from the town itself, Tongli Township, Tuncun Township as well as some villages in Jinjiaba Township, with rural students making up 72 per cent. The majority of the middle school graduates go back to their home villages, many becoming the key members in various rural undertakings. According to the figures from Tongli Township, out of the 299 cadres at the township and village levels, 81 (27 per cent) were graduates from the Tongli Middle School. Some have entered colleges. Since 1978, 25 of its students have been enrolled in universities, among whom 21 are from rural area.

We have presented this brief description of Tongli Town's inception and development in order to make the following points.

First, like many other small towns in the past several decades, Tongli has experienced a cycle of revival and decline, swinging from periods of prosperity to ones of relative penury, and then being revived once again. At the same time, it has also developed from being a town with few functions to one with many functions, and from there, went on to become a multi-functional town with its own characteristics.

Second, like other small towns, Tongli is also a combination of stability and movement, the "lock-gate" of the three "flows" (goods, personnel and information) between the cities and the countryside. The flow of goods can be summarized as the five functions of purchasing, marketing, collecting, distributing and transportation. The flow of personnel means the movement of talented people and manpower. Just as in the past, small towns served as springboards from which learned people launched their careers to serve as officials and to take up residence, they now serve a similar function by giving children of peasants a chance to enter colleges in the cities. At present, many cadres, cultural workers and technicians from the cities who come to work in the countryside settle down in towns. Furthermore, the small towns serve as bases for assembling rural manpower for the expansion of industrial production. The small towns also serve as a medium for the exchange of political, commercial and social information between the rural and urban areas, including such things as fashions in young men's clothing and girls' hair-styles. All these "flows" have to pass through the "lock-gate" of the small town, which is precisely how it functions as a link. Integrated with the transportation and communication network, these three "flows" have bound the villages and the cities into a single entity whose constituent parts constantly interact.

Market towns have an economic and natural agglomerative power with regard to the surrounding villages. Some foreign scholars have referred to cities as "agglomerations", but this term is actually more suited to describe the market towns in the countryside.

III. The Kind of New Tongli the People Aspire to Create

One respect in which small towns differ from big and medium-sized cities is that their rise and decline is closely connected with the conditions in its surrounding villages and their peasants' agricultural production. A small town prospers when agricultural production develops, since then its surrounding villages are affluent and the peasants love to go to town for shopping and entertainment, and it declines and perishes under the reverse circumstances.

At present, small towns have to keep abreast with the two transformations which have emerged in the course of agricultural modernization and rationalization of the production structure: the transformation from agriculture in the narrow sense to that in the broad sense, and the shift of their population from engagement in agricultural labour to non-agricultural labour. They must also realize two transformations within themselves, i.e., to change from towns with few functions to multi-functional ones, and from the state of being closed-off to being open. The first transformation entails that small towns not only change from merely performing commercial and circulation functions, or even from merely performing the function of production, but rather that they actually be transformed into the political, economic and cultural centres of their specific areas. The second transformation means that under the guidance of the principle of "actively developing the small towns", some specific regulations should be altered, and the development of small towns should be included into the general plan for our national economic development, as part of the structural reform of putting counties under the jurisdiction of the cities, so that the policy of "active development" can be materialized and the three flows mentioned above can be facilitated.

These transformations should also be realized in Tongli Town. However, attention should be paid to the town's special characteristics, that is, efforts should be made to preserve its cultural and architectural features as an ancient town in the river and lake region south of the Changjiang River. If these features are carelessly destroyed rather than cherished, the loss to Tongli Town would be inestimable.

In terms of a town as "multi-functional" and "open", we maintain that as the economic and cultural hub of the surrounding townships within an area of approximately 100 square kilometres, Tongli Town has not played such a role yet. To take on more functions, it is necessary for Tongli to assume more duties in education, culture, science and technology, and to play a leading role in the network it forms with the surrounding townships. The performance of these functions is conducive to the realization of the town's general development objective. The achievements of Shazhou County have already furnished us with an example in this regard. With the aim of promoting "megaculture" (not giving the town's residents more opportunities to see dramas and films, but comprehensively developing their educational, cultural, scientific, health and physical culture facilities) and using its constituent townships and villages as bases, this county trained a contingent of activists engaged in educational, cultural works of various sorts, and a number of exemplary personnel who take the lead in his or her field. By effectively making use of them to greatly promote material production, the county simultaneously attained a higher level of cultural life and affluence.

Becoming multi-functional does not mean discarding the special features of the different towns, and still less does it mean giving rise to functional disorder. Since the general objective for a town like Tongli is to become noted for its old culture, its transformation towards becoming multi-functional must be directed towards serving this purpose.

By and large, the transformation from a semi-closed town to an open town is accomplished by speeding up the three flows mentioned above. The focus, however, is on increasing the flow of talented personnel and manpower. A smooth flow of people would promote the flow of goods and information. At present, the township- and town-run enterprises of Tongli Town can only absorb 30 per cent of the surplus manpower of Tongli Township, which shows the volume of flow is still very small. In the Tongli Middle School, a big and comprehensive school, none of the music and fine art teachers have received tertiary normal education or specialized training. Yet as we understand it, the departments of music and fine arts of normal colleges specialized in training qualified teachers for middle schools have difficulty in finding job assignments for their graduates. In the meanwhile, some young people in the town who are good at music or fine arts are vexed at being unable to cultivate their talent, leading people to wonder how such sharp contradictions could exist side by side.

The necessity for a flow of talented people can also be seen from a rough analysis of the 41 leading cadres in the town's 14 factories (3 state-owned, 5 collectively owned and 6 run by the town). (See Table I.)

The table shows that: (1) These cadres are a bit too old; (2) Their educational level is too low; and (3) They lack specialized knowledge. Though this state of affairs is conditioned by historical reasons and the cadres are not to blame, it will no doubt affect the development of the industry in Tongli. The purpose of revealing this situation is to indicate how important and urgent it is to increase the flow of talented personnel.

IV. Contradictions in the Development of an Old Cultural Town

Many contradictions exist in the development of small towns and even more complicated ones arise with regard to the development of old cultural towns.

For instance, there is contradiction between actively developing the town's industry and the preservation of its ancient

Table I

LEADING CADRES IN TONGLI'S FACTORIES

	Number of persons	Percentage
Age group:		
Under 35 years	6	14.6
35-45 years	14	34.1
45-55 years	17	41.5
Above 55 years	4	9.8
Educational level:		
Primary school	10	24.4
Junior middle school	22	53.7
Senior middle school	5	12.2
Secondary specialized school	1	2.4
Specialized college	1	2.4
Qualifications for engaging in the factory's special field of production:		
Demobilized from military services	9	22.5
Transferred during the "cultural revolution"	14	35
Change of occupation	11	27.5
Specially trained	6	15

appearance. The development of small towns should not depend on state investment but mainly on their own strength, that is, they should accumulate funds by expanding production. Therefore, it is imperative to actively develop industry, handicrafts, processing business and service trades and to open up ways for them to earn and amass funds. However, this expansion must still comply with the general objective of Tongli's development plan, and advantages and disadvantages of each move should be weighed carefully. Neither reckless destruction nor so-called destruction for the sake of construction should be allowed. The asbestos factory built in the town proper has already brought industrial pollution to the town. If more factories creating serious pollution were set up and the town's water source were contaminated, the consequences would be disastrous. For a town like Tongli, determined efforts should be made to protect its water source (lakes and rivers) as well as all its buildings and structures (including ancient stone bridges) that are worth preserving. Construction is far more difficult than destruction. Preserving this old cultural town and further transforming it into one which is even more charming and healthier would be a contribution not only to Wujiang County and Jiangsu Province, but also to the state. Endeavours should be made to set up factories with minimal or at least treatable pollution, and to establish more processing industries using local materials and machine-building industries serving agricultural production. The town and the nearby townships should join forces in developing the traditional handicrafts, food processing industries, building industries, various kinds of labour services, and expanding the uses of the watery areas for fishery and agriculture.

The preservation of the Ming and Qing buildings and the improvement of people's living conditions, as well as the improvement of transportation and the protection of the town's ancient stone bridges, are two more contradictions. Ming and Qing buildings provide 37 per cent of the town's residential space, or a total of 112,000 square metres. Constructed with white walls, black tiles and stone door frames, these mansions are joined together in a group, more than 40 of which are still in good condition. Among them are some old residences like the former residence of Chen Boru, one of the founders of the Southern Society and a patriot of the 1911 Revolution; the former residence of Wang Shao'ao, one of the chief founding members of the China Association for the Promotion of Democracy and a fighter during the democratic revolution. Besides, there are the Fuji Mansion* and the Woyun Nunnery**

---

* According to the *Tongli Annals*, the Fuji Mansion used to be the residence of Chen Wangdao, an official of the Ming Dynasty.

** The Woyun Nunnery — a Ming structure. It is said that the nunnery was first built in the Tang Dynasty but the present-day main hall was rebuilt during the Ming.

of the Ming Dynasty and the Wuben Mansion* of the Qing. Though in a dilapidated condition and in need of renovation, the former residence of Jin Songcen, author of the first few chapters of the classical novel *Flowers in the Sinful Sea*, is worth preserving. The town also has more than 20 exquisite stone bridges built in the Song, Yuan, Ming and Qing dynasties. It goes without saying that these structures need to be carefully protected, but this does not mean that the town should be kept as it is without any alteration. Clustered together, these big mansions do not receive sufficient sunlight, and are not equipped with running water and toilets. As there are few two-storeyed buildings among them, they occupy a lot of land. All this must be gradually changed if the living conditions of the people are to be improved. What is important here is to draw a line: to strictly protect those buildings that worth protecting, and to alter in a planned way those structures that have no value for preservation and are not significant to the unified style of the town. As to the question of which are worth preserving and which are not, and how big the area in which the unified style of the old town is preserved, this can be settled by consulting specialists and the mass of town residents themselves. What is needed at present is to perfect the already drawn up overall development plan and to make it more authoritative. It is necessary that a workshop be held in due time to discuss the matter, which should be attended by specialists from the provincial and urban departments of city construction, cultural relics protection, tourism, building and landscape gardening.

We are of the opinion that so long as the aforesaid contradictions are properly solved, the town's economy prospers, the livelihood of the people is gradually improved and the special features of Tongli as an old cultural town are preserved, it will become a charming place, not only loved by the local people

---

* The Wuben Mansion — a well-preserved mid-Qing structure, the place used to be the residence of Ye Yongyi, a member of the Tongli gentry.

but also attractive to city residents, including workers, technical personnel and other intellectuals. In small towns like Tongli, there are things more beautiful than sunshine and green leaves. The present population of Tongli is 9,000, and we are to say that it would be no problem for it to accommodate 10,000 more. If the 20,000 towns and townships throughout the whole country are built up so as to become attractive to city people, they will not only greatly alleviate the burdens which increasing population places on the cities, but more importantly draw large numbers of intellectuals and skilled workers to aid in their development. This flow of personnel would be beneficial not only to the towns and cities but also to the state and the people as a whole.

In the final analysis, the above-mentioned problems are all connected to the relationship between economic development and the protection of historic buildings and structures. In the foregoing paragraphs, we have only discussed the matter with specific reference to Tongli, a relatively narrow, specialized issue. The problems would be much complex if viewed from an overall, historical and developmental viewpoint. Many believe that economic construction and preservation of cultural relics are mutually contradictory. Although this is true in certain cases, the problem is a complicated one and cannot be fully explained just using the term of "contradiction".

From a historical point of view, there would be no cultural treasures had there been no economic construction. The embankments along the quietly flowing rivers crisscrossing the town now present a fascinating scene, but in ancient times they constituted a magnificent feat of engineering, effectively protecting the banks and beds of the rivers and greatly facilitating the navigation and mooring of the boats. They further reflected the level of economic development Tongli attained in ancient times. Without a thriving economy, there would have been no such construction work and the consequent magnificent relics it left behind. This is the essential conformity between economic construction and preservation of relics. If we view the relations between economic construction and

preservation of relics from a specific point on the time co-ordinate, that is, from the present, we see that there are four relationships between them, as is indicated by the following
chart:

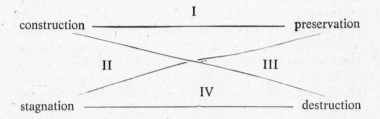

Allow us to explain these four relationships by using Tongli
Town as an example. Everybody admits that the ancient appearance of Tongli has been well preserved. This fact is borne
out by its clear rivers, graceful bridges and numerous Ming
and Qing buildings. Then why has the old face of the town
been so well preserved? In addition to its geographical seclu-
sion and other factors, the fundamental reason lies in the slow
development of the town's modern economy, represented as
relationship III in the chart. Such stagnation is evidence that
the town's development is lagging behind the times. It was
only in early 1980s, when traditional water transportation
could no longer satisfy the economic needs of modern life, that
the town became accessible to trucks and buses. Tongli's prosperity was historically based on the development of commerce
and service trades. After the founding of the People's Republic, the exploitation of the landlord families, who accounted for one quarter of the town's residents, was put an end to,
and consequently the various consumer businesses that catered
to their needs declined. In addition to this, the introduction
of a commercial system based on administrative divisions
greatly reduced the scope of services Tongli used to undertake,
both in collecting and distributing farm and sideline products
as well as in commerce. As a result, the only remaining place

it still served, Tongli Township, constituted only about one-fifth of the original area. Industry started to develop in the 1950s, and in 1982 the industrial output value reached 28.72 million yuan, with a profit of 1.93 million yuan. Of this profit, that created by the town-run industries only amounted to a little more than half a million. Since this was the main source of the town's construction funds, its government could only take a share of only 70,000 yuan, which was utterly inadequate. Such being the case in recent years, the situation in the previous two or three decades can well be imagined.

The slow development of the town's economy and its limited capacity in construction unintendingly resulted in the preservation of its ancient buildings. But this is after all a passive action. Should this state of affairs be allowed to continue, preservation would give way to destruction, i.e., there would be a shift from relationship III to relationship IV. In the long run, old buildings which are not repaired or renovated naturally become ruins, and this has already happened or is going to happen in Tongli. The only existing tea-house in the town is rundown but still in business. Though their main structures are still intact many of the big mansions are a scene of devastation, with their gardens lying in waste, buildings dilapidated, gate-towers collapsed and carved panels stripped away. Members of the town's housing section told us that 405 of the houses under their care are in danger of collapse and that the 35,000 yuan appropriated for maintenance in 1983 were entirely inadequate to salvage them. At present, these collapsing houses are still occupied. It is obvious that if the situation is left unchanged, the ancient appearance of Tongli would not be the same as it is now in a few decades time. At this crucial moment, to make Tongli Town a cultural site under provincial protection will undoubtedly play a decisive role.

Facts in Tongli have proved that cultural sites cannot be effectively preserved without economic development. But can an old town be preserved by way of state appropriations? It is reasonable that Tongli, as a treasure of the whole society, should receive financial assistance from the state in its preservation work.   However, we must also realize that firstly, the state cannot spend too much money for the preservation of relics, as it has a tight budget and must meet large demands for investment in the nation's economic development; secondly, unlike other cultural sites, such as gardens or temples, Tongli is a living town which must be given new vitality beneath old appearance.   Therefore, it is necessary for Tongli to greatly expand its economy, to set up whatever factories and other undertakings it needs.

The expansion of the town's economy might bring about two end results.   During the past few years, a number of people have been appealing for an end to the destruction caused by construction.   An example of this which occurred in Tongli is the renowned Tuisi Garden, which was changed beyond recognition during the "cultural revolution" when it was converted into a factory.   Another example is the foolish act of removing two big mounds which were much prized by the townspeople as scenic spots to fill up two rivers in the town's centre.

The most desirable relationship among the four possible ones is the first, the combination of construction and preservation, namely, preservation in the course of construction and vice versa.   So far as Tongli is concerned, this means dividing up the town's sites into areas of protection on the basis of the three classes mentioned previously, and carrying out the programme in a planned way, step by step.

How can the principle of making the work of construction conform to the needs of preservation be carried out in Tongli? In our opinion, this work should meet the following requirements.

First, the town must be made pleasant to live in.   In the work of Tongli's construction and preservation, primary consideration should be given to the needs of the people, and at the same time the desire of the local residents as well as the nearby peasants should be respected.   There is a big gap between Tongli's present situation and the modern living conditions its residents aspire to, especially in housing.   At present, there are only 30 units of new houses, which account for a mere 3 per cent of the total residential floor space. The majority of the people still live in old-type houses with poor ventilation and lighting. As the private mansions of the Ming and Qing gentry, most of these houses were originally designed to satisfy the needs of one family. With several or even more than a dozen families now living in the same mansion, their structures are no longer rational, and this irrationality will only increase as time goes on. To improve the living conditions of the people, it is imperative for Tongli to build a group of new residential houses, renovate some old ones and vacate some of the buildings. At the same time, public utilities like running water and sewage system should be expanded and facilities for science, education and recreational activities should be set up.

Second, Tongli should be opened up for tourism. It is one of the best preserved old water-country towns in existence. Situated close to Shanghai and Suzhou, it has rich resources for tourism. Its great number of ancient houses present valuable material for the study of our ancient architecture. Therefore, if its special features were better preserved, Tongli would become an attraction to tourists.

Third, so far as town construction is concerned, in order to make the inhabitants comfortable and the tourists happy, efforts should be made to preserve the old and pursue the new. On the one hand, the old look of the town as a whole and some important old buildings should be maintained so as to preserve that "ancient atmosphere" which is pleasing to tourists. On the other hand, the various facilities needed by the people for modern life must also be established. It is too one-sided to object to the presence of anything new in an old town. The point is to harmoniously integrate the old and the new so that Tongli will be old but not shabby and new but not vulgar. To realize the integration of the old and the new, we can draw on the aesthetic principles embodied in the designs of landscape gardens of the ancient times. Here we will cite two examples.

The first is partitioning, which refers to the flexible and opposing ways of applying the art of "borrowing" in landscape gardening. When discussing ways of handling the relationship between the scenes within and without a garden, the famous Ming architect Ji Cheng, a native of Tongli Town, said with regard to those outside, "What is common should be screened out, and what is beautiful should be taken in." In ancient China, the method of screening was often used when building gardens in the city, so that the landscape of the gardens would be independent of the surrounding environment. This method can be extended to city construction. With regard to Tongli, the old town can be separated from the new residential houses and factories by using the rivers and green lands as transitional belts. In this way, not only will the old town be preserved in its entirety as an independent unit, but the emergence and development of the new residential and factory areas will also not be hindered. Modern facilities that must be built within the old town can also be blocked from view by putting up high fences and planting tall trees.

Another is co-ordination, that is to say, there should be a sense of both identity and difference among the town's buildings. New buildings should be harmonious with the old ones in style. The suitable height of the buildings would be two storeys in the old area and no more than four storeys outside the town proper. The new buildings should be built in the Chinese style, with roofs laid with grey tiles in ridges and up-turned eaves, and walls painted white or black, thus maintaining an appearance similar to the old buildings. However, despite their traditional-looking exteriors, these new buildings should have entirely modern interiors. As a matter of fact, ancient architecture also developed with the times. In Tongli one can see buildings of different styles and features — the simplicity of the Ming, the elaborateness of the Qing, and the Western influence in the traditional Chinese architecture since the 1911 Revolution — blending with one another without harming the old look of the town. We must strive to make good use of the old traditions while also boldly creating the new, constructing buildings in Tongli which are endowed with both a national style and characteristics of the time. In addition to ensuring the harmonious blending of the architectural style of its buildings, it is also vital that attention be paid to the overall effect of harmony of the town. To achieve conformity in the general layout of the town, it is necessary to maintain the tradition of building up the town alongside the rivers, letting them play the role of connection and coordination.

Like many other small towns, the main contradiction that Tongli faces is that between its leadership and structure. There are five problems which must be solved in this regard, namely, understanding the role and position of the small towns, the selection of leading cadres for these towns, the structures, the overall plan and the construction fund. As some of the problems have already been discussed above, we would like to focus our attention on the problem of structure.

There are mainly two kinds of structures: the political structure, which is concerned with the ranks of the towns, their personnel, institutional set-up and their relationship between departments and regions, and the financial structure, which is concerned with the source and the use of the funds. Both kinds of structures warrant thorough study.

The first point is how to evaluate the small towns and the work on them. Why are 97 per cent of the 2,077 towns in Jiangsu Province at or below the level of townships? There are various reasons for this, but it is a problem, and an indication that a large number of towns are very low in rank. Being under the leadership of the townships affects their work of appointing cadres and developing production. Yet some of the counties are still reluctant to promote township-run towns to the level of county-run towns. This is a structural problem, and an instance of the financial structure influencing the political structure.

The importance of the work being done in relation to small towns is also worth studying. Guided by the spirit of the Second Plenary Session of the Party's Seventh Central Committee, in 1954, the emphasis of the counties' work was shifted to the small towns. Later, due to the "Great Leap Forward" movement and other factors, there ensued three-year period of economic difficulty. Under the slogans of "the whole Party going all out for agriculture" and "taking grain production as the key link", tens of millions of workers and large numbers of town dwellers were mobilized to settle down in the countryside and the most proficient cadres were transferred to the agricultural front (which was necessary at that time). As a result, the work which was being done and which had just been strengthened, was weakened again. Just when agricultural production and other work were starting to recover, the unprecedented "cultural revolution" was initiated, during which nothing was done to the improvement of small towns. This shows that on the one hand the prosperity of the towns and the work done in them are closely related to the conditions of agriculture, and on the other that work on the small towns has indeed been neglected for many years and must be strengthened by all means.

Another problem is the relationship between the departments and regions in the work carried out in the towns, which is also a problem of administrative structure. To be the magistrate of a town is as difficult as being the magistrate of the capital, as the saying goes. One of the difficulties is to handle the relations between the town and the different departments and enterprises of the county. For instance, the county grain bureau wanted to construct two residential buildings in Tongli Town for its staff near the Fuguan Bridge, an area which was not designated as residential in the town's overall plan. After several months of wrangling, the town had to concede and the construction of the houses were allowed. Another example — a positive one — is that the county's post and telecommunications bureau planned to expand the post office in the town and the town argued that the building should be put back by two metres. After several rounds of consultations the two sides reached agreement. We believe that the contradictions between the departments and regions are unavoidable; they existed in the past, still exist at present and will continue to exist in the future. This problem can only be handled through consultations and negotiations in which the interests of all groups are taken into account. The town's development plan, which represents the overall situation and long-term interests of the people, must be respected.

Still another issue is the relationship between the town and the township. Such a relationship exists between Tongli Town and townships like Tuncun, Jinjiaba, Zhouzhuang, Chefang and Guoxian. Apart from the economic ties between the town and the townships, the former also exerts big influence on the latter in the fields of ideology, moral standards, culture, the popularization of scientific knowledge and customs. Both historically and up to the present the cities (including the towns) have always exerted an influence over the countryside. Whether for good or bad, on fashions in clothing or on articles of daily use, the influence exercised by Shanghai over Suzhou and Tongli, and by Tongli over its surrounding townships has spread like wildfire. Therefore, Tongli Town should play a role in the building of spiritual civilization in its surrounding townships, though the latter are not subordinated to the former administratively.

Here we would like to stress the relationship between Tongli Town and Tongli Township, which is different from that between Tongli Town and other townships. Like two families living on the same lot of land or two riders perched on the same horse, they share the same fate economically and politically, as well as in the fields of culture, education, moral standards and customs. However, for reasons relating to their administrative structures, they are indeed two separate families, neither interfering nor co-ordinating with each other. This shows that in our society, the force produced by administrative structure is tremendous. We should use this as a unifying force to promote production and construction, and not let it become a divisive or containing force. Therefore, from a long-range view, it is imperative to properly settle the administrative relationship between the town and township.

Finally, there is also the problem of financial structure, the most important of its structural problems. In 1982, the revenues of Tongli Town totalled 103,800 yuan, and were derived from three financial sources, as is shown in the following table:

Table II

FINANCIAL SOURCES OF TONGLI

Items	Amount (yuan)
The three surtaxes: water and electricity charges, industrial and commercial taxes, and rentals (70 per cent of the total returned by the county)	28,650
Share from the profit created by town-run enterprises	71,000
Funds collected from county-run enterprises	4,150
TOTAL	103,800

This represents the total financial resources that Tongli Town has at its disposal for such expenditures as the maintenance of roads and sewers, repair of bridges and river embankments, fixing of public toilets, subsidies for secondary and primary schools, and cultural station. The two fundamental causes of the limitedness of Tongli's financial resources lie in the town's slow economic development and its financial structure. Therefore, opening up more sources of income and improving its existing financial structure are urgent problems which must be studied and solved.

September 3, 1983
Nanjing

FORMATION AND DEVELOPMENT OF A RURAL REGIONAL COMMODITY CIRCULATION CENTRE — ZHENZE

Zhang Yulin and Shen Guanbao

In the Chinese history, when *zhen* was incorporated in a place name, it indicated that the place was either a thriving commercial centre or a seat of government and military offices. *Ji* is a general term for a fair. To meet the needs of commodity circulation, a myriad of small towns, or *jizhen* as they are called in Chinese, have come into being and developed into places for trading agricultural and sideline products. Today, China's vast rural area is shifting from their former self-supporting or semi-self-supporting economy to large-scale commodity production, and its circulation channels are being unclogged to cater to the needs of commodity production. In our recent survey of the town of Zhenze in Wujiang County of Jiangsu Province, we made an initial exploration of the development prospects of small towns and of their layout to meet the needs of commodity circulation.

I

Bordered by the city of Suzhou to its north and Zhejiang Province's fertile Hang(zhou)-Jia(xing)-Hu(zhou) plain to the south, Wujiang County is one of the richly endowed, river-traversed areas of the Changjiang River delta. As early as the Tang (618-907) and Song (960-1279) dynasties, this area ranked first in silk industry in China and supplied rice to other areas every year. After the Ming Dynasty (1368-1644), it was among the areas in which the earliest seeds of capitalist industry and commerce were sown. It also had well-developed manual cotton and silk weaving industries. During the reign of Yong Le of the Ming Dynasty, an official named Zheng He went abroad by sailing from the town of Liuhe near Suzhou, thus beginning commercial contacts between China and other countries of Southeast Asia. During the Ming Dynasty, a merchant named Shen Xiu (or Shen Wansan), who was known as the "richest man in the country", also resided in this region. According to the *Annals of Suzhou Prefecture*, Shen made a big fortune through trading with foreign countries. Commodity production and growing domestic and foreign trade not only transformed Suzhou into the biggest city in the south of the lower reaches of the Changjiang River at a time, but also created a large number of prosperous towns around Suzhou. Zhenze is an example of one such town.

Located in the southwest part of Wujiang County, 60 km. away from Suzhou, the town is the centre of a small economic zone with a network of waterways. Within an area not exceeding five kilometres from the town, there is an even distribution of agriculture and sideline production. The Ditang River which runs through the area connects with the Grand Canal, linking Beijing in the north with Hangzhou in the south, which flows southward through Wujiang County. Zhenze thus became a centre for trading agricultural and sideline products in this area. Historical records concerning the town state that "during the Yuan Dynasty (1271-1368) it was only a desolate village with several dozen households. During the reign of Cheng Hua (1465-87) of the Ming Dynasty, it contained 300 to 400 households, and during the reign of Jia Jing (1522-66) of the same dynasty, the number of households was more than doubled." During the reign of Qian Long (1736-95) of the Qing Dynasty, "goods and materials were collected there and households numbered 2,000 to 3,000".* This account shows

---

* See the *Annals of Zhenze County.*

that since the Ming Dynasty Zhenze has gradually expanded to meet the needs of commodity production.

Rice and silk are the main farm and sideline produce of this area. Silk production reached its peak in the 1920s, with an annual output of 1,000 tons of dry silk yarn. Later, silk production declined gradually due to the competition posed by the raw and artificial silk produced by Japan. By 1937, the annual output dropped to 250 tons. Shortly after occupying China's Jiangsu and Zhejiang provinces, the Japanese aggressors blew up the Zhenfeng Reeling Mill — the sole mechanized industry then in the town of Zhenze, which had been set up in 1929. They also blocked China's trade with foreign countries. As a result, silk prices plummeted, and local peasants very reluctantly gave up growing mulberries and turned to producing grain. By 1945, the year of the victory in the War of Resistance Against Japan, the annual output of dry silk yarn was only 100 tons, or one-tenth of what it had been during the peak years. Although production was restored to a certain extent, no substantial progress was made.

There were five or six kinds of commercial businesses and handicrafts in the town which corresponded with mulberry-growing and silkworm-raising in its surrounding rural areas, including silk firms, silk yarn workshops, merchants specializing in purchasing silk waste, handicraft workshops making silk wadding using floss as a raw material, and firms selling mulberry trees as firewood. Among these, the silk firms and silk yarn workshops were the principal trades. Traditionally, the silk reeled by peasants themselves were called "home-made silk", so as to distinguish it from "factory-produced silk" reeled by machines. The town had more than 20 native silk firms of different sizes engaging in the purchase of home-made silk. They resold the bulk of their purchases to the town's silk yarn workshops, and the rest to silk factories and silk shops. The silk yarn workshops then contracted with local peasants, who processed the workshops' natural silk into silk yarn in their homes in return for processing fees. The workshops then shipped their yarn to Shanghai, where it was exported by

foreign firms and compradors. The way the silk yarn workshops operated was a special form of transition from commercial capitalism to industrial capitalism. During the heyday of
silk yarn trade in the 1920s, rivers running through the town
were crowded with boats loaded with silk, and boxes of silk
yarn were stored in many places in the town. According to
estimate, the annual income earned by local peasants from processing silk yarn alone totalled 500,000 to 1,000,000 silver
coins at the time. Although the market later became increasingly dull because of decreased silk production, silk yarn trade
was still the main business on the market.

Rice was the second major product. There were a number
of commercial and handicraft businesses in the town related
to the rice trade including rice firms, distillers and sauce and
pickle shops. Before the founding of the People's Republic
in 1949, the town had a dozen of rice firms of considerable
size, six of which were also engaged in husking rice. Besides
these, there were a large number of rice stalls. During years
of bountiful harvest, the biggest rice firm ground a daily average of 65 tons of rice. The thriving rice firms also brought
prosperity to the distillers. According to recollections of some
veteran wine-makers during bumper harvest years Zhenze and
its adjacent areas consumed 20 to 30 tons of grain every day
for making wine (during the winter-time). These rice firms
and distilleries also helped the growth of a large number of
other commercial and service trades; rice husk and chaff and
distiller's grains — by-products of the rice firms and distilleries
— became major commodities circulating in large quantities
in the town.

The circulation of silk, silk yarn, rice and other agricultural
and sideline products as well as several thousand kinds of industrial and handicraft products facilitated the establishment
of economic links between capitalists in Shanghai and Suzhou,
the proprietors in the town, and the peasants in the rural areas.
There were two principal mediums linking these three groups.
One was boats that plied regularly between inland towns.
They shipped farm and sideline produce from rural areas to

the town and transported industrial and handicraft products from the town to rural areas, their owners serving as the commercial agents of both the peasants and the proprietors in the town. The other medium included resident buyers, salesmen and their auxiliary staff members. These resident buyers, who were local traders stationing in Shanghai and Suzhou, wrote letters every day to inform Zhenze businessmen of the market quotations; while salesmen served as brokers in buying farm and sideline produce and selling industrial products in the town. Their activities constituted a network of interflows of people, material and information between cities and the town, whereby silk and silk yarn produced by peasants were exported and foreign goods were sold in the town. Both peasants and foreign and local business owners needed this network, the former for realizing the value of their commodities, and the latter for gaining profits through exploitation. The greedy rice firm owners were not satisfied with this form of exploitation, and so they also practised usury, lending peasants rice during periods of temporary shortage at interest rates generally ranging from 20 to 50 per cent, and even running as high as 100 per cent.

The exploitation at these two different levels resulted in the impoverishment of the rural areas. In the years shortly before the founding of the People's Republic in 1949, there was galloping inflation in the areas under the Kuomintang rule. Under these circumstances, the two banks in the town of Zhenze closed down one after the other, and the owners of silk yarn workshops, rice firms and other businesses transferred their capital to speculatory activities. Quantities of rice became the yardstick for measuring prices on the market, and some people even bartered rice for other goods. The serious economic depression of this period almost reduced the town to the level of a rural village.

After the founding of the People's Republic, the people's government adopted prompt measures to maintain social order and cracked down on the speculators and capitalists who had driven up prices. By 1950, prices had by and large achieved stability. In the same year, the imperialist blockade was broken and silk once again found a market abroad. At the same time the government energetically encouraged the development of silkworm and mulberry, grain, and other agricultural and sideline production. In August 1951, Wujiang County held a meeting on native products, thus further promoting trade between town and country. As a result, the market in Zhenze was gradually restored to normal. In December 1950, registration of industry and commerce was commenced for the first time. On page 348 appears the table for Zhenze.

II

Immediately after the founding of the People's Republic, reforms began to be instituted in the field of circulation. The reform was characterized by gradually cutting off the economic links between capitalists and peasants and establishing economic ties between the peasants and the state sector and other socialist sectors of the economy.

As mentioned above, before the founding of the People's Republic, silk and silk yarn were exported mainly through comprador capitalists in Shanghai. Following the victory in the War of Liberation foreign firms were driven out of the country and the links between comprador capitalists and the rural areas were cut off. The state-run China Silk Corporation took the place of these firms and flourished. The supply and marketing co-operative in the Zhenze area was entrusted by this corporation to purchase silk cocoons and have them processed in Suzhou and Wuxi. The original capital invested in the silk yarn trade was gradually transferred to Shanghai and Suzhou or to other trades in the town. The "Long Chang Zhen", formerly the biggest silk yarn firm in the town, transferred its operations to Suzhou and ran a silk-weaving factory there. The "Chen Ji", formerly the smallest silk yarn firm, changed its line of business running a printing house in the town. Still more capital from silk and silk yarn trade was

Table I

GENERAL SITUATION OF ZHENZE'S PRIVATELY-OWNED INDUSTRY AND COMMERCE

Name of trade	Number of households			Number of persons involved*	Total capital (yuan)	Number of lines of production	Name of principal lines of production
	Run by a single person's capital	Run with joint capitals	Total				
Handicraft	14	14	28	224	220,526	4	Rice-processing, wine-making, silk yarn spinning,** and cloth weaving
Small handicraft	146	1	147	226	22,193	22	Bamboo, wooden, stone, iron, copper and tin articles, and cotton fluffing
Commerce	258	73	331	1,146	444,259	33	Rice, silk, and furs
Catering trade	95	4	99	196	13,526	5	Tea-houses and restaurants
Service trade	42	3	45	121	12,907	9	Washing and dyeing, haircutting, hotels public bathrooms, and storytelling houses
Communications and transportation	5	6	11	24	785	1	Dock
TOTAL	560	101	661	1,937	714,196		

* All those listed were licensed resident traders, not including street pedlars.
** Although silk yarn production is listed in the category of handicraft, it has some commercial nature.

transferred to Shanghai and Suzhou for investment in other lines of production. According to available statistics, all of the privately-owned silk and silk yarn businesses in the town had disappeared by 1954.

Rice firm capital had long been closely connected with the landlord economy, and some rice firm owners were indeed landlords who concurrently engaged in industry and commerce. While the agrarian reform was carried out in the country, transformation was made for rice firms run by landlords in the town. Through the Associations of Industry and Commerce, the government helped small rice shops organize joint grain distribution centres, so as to meet the needs of the market, while big purchases and sales were handled by the supply and marketing co-operatives entrusted with this work by the China Cereals and Oils Corporation or by its own branches. After the state monopoly of the purchase and marketing of grain was set up in 1953, the grain business was basically run by the state, and privately-owned firms were allowed to operate only as "commission agents". In Zhenze, however, no private firm was willing to engage in the commission business. Thus, the town's entire grain business was taken over by the state commercial departments or the supply and marketing co-operative, and private capital withdrew from the town's grain market completely.

Since the establishment of joint state-private ownership in all trades in 1956 (the principal form of state capitalism adopted during the socialist transformation of capitalist enterprises in China), fundamental changes have taken place in the nature of the town's commerce. After the transformation, Zhenze then had a total of 332 enterprises, including 68 joint state-private enterprises, 139 co-operative shops, 103 handicraft producers' co-operatives, and 22 households operating on a self-employed basis. This transformation was both necessary and successful, but it was carried out a bit impetuously, and too many shops were merged. As a result, the number of commercial establishments was cut by nearly 50 per cent as compared with 1951.

In the course of this transformation, extensive changes took place in the economic composition of commerce and the nature of the relationship between town and country. At the same time, the number of commercial workers was reduced, and the volume of business doubled as compared with that in 1949, maintaining the level it had reached in 1952, the year which saw the end of the period of economic restoration. This is shown in the following table:

Table II

COMPARATIVE COMMERCIAL STATISTICS OF ZHENZE

Year	Number of workers of commerce, catering and service trades	Total volume of business (yuan)	As % of 1949
1949	1,489	2,997,329	100
1950	1,751	6,373,950	212.7
1951	1,821	6,579,828	219.5
1952	1,825	8,730,906	291.3
1953	1,667	9,063,285	302.4
1954	1,514	8,552,634	285.6
1955	1,489	7,308,785	243.8
1956	1,550	6,812.474	227.3
1957	1,162	6,501,093	216.9

After the transformation of privately-owned enterprises, commerce ought to have thrived in the towns. However, major setbacks occurred in the fields of circulation and production because of the influence of the wrong ideas of "Left" deviation which appeared shortly after the transformation. In 1958, people's communes were organized in a rash way, and towns ceased to exist as a level of administration. Apart from state-run wholesale departments, all the commercial establishments in the town were placed under the administration of the commune's supply and marketing department. As a result, the town's establishments were placed on a par with nearby communes' commercial establishments, and the town's role as a regional circulation centre was reduced.

Afterwards, commercial set-ups were further merged and small retail businesses were amalgamated to form co-operative shops. In 1959, the number of commercial establishments was further reduced, and by 1961, they numbered only 106, about half of that in 1956. During the "Great Leap Forward" in 1958, a large number of commercial workers were organized to join industry. Records preserved by the town's supply and marketing co-operative note that at this time, "a large number of commercial workers took part in steelmaking," "commercial departments set up 79 factories in a very short period," "the joint state-private department store produced 1,734 dozen gauze coverings for rural areas," "ten shops dealing in tobacco, paper, soy sauce and other goods began to run a soap factory," and "92 workers from commercial enterprises were transferred to run or work in factories". The reduction of commercial set-ups and workers naturally resulted in a commercial depression.

In 1961, commercial restructuring began. Excessively large co-operative shops were divided into smaller ones, and more commercial establishments were set up. In 1962, towns were separated from people's communes, and the system of placing towns directly under the administration of relevant counties was reinstated. Not long after this, state-run shops and department stores were set up in the towns, thus forming a commercial system whereby three economic forms — state-run stores, supply and marketing co-operatives and co-operative shops — co-existed.

The practice of using a single circulation channel had a more adverse effect on commerce than the merger of commercial establishments. During the three years of difficulty following the "Great Leap Forward", there was a serious shortage of materials and commodities. This, coupled with the ideological influence of the supply system (a system of payment in kind practised during the war times and in the early days of the People's Republic, providing working personnel and their dependents with the primary necessities of life), gave rise to the practice of forming circulation channels based on administrative structures rather than on the laws of commodity circulation.   When commercial establishments needed to replenish their stock, they had no other choice but to turn to the corporation to which they belonged, and could only take in what the corporation had on hand.   On the other hand, peasants could only sell their farm and sideline produce to the designated purchase centres, and had no other sales outlet for them.   As a result, the circulation channel became seriously clogged.

As mentioned in the first part of this article, it was natural that the capitalist and pre-capitalist exploitation which existed in the circulation system in pre-1949 days was abolished in the course of socialist transformation.   But, the network of interflows of people, material and information formed in the commodity circulation before the founding of the People's Republic should not be dealt with in an over-simplified way.   We should transform and utilize them, and retain their flexible and rational aspects while eliminating their defects of spontaneity and anarchism.   During a certain period in the past, we handled these questions in an over-simplified way, thereby making mistakes in our work.   Although some minor readjustments were made in this field, no fundamental changes were made until after the Third Plenary Session of the Eleventh Party Central Committee held in December 1978.

III

The current commercial reform is being carried out against the above-mentioned historical background.

After the Third Plenary Session of the Eleventh Party Central Committee, the agricultural responsibility system of linking rewards to production output was implemented, and policies concerning the flow of funds, technology and labour force have become flexible.   As a result, commodity production has grown vigorously in Zhenze and its surrounding rural areas, and unclogging the circulation channels has become an even more pressing task.

The growth of commodity production finds expression in the following two ways:

(1) Rapid development of the town-based county- or town-run industrial enterprises and of enterprises in the surrounding rural areas run by people's communes or production brigades. Zhenze now has 24 industrial enterprises, of which 11 commenced operation after 1979. The combined output value of these enterprises amounted to 55,068,500 yuan in 1983, an 81.6 per cent increase over the 1978 figure of 30,324,000 yuan. The production of enterprises in the surrounding rural areas run by people's communes or production brigades increased even faster. Take, for example, the enterprises of the Zhenze Commune, located adjacent to the town of Zhenze. The output value of its commune- and brigade-run enterprises reached 26,260,000 yuan in 1982, or 5.5 times the 1978 figure of 4,780,000 yuan. Their profits amounted to 2,806,000 yuan in 1982, or 2.5 times the 1978 figure of 1,110,000 yuan. In 1983, further progress was made.

(2) Fairly big increases were registered in both output and output value of the production of major commodities in the surrounding rural areas. Table III shows the situation in the Zhenze Commune.

The process of reproduction consists of the processes of direct production and circulation. Production determines circulation, while the latter can also in turn influence the former. The vigorous growth of commodity production made the incongruity between circulation and production even more conspicuous, and it became a pressing task to restructure and unclog the channels of circulation. In Zhenze, some measures of restructuring were carried out to cope with the rapid expansion of commodity production. This has brought about gratifying changes in Zhenze's commerce.

Various new economic forms have come into being. Apart from the progress which has been made by the original three

Table III

INCREASE IN OUTPUT AND OUTPUT VALUE OF MAJOR COMMODITIES IN ZHENZE COMMUNE

	1978	1982	Increase rate (%)
Cereals and soybean (ton)	25,638.7	29,362.4	14.5
Silkworm cocoons (ton)	235.436	421.724	79
Oil crops (ton)	950.6	2,049.45	116
Brigades' income from selling products (yuan)	4,000,000*	8,010,780	100

economic forms, state-run stores, supply and marketing co-operatives and co-operative shops, the following economic forms have also emerged:

(A) Commune-run commerce. As early as the late period of the "cultural revolution" (1966-76), when the local commune-run commerce was criticized as being "capitalist", this form of economy had already begun making its way by breaking through obstructions. At that time, the existing commune- and brigade-run industrial enterprises had to do all their purchasing and marketing themselves, because their raw materials supply and product marketing was not included in the plan of state-run commerce and supply and marketing co-operatives. This, coupled with the fact that planned supply of agricultural means of production and building materials in rural areas fell short of demand, gave rise to the growth of commune-run commerce.

Since 1978, this channel has been widened. Thanks to the Party's encouragement of the comprehensive operation of agriculture, industry and commerce, commune-run commerce has grown rapidly. The Zhenze People's Commune formally established a "department of industrial management" in 1981

* This is the figure for 1979. The increase rate of income from selling products roughly shows the growth rate of commodity production in agriculture and sideline occupation.

and a diversified economy service corporation the following year. As a result, the purchases and sales of various commune- and brigade-run factories have markedly increased. Take the garment factory and the knitting mill of the Zhenze People's Commune as an example. Apart from establishing sales stations in neighbouring Anhui Province according to the arrangements made by the Management Department of the county's Commune- and Brigade-Run Enterprise Bureau, the two factories have themselves also set up sales stalls in Suzhou and Huzhou besides Zhenze. In recent years, the improved quality of their products has attracted state-run stores, and the knitting mill's products are now sold in the Nanyang Shirt Shop on Nanjing Road in Shanghai. This favourable situation shows that products of commune- and brigade-run enterprises have entered the circulation channel of the state-run commerce.

Commune-run commerce made fairly big progress in 1983. Retail shops were set up in Zhenze by the commune to sell products of commune- and brigade-run enterprises as well as cigarettes, wine, sweets and pastry. The commune's Diversified Economy Service Corporation set up a hatchery and vegetable processing factory. It purchased such raw materials as eggs and vegetables, supplied young domestic fowls to specialized households, and directly sold preserved eggs and pickles to other parts of China, including Jilin Province in northeast China. The rising commune-run commerce is developing into a potent force.

(B) Country fair trade. Apart from commune-run commerce which started from scratch, country fair trade has expanded the most rapidly of all of the economic forms. In 1978, the volume of transactions of Zhenze's country fair trade was only 144,800 yuan, or 1.5 per cent of the town's annual volume of retail sales. In 1982, the figure rose to 3,790,391 yuan, 26 times that for 1978, or 17 per cent of the town's annual volume of retail sales. It has thus become a major supplementary channel of the town's commodity circulation. The variety of goods available on the market has also increased considerably. Before 1978, the market only offered a small amount of vegetables and aquatic products, while today, by contrast, it offers edible farm and sideline produce, including cereals, oil crops, meat, poultry, eggs, aquatic products, vegetables, fruit, means of production, industrial products, as well as sundry goods for daily use, such as bamboo products, garments and knit goods. This shows that the present country fair trade has far surpassed its traditional scope of merely offering a small amount of trade of farm and sideline produce, and is changing into small commodity market offering a wider variety of goods. People attending it include pedlars from rural areas and towns a dozen kilometres away from Zhenze, persons from the cities of Shanghai, Huzhou and Jiaxing, travellers and motor vehicle drivers, as well as residents of Zhenze and peasants from its surrounding areas. In normal times, people attending the fair average 1,000-2,000 per day. During festivals, the figure rises to 4,000-5,000, and the place is so jam-packed that even bicycles can hardly pass through. In order to further improve conditions for country fair trade, the Town Industrial and Commercial Administration Department has invested a sum of 28,000 yuan in building a trading place with a floor space of 1,035 square metres roofed with plastic sheets.

(C) Households engaged in self-employed businesses. During the period of socialist transformation of privately-owned enterprises, too many privately-owned establishments in the fields of commerce, handicraft and service trade were merged, causing the people a lot of inconvenience. During the "Great Leap Forward", this shortcoming accentuated a result of further amalgamation. Things became even worse during the "cultural revolution" when some self-employed households engaged in business were sent to settle down in the country to work as peasants. By 1972, there were only 81 self-employed households in the town, including 40 engaged in commerce, 28 in handicraft and repair service and 13 in catering trade. These privately-owned establishments were also regarded as "capitalist remnants" and were all annexed to collective industrial and commercial enterprises. Up to that time, this important supplementary circulation channel was completely blocked. It is only in the past few years that new self-employed households have come into being. Despite the obstructions of "Left" ideology, such households have made progress as a supplementary form of circulation channel. In 1982, there were 43 such licensed households in the town. Zhenze and the Zhenze People's Commune had a total of 204 such households, including 89 engaged in commerce, 26 in handicraft and repair service, 34 in catering trade, and 48 in transportation. Statistics made by the town's Industrial and Commercial Administration Department show that in 1982 the volume of business of self-employed households reached 211,700 yuan, or one per cent of the town's annual volume of retail sales.

As a result, in the field of circulation, a structure composed of several economic forms has arisen, with state-run commerce and supply and marketing co-operatives constituting the main body, and the number of commercial establishments has also increased. This is shown in Tables IV, V and VI.

2. Increased channels and reduced intermediate links have helped to invigorate commodity circulation. In the past few years, efforts have been made to change the situation in which commodity circulation was seriously blocked because it only had one channel available to it. Now, there are three main channels for obtaining goods: (1) Purchasing from wholesale stations at a higher level; (2) Purchasing directly from nearby big and medium-sized cities or even from distant cities; and (3) Purchasing directly from places of origin or factories. The channels for selling goods have also become diversified. Goods are now sold not only in town but also in nearby areas as well. A large amount of farm and sideline produce is supplied directly to retail shops and vegetable markets in cities. Great achievements have also been made in trading vegetables and fruit. The town has now been given a free hand in purchasing goods from producing areas throughout the country. In Zhenze, people can buy apples from Yan-

tai in Shandong Province, dried persimmons from Linxian
County in Henan Province, sunflower seeds from Baotou City
in Inner Mongolia, and watermelons from Pinghu in Zhejiang
Province. Apart from selling these goods locally, the town
also resells them to nearby cities and towns, including Jiaxing
and Huzhou in Zhejiang Province. In the past, only two veg-

Table IV

COMPOSITION OF ZHENZE'S TOTAL COMMODITY SALES

(Unit: yuan)

		1978	1982	Percentage difference (1982 compared with 1978)
State-run commerce	sum	33,740,520	53,193,925	+57.6
	%	76.6	69.5	—7.1
Supply and marketing co-operatives	sum	7,693,010	11,147,614	+44.9
	%	17.5	14.6	—2.9
Collective commerce run by the town and the Zhenze Township	sum	2,450,964	7,303,621	+198
	%	5.6	9.5	+3.9
Commerce run by the Zhenze People's Commune	sum	—	927,766	—
	%	—	1.2	+1.2
Country fair trade	sum	144,833	3,790,391	+2,500
	%	0.3	4.9	+4.6
Self-employed businesses in the town and the Zhenze Township	sum	—	211,700	—
	%	—	0.3	+0.3
TOTAL		44,029,377	76,557,017	+73.9

Note: 1. Sales done by factories (including commune- and brigade-run
        enterprises) themselves were not counted.
      2. Total sales include the volume of wholesale and retail.

Table V

COMPOSITION OF THE VOLUME OF RETAIL SALES OF ZHENZE AND THE ZHENZE TOWNSHIP

(Unit: yuan)

		1978	1982	Percentage difference (1982 compared with 1978)
State-run commerce	sum	3,895,565	5,545,818	+42.4
	%	40.7	24.9	—15.8
Supply and marketing co-operatives	sum	3,089,000	4,474,000	+44.8
	%	30.2	20.1	—12.1
Collective commerce run by the town and the Zhenze Township	sum	2,450,964	7,303,621	+198
	%	25.6	32.8	+7.2
Commerce run by the Zhenze People's Commune	sum	—	927,766	—
	%	—	4.2	+4.2
Country fair trade	sum	144,883	3,790,391	+2,500
	%	1.5	17	+15.5
Self-employed businesses in the town and the Zhenze Township	sum	—	211,700	—
	%	—	1	+1
TOTAL		9,580,412	22,253,296	+132.3

Table VI

CHANGES IN THE NUMBER OF COMMERCIAL ESTABLISHMENTS AND WORKERS

	1978	1982
Number of establishments	130	308
Commercial workers	1,114	1,555

Note: The country fair trade was taken as one unit and the people engaged were not counted.

etable markets in Shanghai had business links with Zhenze's vegetable and fruit shops in trading the vegetables, pickles and smoked green peas produced in Zhenze. Now, Shanghai's 24 vegetable markets, one sauce and pickle shop, one dairy farm and four other shops sell Zhenze's products. Flexible ways have also been adopted in purchasing daily use articles. Since Zhenze is only 118 km. away from Shanghai, consumers in the town prefer to buy Shanghai-produced goods. In the past, people complained frequently about the shortage of Shanghai goods, which resulted from regulations to the effect that goods should be supplied on the basis of administrative division. In recent years, restrictions concerning the supply of goods have gradually been removed. Apart from some badly-needed commodities, which are distributed according to plan by the wholesale departments at provincial and county levels, other goods can be purchased from Shanghai according to need. Retail shops also purchase goods from other cities. Guangzhou-produced folding umbrellas are sold in Zhenze at 11 yuan in the town's wholesale departments, but are sold at 9.7 yuan each by the town's Yimin (Benefit the People) Store, which takes stock directly from Guangzhou. In addition, retail and wholesale shops have also established ties with factories and purchase those products which the factories can dispose of freely after fulfilling their production quotas.

In 1983 a major step was taken to unclog circulation channels. To meet the needs of increased commodity production and trade between rural and urban areas, wholesale corporations in the county began to allow the wholesale stations in the town to share the right of the county corporations (third-grade wholesale stations). Thus, the town's wholesale stations can, without going through the county corporations, directly take stock from the second-grade wholesale stations the province has established in some big cities nearby, including Nanjing, Changzhou, Wuxi, Suzhou and Xuzhou. This has had the effect of eliminating one intermediate link in the circulation process, thus greatly raising economic results of commodity circulation. According to an estimate made by Zhenze's

General Merchandise Wholesale Station, this method can lessen the annual commodity circulation period by one to two weeks, save 20,000 yuan annually on transportation expenses, and reduce commodity spoilage. Take the purchase of detergent powder from Xuzhou as an example. Through direct purchase the town has reduced commodity spoilage to 1 per cent, as compared with spoilage of 5 to 6 per cent which occurred in the past when the town took stock through the county's third-grade wholesale station. A statistical survey made by the Zhenze office of the People's Bank of China shows that after unclogging circulation channels and reducing intermediate links, both circulation costs and the amount of circulating funds used for each 100 yuan of sales have dropped, and profits have increased accordingly. This is shown in the table on page 362.

3. The process of circulation is evolving from being a simple matter of purchase and sales, into being a comprehensive service which includes supplying the means of production and technical guidance, and the processing and marketing of products. Today, such comprehensive services are organized by the Joint Economic Association of People's Communes established at the town level. The Diversified Economy Service Corporation, which is under the administration of the association, is active in these undertakings. It has recently set up a hatchery, which purchases eggs, supplies young poultry and gives technical guidance to households specializing in raising poultry. It also purchases duck eggs and produces preserved eggs for sale in other areas. This corporation has reached an agreement with the rural commune according to which, the commune shall grow rutabaga and melons, while the corporation shall, in co-operation with the town's supply and marketing co-operative, purchase the rutabaga and process it. The corporation has also contacted organizations concerned in Shanghai, Suzhou and Jiaxing and signed contracts with them for supplying and marketing 2,500 tons of melons. State-run commercial establishments, supply and marketing co-operatives and

Table VII

CHANGES OF ECONOMIC RESULTS IN CIRCULATION FIELD

	Circulating funds for each 100 yuan of sales		Circulation costs for each 100 yuan of sales		Profits from each 100 yuan of sales		Profits from each 100 yuan of circulating funds	
	1982	1983	1982	1983	1982	1983	1982	1983
Wholesale of general merchandise	23.14	16.93	2.92	2.71	2.68	3.78	11.59	63.90
Wholesale of vegetables	9.92	6.37	5.05	3.30	3.69	3.64	63.90	86.39
Wholesale of metals, transport and electrical appliances, and chemical products	17.14	13.32	2.70	2.64	5.62	3.63	33.51	27.27
Wholesale of medicines	19.58	17.91	4.38	3.96	1.76	2.06	11.52	13.76
Wholesale of tobaccos, wine and sweets	13.60	8.15	1.99	1.41	3.14	1.87	21.95	22.92

Note: (1) Figures listed were for the first 11 months of 1982 and 1983 respectively.
(2) The table shows the reduction of circulating funds and circulation costs for ecah 100 yuan of sales and the increase of profits. Some figures, however, do not accord with this tendency, due to factors not related to circulation channels.

other commercial set-ups are also beginning to offer such comprehensive services.

Today, the vigorous commercial activities going on in Zhenze are entirely unlike those which went on in the past in terms of their contents, character and level of vitality. However, they still fall far short of the needs of the current urban and rural economic development. The commodity circulation network is still imperfect, posing the question of how to build a circulation network of small towns which will promote further growth of rural commodity production.

IV

The basic requirement for socialist socialized mass production is to achieve maximum economic results with minimum consumption of materials. In field of circulation this means using minimum circulation costs and time to enable producers to realize the value of their products and consumers to obtain the proper use value from them. To fulfil this requirement, it is necessary to establish a rational circulation network. Such a network would include channels for commodity circulation; channels and measures for information collection and dissemination; and such necessary facilities as transport, warehouses and places for exchanging goods. In rural areas, apart from roads and telecommunication wires, the above-mentioned things are mainly concentrated in small towns. Hence, the various closely-linked towns have become the key points in the rural circulation network.

Chen Yun, a veteran economist and a member of the Party's Political Bureau, put the matter plainly in his statement: "Industrial products do not go directly from big cities to rural villages, but rather from big cities to medium-sized cities, from medium-sized cities to small cities, and from small cities to primary markets." What Chen Yun is talking about here is precisely the circulation network. Of course, he was describing the general situation in the country as a whole. In areas not far from big and medium-sized cities, industrial products naturally go directly from the big and medium-sized cities to primary markets without relying on the intermediate link of small cities. However, the circulation process of farm and sideline produce is exactly the opposite, namely, from the countryside to primary markets, and from there to the small, medium-sized and big cities. What must be further explored is how to realize the rational distribution of primary markets in rural areas. The history of commodity circulation in Zhenze and the tendency towards the on-going restructuring of its administration show that the rationalization of distribution channels does not mean that all the primary markets within a county should rely on one same centre (such as the county seat), with this sole centre making contacts with cities. Neither does it mean that all primary markets should enjoy equal status in making contacts with cities. Instead, it means that several circulation centres should be set up, in accordance with economic, administrative and transport conditions of a given locality, all of which should be linked with surrounding primary markets and have close ties with cities of different sizes. Zhenze, for example, has links with the small towns in its seven surrounding townships. There is general consensus that four such regional circulation centres should be established in Wujiang County: at Pingwang in the county's centre, Songling in the north, Luxu in the southeast and Zhenze in the southwest. Contacts with cities will be carried out primarily by these four centres. Such layout can raise economic results of circulation considerably.

Why should the system of circulation be laid out in this manner?

If a county has only one centre which makes contacts with big and medium-sized cities, all industrial products will be distributed by the county's "third-grade wholesale station" based on its administrative divisions, as was done in the past, thus blocking circulation channels and lowering economic results. Take Wujiang County for example. It is naturally more costly and time consuming if industrial products from Shanghai are first sent to the county seat of Songling, which is relatively far from Shanghai, and from there are distributed to Pingwang and Luxu, which are relatively near by Shanghai, or to Zhenze, which is almost the same distance from Shanghai as Songling and has direct transport links with Shanghai. Although it is necessary that goods pass through Songling when they are shipped from Suzhou to Zhenze, they need not make a "stopover" at Songling. In addition, it is difficult for a county's "third-grade wholesale station" to take into consideration the different needs of various areas of the county. If there is only one centre, this will inevitably not only give rise to a discrepancy between supply and demand, with some goods being overstocked and consumers' specific needs not being satisfied, but will also cause waste of social labour and diminishment of economic results.

On the other hand, economic results are likewise low if the supply and marketing departments of each township make direct contacts with cities, because the townships are small in scale and short of circulating funds and circulation equipment. In addition, they need only small quantity of goods each time they take stock. Therefore, it is difficult for them to lay in stock directly from cities. Supply and marketing departments of the rural communes surrounding Zhenze prefer to make purchase from the town according to their needs, instead of from cities like Shanghai and Suzhou. They can order small quantity of goods over the telephone, and wholesale departments in Zhenze will send goods to them by boats which are shuttling through the area. This is the most economical way for them.

Through practising of commodity circulation, people are inclined to choose a layout pattern like that of Zhenze: In an economic area of a certain scope, a regional circulation centre should be established in a place that is centrally located and easily accessible. In the area surrounding the centre there should be several centres at the commune level. Rural communes are entities of the co-operative economy. Because they practise comprehensive operations covering agriculture, industry and commerce, they will inevitably have one or more circulation and comprehensive service centres. Under the commune, there are such centres at the village level. Thus, in an economic district, a multi-levelled circulation network will be formed. Today, such a network is considered rather ideal for rural commodity circulation.

In most cases, rural regional circulation centres coincide with rural regional industrial centres. The relative concentration of rural industry can save investments in energy, transport, warehouse construction, water supply and sewage drainage. Generally speaking, the places where rural industries are concentrated have favourable circulation conditions. At the same time, the relative concentration of population engaging in industry and the turnover of large quantity of industrial raw materials and waste inevitably promotes the growth of commodity circulation. Just like a circulation network with different layers, industrial productive forces also have different layers. From handicraft industry and simple processing industry to rather well-developed machine industry, their distribution is by and large in keeping with the different layers of circulation network. Industrial and commercial development can also promote the growth of cultural, educational and service undertakings, thus making industrial and commercial centres at different levels gradually become rural economic and cultural centres at various levels.

Unlike the capitalist countries which practise spontaneous market economy, China practises a planned economy. Thus, there arises a question: At what level should we set the basic point for planning and guiding commodity circulation? In the past, the basic point was set at the county level, in accordance with administrative structure and the existing commercial system. Today, along with the development of commodity production, a great deal of circulation activities are concentrated in rural regional circulation centres. This gives rise to a negative phenomenon, which has been reported by commercial workers in Zhenze, namely, that township government and commercial bodies, which have close contacts with rural circulation centres, have not been invested with the power to administer the centres, while county industrial and commercial administrative departments, which have been invested with the power to administer the centres, have no direct contact with them. This is obviously detrimental to market control. In view of the actual situation, it is advisable that we should take the rural regional circulation centres as the basic point for rural market management and strengthen the centres' co-ordinating and administrative organs, while making the county the unit for planning overall balance and adjustment. However, how this should be done is a question concerning the restructuring of rural commerce and merits further study.

Zhenze's status and role as a rural regional circulation centre is being strengthened. But its existing circulation facilities (including transport facilities, warehouse equipment and carriage organization and equipment) do not suit its status and role. For example, the bus station in the town is just an ordinary rural bus station, which does not undertake consignment work, so goods shipped in from other areas have to be fetched from the Pingwang station 16 km. away from the town. Steamboats sailing between Shanghai and Huzhou do not stop at the town for loading and unloading goods. This, coupled with the insufficiency of warehouses and backwardness of storage equipment, has restricted the role of Zhenze as a rural regional circulation centre. Thus the conclusion we draw from our initial survey of the town of Zhenze is that with the growth of rural commodity production, the speeding up the construction of towns has become a pressing task.

INDEX

agriculture, industry's aid to, 223, 276

agro-industrial households 77

Bachi (town) 54

"big pot" egalitarianism 69, 109, 144, 145

"capitalist tails" 30, 356

Changzhou (city) 63-66, 72-74, 77, 79

Chen Yun 363

commodity circulation 53-56, 81, 254, 278, 284, 357, 367

commodity economy 222

commodity production 353

C.P.C. 7th Central Committee, 2nd Plenum of, 339

C.P.C. 11th Central Committee, 3rd Plenum of, 28, 41, 42, 64, 69, 92, 151, 152, 153, 174, 211, 212, 213, 214, 273, 280, 302, 303, 352

C.P.C. 12th Central Committee, 3rd Plenum of, 134, 144

"cultural revolution" 29, 38, 40, 42, 69, 98, 106, 152, 231, 247, 318, 322, 335, 339, 354, 356

Dagang (town) 124

Deng Xiaoping 10, 161

"dragon-like" production process 72

economic pattern, change of, 216

Gaochun (county) 24

Great Leap Forward 351, 356

Hengshan (town) 54

Hu Yaobang 11

Huaiyin (city) 86, 89, 95, 99, 100, 101, 112, 113

Jinjinba (town) 54

labour shift, economic basis for, 175; two features of, 178

"Left" deviationist thinking 29, 41, 119, 173, 212, 273, 322, 350, 357

Lianyungang (city) 88, 89, 92, 100, 108, 112

Miaogang (town) 31, 32, 44, 53, 58, 60

modernization, big stride towards, 154; key to, 280

Nanku (town) 34

Nantong (city) 63, 73, 74, 81

new city-country links 149

open social system 164

peasant workers 50, 76, 79, 196

Pingwang (town) 24, 44

planned and market economies 147

population "chess game" 108

population distribution 220

productive force 211, 214, 280

rural fairs 56, 95, 97, 128, 274, 355

rural industrialization, new pattern of, 74; conditions exist for, 126

rural industry, driving force for, 38; as source of wealth 66; growth of, 123, 150; spreading of, 125; need for stabilization of, 184; extension to villages 141, 212, 214, 215

rural market 323

science and technology 155, 279, 280

Shanghai economic zone 89

Shengze (silk town) 21, 22, 26, 27, 290

silver triangle area 133

socialist road, novel characteristic of, 66, 67, 69

socialized production 187

Songling (town) 22, 31, 54, 227

specialized households 113

state grain monopoly 349

surplus labour, jobs for, 75; export of, 106; shift of, 188, 191

Suzhou (city) 63, 64, 65, 69, 71, 72, 73, 75, 83

Tangqiao (town) 211, 212, 215

Tongli (cultural town) 23, 26, 316

Tongluo (town) 27, 33, 39, 54

urban construction 313

urbanization, way to, 195

urban-rural economic entities 148

Waiyi (village) 172

Wanping (town) 34

working class, new members of, 50

Wujiang (county) 26, 40, 60

Wuxi (city) 63-68, 72, 73, 75, 77, 79, 86

Xinta (town) 35, 36

Xuzhou (city) 88, 89, 92, 95, 100, 101-106, 112, 228, 231

Yancheng (city) 88, 89, 100, 102, 112, 117, 118, 122, 123, 128

Yangzhou (city) 88, 89, 100, 102, 107, 112, 119

Yiling (village) 271, 280

Zhenze (town) 18, 22, 37, 53, 55, 58, 342

SMALL TOWNS, GREAT SIGNIFICANCE

Small towns described

Bachi 54

Hengshan 54

Jinjiaba 34

Miaogang 31, 32, 44, 53, 58, 60

Nanku 34

Pingwang 24, 44

Shengze 21, 22, 26, 27

Songling 22, 31, 54, 227

Tongli 23, 26

Tongluo 27, 33, 39, 54

Wanping 34

Xinta 35, 36

Zhenze 18, 22, 37, 53, 55, 58

Small towns in South Jiangsu

"capitalist tails" 30

common characteristics of, 25

"cultural revolution" 38, 40, 42

decline of role as economic centres 29

different roles of, 53

diversified rural economy, Party policy on, 28

five types of, 18

"Left" deviationist policies 29, 41

meaning of classification 26

reasons for population decrease 28

Small towns in Wujiang County

cause of town revival 35

cause traced to "Left" deviation 29

changes in commercial channels 30

commodity circulation 53, 54, 55, 56

consequences of small towns' decline 29

contradictions in agricultural society 36

driving force for industries 38

emerging of "peasant-workers" 50

expansion of factories 40

future of rural economy 42

illiteracy in Wujiang 60

little population flow 51
major changes in, 26
need for cultural centres 59
new members of working class 50
population growth at Shengze 27
reasons for decline at Tonglou 27
recovery of rural industries 41

social changes 51
three types of rural factories 44
thriving business of fairs 56
two types of factories in Wujiang 40
villages' turn into commercial town 34

PROBING DEEPER INTO SMALL TOWNS

In four municipalities

agro-industrial households 77
"big pot" egalitarianism 69
burgeoning rural industry 67
change in rural economic structure 66
changes in business activities 80
Changzhou 63, 64, 65, 66, 72, 73, 74, 77, 79
contract production system 69
countryside industrialization system 74
current administrative system 85
development of regional economy 74
"dragon-like" production process 72
industry as source of wealth 66
jobs for surplus labour 75
labour teams to frontiers 79

Nantong 63, 73, 74, 81
new look in countryside 65
new pattern of industrialization 74
novel characteristic of socialist road 66, 67, 69
"peasant-workers" 76, 79
problems and difficulties 74
problems in commodity circulation 81
production for urban plants 72
reasons for development 68
reform advocated 86
resurgence of small towns 64
small town reconstruction 83
Suzhou 63, 64, 65, 69, 71, 72, 73, 75, 83
three sectors in trade 81
traditional structure destroyed 68
two industries in co-operation 73
Wuxi 63, 64, 65, 66, 67, 68, 72, 73, 75, 77, 79, 86

SMALL TOWNS IN NORTH JIANGSU

Tour in five municipalities

bright prospects 94
conditions exist for rural industrialization 126
effect of Huaihe conservancy 92
export of labour 106
fair activities 97
fair and town — the difference 111
farm production expansion at Lixiahe 130
forerunners of towns 99
growth of rural industry 123
high crop yields 92
Huaiyin 88, 89, 95, 99, 100, 101, 112, 113
improvement at Dagang 124
improvement of economic standing 93
industry spreading to villages 125
Lianyungang 88, 89, 92, 100, 108, 110
nature of Xuzhou industry 104
new life at Yancheng 118
peasants investing in production 116
pioneering work at Jianggang 121
population "chess game" 108
pre-1949 economic backwardness 89

role of Grand Canal 90
rural industrialization — a major problem 130
Shanghai economic zone 89
situation at Xuzhou 102
specialized households 113
towns at Lianyungang 109

transformation of fairs 128
Xuzhou 88, 89, 92, 95, 100, 101, 102, 103, 104, 105, 106, 112
Yancheng 88, 89, 100, 102, 112, 117, 118, 122, 123, 128
Yangzhou 88, 89, 100, 102, 107, 112, 119

SMALL TOWNS IN CENTRAL JIANGSU

Trips in silver triangle area

activities in market 148
administrative division to be adjusted 168
big stride towards modernization 154
change from closed character 140
contract responsibility system 166
effect on regional economies 164
efficient management needed 164
extension of industry to villages 141
growth of industry 150
independent commodity producers 165

industrial distribution 138
measures for consolidation 145
new city-country links 149
open social system 164
planned and market economies 147
role not fully played 139
science and technology in rural areas 155
six levels of industry at Yangzhong 142
stress on information 158, 164
three cities linked in area 133
three stages of development 150
two-way links 147
urban-rural economic entities 148

SHIFT OF SURPLUS LABOUR FORCE

Investigations at four villages

changes in economy 174
collectively-owned enterprises 194
contract responsibility system 174
doubly engaged labourers 188
economic basis for labour shift 175
economy on collective basis 184
favourable conditions of Waiyi 173
help between two industries 183
increased output value 175

labour and household switch 180
labour division among households 179
rural industry to be stabilized 184
shift of surplus labour 188, 191
social division of labour 176
socialized production 187
two administrative levels 179
two features of labour shift 178
Waiyi Village as typical case 172
way to urbanization 195

PEASANT WORKERS IN COUNTY TOWNS

Survey at Tangqiao Town

building of small towns 209
city-country integration 209
distribution in trades 202
division into four categories 200
effect on town construction 208

flourishing towns 198
gradual shift needed 209
peasant workers on increase 196
socialist labour form 210
trend of Wujiang development 197
Zhenze specialized in industry 199

RISE OF RURAL INDUSTRY AND PROSPERITY OF TOWNS

Development of Tangqiao

better living standards 221
change of economic pattern 216
expansion of industries 215
growth of commodity economy 222
growth of rural industries 212, 214
imbalance in population distribution 220
improvement of leadership needed 226
"industry subsidizes agriculture" 223

links with cities 218
need for vegetable growing 224
population transformation 219
pressing task ahead 220
problems awaiting solution 223
prospects of technical exchange 219
prosperity at Tangqiao Town 211, 212
role of productive force 211, 214
significance of Beijing directives 222
Tangqiao's characteristics 215

TOWN-CITY ECONOMIC CONNECTIONS

Survey conducted at Songling

bright future of economic links 242
connections with cities 229
different forms of co-operation 242
economic links with Suzhou 228, 231
evolution of spare-time school 245

expansion of Songling industry 240
five forms of connections 233
needs of two sides met 231
other links 243
school's role in aiding production 246
three groups of factories 241
three stages of links 232

DISTRIBUTION OF VILLAGES AND TOWNS

Study of situation at Gaochun County

commodity circulation 254
contrast with diked region 251
different functions of towns 254
diked region type 249
distribution of residential areas 252
economic activities 252

formation of inhabited areas 249
four grades of towns 255
grade I villages be increased 266
grade II villages be expanded 268
hilly land type 251
location of towns — a problem 262
types of villages 257
village-town dividing line 260
small towns be developed 265

GIVE FULL PLAY TO ROLE OF SMALL TOWNS

Investigation of Yiling

a great turning point 273
a positive cycle 283
blindfold development — a lesson 284
bodies for popularizing science 279
bridge for goods circulation 278
change in economic structure 277

commodity circulation be transformed 284
conversion into market fair 274
development into commodity production 278
economic and cultural centres 279
free flow of commodities 285
growth of productive force 280
help to modernize agriculture 283

how to develop small towns 280
industry's support to agriculture 276
key to realize modernizations 280
market transactions 278
need for education 287
new look of Yiling 280
outlet for surplus labour 275
problems in organization 288
problems in planning work 287
reliance on small towns 277
rise and decline of village 271
study of science 286
way out for agriculture 276

FORMATION AND DEVELOPMENT OF SHENGZE

Situation at silk town

decline of silk industry 300
development into industrial town 298
development recounted 307
entrepot of handicraft products 293
favourable conditions for expansion 303
flourishing trade explained 297
foundation for town construction 309
recovery of production 301
rise of cottage handicraft 291
role of Shengze silk industry 305
shift to non-agricultural work 309
silk trade centre 294
small industrial town 290
two problems faced 310
urban construction 313
workshop handicraft production 291

DEVELOPMENT OF TONGLI

Study of ancient cultural town

classification of industries 321
contradictions in development 329
damage by "Left" thinking 322
development plan be respected 340
features of cultural town be preserved 332
future of Tongli 317
link for urban-rural area 319
"multi-functional" town 327
need for talented people 328
relationships deserve attention 333
responsibility system introduced 323
revival of rural market 323
small town transformation 326
Tongli's functions in three stages 319
towns be attractive to city folk 332
two structures need study 338
typical river-lake region town 316
views on construction work 334

FORMATION AND DEVELOPMENT OF ZHENZE

As commodity circulation centre

business of households merged 356
"capitalist remnants" 356
circulation channel clogged 352
circulation reform 347
circulation structure 357
commercial depression 351
country fair trade 355
emerging of economic forms 355
growth of commodity production 353
ideal multi-levelled network 365
impetuous transformation 349
less intermediate links 359
necessary network 346
progress of commune commerce 355

rational network needed 363
responsibility system 352
shift to commodity production 342
silk and rice as major products 345
supplementary circulation channel 357

three main channels 359
town construction, a pressing task, 367
Zhenze as prosperous town 342
Zhenze layout pattern 365
Zhenze's role as circulation centre 367

中 国 小 城 镇

费孝通　等著

*

新世界出版社出版（北京）

外文印刷厂印刷

中国国际图书贸易总公司发行

（中国国际书店）

北京399信箱

1986年第一版

编号：（英）17223—172

00980（精）

00730（平）

4—E—1726